# MIGRATION TO
# SOUTH CAROLINA – 1850 CENSUS

## from
## England, Scotland, Germany, Italy, France, Spain, Russia, Denmark, Sweden, and Switzerland

*Abstracted by*
*Margaret Peckham Motes*

Clearfield Company
Baltimore, Maryland

Other books by the author:

*Laurens & Newberry Counties, S.C.: Saluda and Little River Settlements 1749-1775*, co-authored with Jesse H. Motes, III. Winner of the National Genealogical Society 1995 Award for Excellence (Methods and Sources).

*South Carolina Memorials: Abstractes of Land Titles - Vol. 1, 1774-1776*, co-authored with Jesse H. Motes, III.

*Free Blacks and Mulattos in South Carolina - 1850 Census.*

*Blacks Found in the Deeds of Laurens and Newberry Counties, S.C.: 1785-1827: Listed in Deeds of Gift, Deeds of Sale, Mortages, Born Free and Freed.*

*Butcher, Baker, Candlestick Maker and Other Occupations in Newburyport, Massachusetts - 1850 Census.*

*Irish in South Carolina - 1850 Census.*

*Migration to South Carolia: Movement from the New England and Mid-Atlantic States - 1850 Census.*

ISBN: 978-0-8063-5277-0

# CONTENTS

**Surnames** (Alphabetical by Country)

**Index**

# INTRODUCTION:

This is the fourth book in a series on migration into South Carolina by 1850. The first book dealt with *Free Blacks and Mulattoes, South Carolina– 1850 Census.* This was followed by *Irish in South Carolina–1850 Census* and *Migration to South Carolina: Movement from the New England and Mid-Atlantic States, 1850 Census.* This book covers people found in the 1850 South Carolina census who were born in England, Scotland, Germany, Italy, France, Spain, Russia, Denmark, Sweden or Switzerland.

Ths first migration into South Carolina began during its colonization under King George II of England and continued to grow with the opening of new lands for farmers. Many of those who migrated from Great Britain and Europe tended to settle in the more populated areas, like Charleston. They brought with them their various trades, religious beliefs and values to this new frontier.

The 1850 census is important for researchers since it is the first census which sheds light on the family, family grouping, place of birth, occupations in the household, and areas in which the families settled together.

There are over 3,700 names listed, with over 1900 Germans, followed by the English (861) and those from Scotland (579). The largest German settlement was in Charleston, where immigrants worked as bakers, carpenters, cabinet makers, clerks, jewelers, merchants, musicians, shoemakers and shop keepers.

People were moving for many reasons: political unrest, changing country boundaries, new job opportunities, land, weather, economic growth, education and/or religious movements. They brought with them new cultural ideas, foods, religious ideals, and trades which resulted in continued change and growth in each community where they settled.

Many of the same occupations found in the previous books on the migration into South Caroline by the 1850's appear in this work.

These trades include blacksmiths, bricklayers, brick masons, boot and shoe makers, carpenters, coach makers and trimmers, coopers, farmers, fruiterers, laborers, mariners, mechanics, painters, peddlers, saddlers, saw mill operators, servants, stone cutters, silversmiths, tailors watchmakers and wheelwrights.

There were also many new occupations which appeared with each group of immigrants; some of which were artists, clergymen, custom house inspectors, daguerreotype artists, engravers, book dealers, book keepers, clerks, dance masters, dentists, druggists, editors, engineers, grocers, inn and hotel keepers, merchants, musicians, ship masters, professors of language and music, physicians, teachers, shop keepers, and U.S. Army personnel.

Thirteen reels of microcopy were read covering the twenty-nine countries in the 1850 South Carolina Federal Census. The information for this book was abstracted and sorted by place of birth, name and age. If an individual is listed in another household, then that head of household is stated below, even if that individual was born in South Carolina.

Every effort has been made to keep the spelling for first and last names as they appear in the census record. The spelling of names is always difficult, and variations do appear for the same surname.


Margaret P. Motes
Newburyport, Massachusetts
January 2005

## MICROCOPY RECORDS:

The 1850 South Carolina Census Reels

| | |
|---|---|
| M432-848 | Abbeville and Anderson Counties |
| M432-849 | Barnwell and Beauford Counties |
| M432-850 | Charleston County |
| M432-851 | Chester, Chesterfield, Colleton and Darlington Counties |
| M432-852 | Edgefield and Fairfield Counties |
| M432-853 | Georgetown and Greenville Counties |
| M432-854 | Horry, Kershaw and Lancaster Counties |
| M432-855 | Laurens and Lexington Counties |
| M432-856 | Marion, Marlboro and Newberry Counties |
| M432-857 | Orangeburg and Pickens Counties |
| M432-858 | Richland and Spartanburg Counties |
| M432-859 | Sumter and Union Counties |
| M432-860 | Williamsburg and York Counties |

The Microcopy used was purchased from American Genealogical Lending Library, Bountiful, Utah.

## ABSTRACT FORMAT:

Last name, first name, age, sex, occupation (if indicated), color, ( - ) all are white unless listed as m for mulatto, birthplace, dwelling #, family #, county. Notes if any apply. See examples below.

Example: **HUNTER, WILLIAM**, 48, M, Brick mason, -, Scotland, 938, 936, SPART. In HH of William White M 50, born SC.

# COUNTY CODES:

Abbreviation, county and the date the census was taken.. Two censuses were recorded in January 1851.

| | |
|---|---|
| ABB: | Abbeville. 20 July to 14 December 1850. |
| AND: | Anderson. Western Division.17 July to 12 Octtober 1850. |
| AND*: | Anderson. Easter Division. 22 July to 19 October 1850. |
| BARN: | Barnwell. 16 July to 22 November 1850. |
| BEAU: | Beaufort, St. Helena Parish: 3 October to 10 December 1850. (Note: last page out of order) |
| BEAU*: | Beaufort, Prince Williams Parish (Whites). 6 September to 16 December 1850. |
| BEAU#: | Beafort, Prince Williams Parish (Free Black). 6 September to 16 December 1850. Pages 35-36) |
| BEAU+: | Beaufort, St. Lukes Parish. 16 September to 16 November 1850. |
| BEAU-: | Beaufort, St. Peters Parish. 12 July to 12 September 1850. |
| CHAS: | Charleston. City of Charleston, Ward 1, Parishes of St. Philips & St. Michael's. 1 August to 16 August 1850. |
| CHAS*: | Charleston. City of Charlteston, Ward 2. The Parish of St. Philips & St. Michael's. 20 August to 18 Auuust 1850. |
| CHAS-: | Charleston. City of Charleston, Parishes of St. Philips and St. Michael's, Ward 4. 10 October to 12 November 1850. |
| CHAS%: | Charleston. Charleston Neck, Parish of St. Philips & St. Michael's. 9 November to 22 December 1850. |
| CHAS#: | Charleston, Parish of St. James Santee. 23 July to 18 August 1850. |
| CHAS!: | Charleston, St. Andrews Parish. 26 August to 18 October 1850. |
| CHAS$: | Charleston. Christ Church Parish. 1 August to 20 September 1850. CHAS & Charleston, Parish of St. |

September 1850. CHAS & Charleston, Parish of St.

Thomas and St. Dennis. November to 16 November 1850.

CHAS^:          Charleston, Parish of St. Johns, Colleton. 13 August to 23
                October 1850.

CHAS-:          Charleston, St. Johns Berkley. 2 September to 12 October
                1850.

CHAS2:          Charleston, St. Stephens Parish. 21 August to 19
                November 1850.

CHAS3:          Charleston, St. James Goosecreek. 25 July to 26 November
                1850.

CHES:           Chester. 22 July and 16 November 1850.

CHFD:           Chesterfield. 30 July to 13 January 1851.

COLL:           Colleton, St. Bartholomew's Parish. 14 August and 25
                December 1850.

COLL*:          Colleton, St. George's Parish. 28 October to 16 November
                1850.

COLL+:          Colleton, St. Paul's Parish. 21 October to 24 December
                1850.

DARL:           Darlington, First Division. 26 July to January 1851.

EDGE:           Edgefield. 11 July to 19 December 1850.

EDGE*:          Edgefield. 23 October to 19 December 1850.

FAIR:           Fairfield. 13 July and 23 November 1850.

GEOR:           Georgetown, City of George Town. 19 August 1850.

GEOR*:          Georgetown, Prince George, Winyaw. 20 August to 22
                August 1850.

GEOR+:          Georgetown, Lower All Saints. 23 August to 23 August
                1850.

GREE:           Greenville. 22 July to 13 December 1850.

| | |
|---|---|
| HORR: | Horry. 24 July and 4 November 1850. |
| KERS: | Kershaw. 19 July and 16 December 1850. |
| LANC: | Lancaster. 11 November to 16 November 1850. |
| LAU: | Laurens. 23 July to 13 December 1850. |
| LEX: | Lexington. 27 July to 13 October 1850. |
| MAR: | Marion. 19 July to 26 November 1850. |
| MARL: | Marlboro. 29 July and 15 October 1850. |
| NEWB: | Newberry. 18 July to 16 November 1850. |
| ORNG: | Orangeburg, between the River Road from Orangeburgh CH to Branchville and Four Hole Swamp. 13 December to 18 January 1851. |
| ORNG*: | Orangeburg, between Santee and Edisto North of Bellville Road. 12 November to 26 December 1850. |
| ORAN+: | Orangeburg, Orangeburg District. 29 July to 25 Dec. 1850. |
| PICK: | Pickens, Western Division. 26 July to 25 December 1850. |
| PICK+: | Pickens, Eastern Division. 19 July to 12 October 1850. |
| RICH: | Richland, Town of Columbia. 3 October to 28 October 1850. |
| RICH+: | Richland. 20 July to 1 October 1850. |
| SPART: | Spartanburg. 15 July to 18 December 1850. |
| SUMT: | Sumter. 19 July to 22 November 1850. |
| UNION: | Union. 17 July to 23 November 1850. |
| UNN+: | Union: 29 October to 21 November 1850. |
| WILL: | Williamsburg. 22 July to 22 November 1850. |
| YORK: | York. 29 July to 22 October 1850. |
| YORK*: | York. 22 July to 10 December 1850. |

# BORN IN ENGLAND - ( 861)

## A

**ABRAHAMS, ELIAS**, 63, M, Merchant, -, England, 78, 72, CHAS-.

**ADLIN, GEORGE**, 28, M, Boot maker, -, England, 391, 355, CHAS. In HH of F.W. Theus, M, 28, born Germany.

**AIMSBERRY, MARY**, 50, F, None listed, -, England, 388, 371, CHAS-. In HH of W.L. Daggett, M, 35, born SC.

**ALAWINE, SARAH**, 34, F, None listed, -, England, 962, 962, ABB.

**ALEXANDER, ALEXANDER**, 53, M, Merchant, -, England, 225, 230, RICH. {Page out of order, follow HH 177/181.}

**ALEXANDER, ANN**, 28, F, None listed, -, England, 65, 64, CHAS*. In HH of Charles Start, M, 35, born Ireland.

**ALEXANDER, CHARLES**, 31, M, Rigger, -, England, 65, 64, CHAS*. In HH of Charles Start, M, 35, born Ireland.

**ALEXANDER, MARY ANN**, 24, F, None listed, -, England, 65, 64, CHAS*. In HH of Charles Start, M, 35, born Ireland.

**AMIEL, FANNY**, 18, F, None listed, -, England, 52, 52, CHAS^. In HH of John Amiel, M, 54, born England.

**AMIEL, JOHN**, 54, M, Blacksmith, -, England, 52, 52, CHAS^.

**ANDERSON, ANN**, 17, F, None listed, -, England, 1115, 1093, CHAS%. In HH of John Anderson, M, 44, born England.

**ANDERSON, FRANCES S.**, 31, F, None listed, -, England, 310, 286, CHAS. In HH of James Anderson, M, 36, born England.

**ANDERSON, JAMES**, 36, M, Clerk, -, England, 310, 286, CHAS.

**ANDERSON, JOHN**, 44, M, Engineer, -, England, 1115, 1093, CHAS%.

**ANDERSON, MARY**, 37, F, None listed, -, England, 1115, 1093, CHAS%. In HH of John Anderson, M, 44, born England.

**ANDERSON, SUSAN**, 12, F, None listed, -, England, 1115, 1093, CHAS%. In HH of John Anderson, M, 44, born England.

**ANDERSON, THOMAS**, 80, M, Planter, -, England, 548, 557, RICH+.

**ASHTON, ANN**, 14, F, None listed, -, England, 846, 826, CHAS-. In HH of William Ashton, M, 38, born England.

**ASHTON, ANN MARGARET**, 58, M, None listed, -, England, 846, 826, CHAS-. In HH of William Ashton, M, 38, born England.

**ASHTON, ELIZABETH**, 39, F, None listed, -, England, 846, 826, CHAS-. In HH of William Ashton, M, 38, born England.

**ASHTON, ELIZABETH**, 12, F, None listed, -, England, 846, 826, CHAS-. In HH of William Ashton, M, 38, born England.

1

ASHTON, MARTHA SCOTT, 55, F, None listed, -, England, 846, 826, CHAS-. In HH of William Ashton, M, 38, born England.

ASHTON, MARY, 16, F, None listed, -, England, 846, 826, CHAS-. In HH of William Ashton, M, 38, born England.

ASHTON, WILLIAM, 38, M, Watch maker, -, England, 846, 826, CHAS-.

ASHTON, WILLIAM, 11, M, None listed, -, England, 846, 826, CHAS-. In HH of William Ashton, M, 38, born England.

ASTON, GEORGE, 29, M, Dairyman, -, England, 222, 199, CHAS*.

ASTON, MARTHA, 26, F, None listed, -, England, 222, 199, CHAS*. In HH of George Aston, M, 29, born England.

ATHERTON, THOMAS, 24, M, Superintending carding machine, -, England, 1628, 1628, EDGE.

AUSTIN, AMBROSE, 25, M, Clerk, -, England, 846, 826, CHAS-. In HH of William Ashton, M, 38, born England.

**B**

BABBAGE, GEORGE F., 31, F, Clerk, -, England, 374, 383, RICH. In HH of Edmund Walsh, M, 28, born England.

BAILY, ROBERT S., 56, M, Physician, -, England, 63, 54, CHAS$.

BALL, ANN G., 40, F, None listed, -, England, 68, 66, CHAS*.

BALLARD, ELIZA, 60, F, None listed, -, England, 219, 196, CHAS*. In HH of Joseph Ballard, M, 49, born MA.

BALLENTINE, MARIA, 25, F, Servant, -, England, 882, 840, CHAS+. In Charleston Hotel.

BALLS, JOHN, 30, M, Labourer, -, England, 201, 201, BEAU+.

BARBER, F.C., 48, M, Broker, -, England, 463, 420, CHAS.

BARING, CHARLES, 75, M, Planter, -, England, 118, 118, COLL+.

BARNES, JAMES, 27, M, Butcher, -, England, 948, 925, CHAS%. Born : London {England}.

BARNES, JANE, 26, F, None listed, -, England, 948, 925, CHAS%. Born : London {England}. In HH of James Barnes, M, 27, born London {England}.

BARNETT, JOHN, 32, M, Merchant, -, England, 267, 272, RICH.

BARNETT, RACHEL, 24, F, None listed, -, England, 267, 272, RICH. In HH of John Barnett, M, 32, born England.

BARRETT, JOHN P., 55, M, MD, -, England, 1773, 1773, ABB.

BARTLEY, THOMAS, 92, M, Farmer, -, England, 84, 84, EDGE*. In HH of Thos. Bartley, M, 57, born NC.

BATTLE, JAMES, 24, M, Clerk, -, England, 728, 708, CHAS-. In HH of Maria Spencer, F, 63, born England.

BAXTER, JOHN W., 27, M, None, -, England, 895, 895, LEX.
BEARDEN, CHARLES, 22, M, Clerk, -, England, 87, 79, CHAS+. In HH of
Thos. Randalls, M, 40, born Ireland.
BEASLEY, C., 35, F, Tailor, -, England, 75, 73, CHAS*.
BEASLEY, JAMES J., 33, M, Comm Merchant., -, England, 115, 107,
CHAS+. In HH of Thomas Gleave, M, 32, born England.
BEASLEY, MARIA, 28, F, None listed, -, England, 75, 73, CHAS*. In HH of
C. Beasley, M, 35, born England.
BEATEY, ELIZABETH, 24, F, None listed, -, England, 195, 179, CHAS*. In
HH of James Nichols, M, 34, born ME.
BEATSEN, DAVID, 42, M, Blacksmith, -, England, 693, 693, SUMT.
BECK, THOMAS, 34, M, Mariner, -, England, 337, 311, CHAS. In HH of
William H. Fowler, M, 38 running Boarding House, born England.
BECO, ANN, 41, F, None listed, -, England, 567, 568, AND*. In HH of
Antwanrn Beco, M, 44, born West Indies.
BEE, CHARLOTTE, 30, F, None listed, -, England, 173, 159, CHAS*. In HH
of John P. Bee, M, 40, born SC.
BELTON, ALICE, 45, F, None listed, -, England, 481, 438, CHAS. In HH of
George Belton, M, 50, born England.
BELTON, GEORGE, 50, M, Tailor, -, England, 481, 438, CHAS.
BIRD, J.S., 53, M, Merchant, -, England, 695, 675, CHAS-.
BLACK, THOMAS, 20, M, Apprentice, -, England, 66, 66, NEWB. In HH of
William Morris 45, M, born TN.
BLACKLEY, JAMES, 17, M, Carpenter, -, England, 387, 351, CHAS. In HH
of Wm. Parker, M, 48, born MA.
BLACKMAN, SARAH, 50, F, None listed, -, England, 299, 283, CHAS-. In
HH of Joseph Blackman, M, 28, born SC.
BLADEN, GASSNELL, 2, M, None listed, -, England, 1144, 1144, DARL. In
HH of Ones Bladen, M, 32, born England.
BLADEN, HANNIBAL, 4, M, None listed, -, England, 1144, 1144, DARL. In
HH of Ones Bladen, M, 32, born England.
BLADEN, LUCY, 24, F, None listed, -, England, 1144, 1144, DARL. In HH of
Ones Bladen, M, 32, born England.
BLADEN, ONES, 32, M, Labourer, -, England, 1144, 1144, DARL.
BLAKE, A., MRS., 22, F, None listed, -, England, 56, 56, CHAS#. In HH of
Mr. Ar. Blake, M, 36, born GA.
BLAKE, DANIEL, 48, M, Planter, -, England, 726, 726, COLL.
BLEASE, ORATIO, 46, M, Painter, -, England, 60, 60, EDGE.
BLUETT, ABSOLUM, 10, M, None listed, -, England, 24, 19, CHAS+. In HH
of John Bluett, M, 45, born England.

3

BLUETT, ELIZABETH, 14, F, None listed, -, England, 24, 19, CHAS+. In HH of John Bluett, M, 45, born England.

BLUETT, JOHN, 45, M, State Constable, -, England, 24, 19, CHAS+.

BLYTHE, JOHN, 17, M, Clerk, -, England, 1022, 1022, UNION. In HH of William Cleveland, M, 27, born SC.

BRACKENRIDGE, ELLENER, 62, F, None listed, -, England, 347, 348, AND*. In HH of Robert Brackenridge, M, 69, born Ireland.

BRENT, JOHN, 21, M, Mariner, -, England, 341, 305, CHAS+. In HH of Jane Hamilton, F, 49, born England.

BRINGLOW, RICHARD, 59, M, Custom House, -, England, 109, 121, CHAS.

BROADFOOT, FRANCES L., 75, F, None listed, -, England, 25, 30, CHAS.

BROCKWELL, WILLIAM H., 29, M, Merchant, -, England, 882, 840, CHAS+. In Charleston Hotel.

BROWN, BENJAMIN, 40, M, Merchant, -, England, 861, 819, CHAS+.

BROWN, E.H., 35, M, Miller, -, England, 1068, 1046, CHAS%.

BROWN, EMMELINE, 25, F, None listed, -, England, 861, 819, CHAS+. In HH of Benjamin Brown, M, 40, born England.

BROWN, JAMES, 31, M, Painter, -, England, 651, 670, RICH.

BROWN, JOHN, 27, M, Seaman, -, England, 326, 301, CHAS. In HH of William Rollins, M, 40, born {-}.

BROWN, MARY H., 30, F, None listed, -, England, 1068, 1046, CHAS%. In HH of E.H. Brown, M, 35, born England.

BRUNSE, JOSEPH B., 26, M, Machinist, -, England, 1675, 1675, EDGE.

BUGGS, THOMAS, 36, M, Pilot, -, England, 15, 15, GEOR.

BULL, WILLIAM, 34, M, Farmer, -, England, 747, 747, GREE.

BURKLEY, CHARLOTTE, 35, F, None listed, -, England, 512, 470, CHAS+. In HH of John Burkley, M, 36, born England.

BURKLEY, JOHN, 36, M, Engineer, -, England, 512, 470, CHAS+.

BURNET, JAMES, 48, M, Farmer, -, England, 31, 31, YORK.

BURNHAM, ELIZA, 55, F, None listed, -, England, 595, 553, CHAS+. In HH of William Burnham, M, 50, born England.

BURNHAM, WILLIAM, 50, M, Locksmith, -, England, 595, 553, CHAS+.

BURROWS, ED., 54, M, Mariner, -, England, 219, 197, CHAS. In HH of A. Fink, M, 30, born Hanover.

BURTON, ELIZA, 47, F, None listed, -, England, 639, 657, RICH.

BURTON, WILLIAM, 26, M, Machinist, -, England, 639, 657, RICH. In HH of Eliza Burton, F, 47, born England.

BURTWHISTLE, AUGUSTA, 34, F, None listed, -, England, 365, 365, ABB. In HH of Alexander Houstonh, M, 72, born SC.

BUSHBY, JOHN, 38, M, Spinner, -, England, 1619, 1619, GREE.

BUSSELL, JOHN, 36, M, Carpenter, -, England, 881, 861, CHAS-. In HH of R. Chrietzberg, M, 36, born SC.

BUTLER, FRANCES, 20, F, None listed, -, England, 821, 801, CHAS-. In HH of August Pelerun, M, 31, born France.

BUTTERFIELD, H.M., 22, F, None listed, -, England, 438, 421, CHAS-. In HH of H.L. Butterfield, M, 35, born VT.

# C

CADLE, HARRIET, 30, F, None listed, -, England, 120, 113, CHAS*.

CAHAL, CATHERINE, 25, F, None listed, -, England, 33, 29, CHAS$. In HH of James Cahal, M, 35, born Ireland.

CARNAGHAM, JOHN, 45, M, Mariner, -, England, 212, 190, CHAS.

CARNAGHAM, MARY, 36, F, None listed, -, England, 212, 190, CHAS. In HH of John Carnagham, M, 45, born England.

CARRERE, CATHARINE, 60, F, None listed, -, England, 856, 833, CHAS%.

CARRINGTON, A., MISS, 18, F, None listed, -, England, 56, 56, CHAS#. In HH of Mr. Ar. Blake, M, 36, born GA.

CARRINGTON, CATHERINE, 40, F, None listed, -, England, 714, 694, CHAS-. In HH of William Carrington, M, 48, born England.

CARRINGTON, WILLIAM, 48, M, Watch maker, -, England, 714, 694, CHAS-.

CARROLL, ALEXANDER, 32, M, Editor, -, England, 592, 609, RICH.

CASH, ESTHER, 21, F, Servant, -, England, 882, 840, CHAS+. In Charleston Hotel.

CASTEN, BRIDGET, 33, F, None listed, -, England, 167, 153, CHAS*. In HH of Lawrence Haberson, M, 38, born Germany.

CHALK, J.G., 27, M, Engineer, -, England, 847, 805, CHAS+.

CHARELL, EDWARD, 28, M, Shopkeeper, -, England, 680, 660, CHAS-.

CHARELL, MARY ANN, 27, F, None listed, -, England, 680, 660, CHAS-. In HH of Edward Charell, M, 28, born England.

CHARLESWORTHE, JOSEPH, 57, M, Merchant, -, England, 22, 22, KERS.

CHARLESWORTHE, M., 61, F, None listed, -, England, 22, 22, KERS. In HH of Joseph Charlesworth, M, 57, born England.

CHEESEBORO, ELIZA, 54, F, None listed, -, England, 423, 381, CHAS.

CHESTER, THOMAS, 51, M, None, -, England, 237, 222, CHAS-. Works in Poor House.

CHILDORE, EDWARD, 28, M, Engineer, -, England, 57, 52, CHAS-. In HH of George Garrett, M, 41, born England.

CHILDORE, MARY, 23, F, None listed, -, England, 57, 52, CHAS-. In HH of George Garrett, M, 41, born England.

5

**CLARK, RICHARD**, 64, M, Pilot, -, England, 517, 467, CHAS.

**CLINTON, CHARLES**, 30, M, Clerk, -, England, 393, 403, RICH. In Hotel.

**CLINTON, CHS. C.**, 30, M, Merchant, -, England, 378, 343, CHAS. In HH of John McMullan, M, 65, born Scotland.

**COBIER, ANN**, 58, F, None listed, -, England, 889, 866, CHAS%. In HH of John J. Lafar, M, 27, born SC.

**COCKEROFT, ABRAM**, 52, M, Carpenter, -, England, 127, 127, BEAU.

**COCKEROFT, LOUSIA**, 19, F, None listed, -, England, 127, 127, BEAU. In HH of Abram Cockeroft, M, 52, born England.

**COCKEROFT, MARY**, 50, F, None listed, -, England, 127, 127, BEAU. In HH of Abram Cockeroft, M, 52, born England.

**COCKEROFT, MARY ANN**, 24, F, None listed, -, England, 127, 127, BEAU. In HH of Abram Cockeroft, M, 52, born England.

**COCKEROFT, ROBERT**, 21, M, None listed, -, England, 127, 127, BEAU. In HH of Abram Cockeroft, M, 52, born England.

**COHEN, AARON N.**, 74, M, Merchant, -, England, 291, 297, RICH.

**COHEN, ELIZABETH**, 50, F, None listed, -, England, 275, 252, CHAS. In HH of Nathan A. Cohen, M, 45, born England.

**COHEN, HENRY S.**, 34, M, Merchant, -, England, 259, 264, RICH.

**COHEN, NATHAN A.**, 45, M, Merchant, -, England, 275, 252, CHAS.

**COHEN, RACHEL**, 61, F, None listed, -, England, 291, 297, RICH. In HH of Aaron N. Cohen, M, 74, born England.

**COHEN, REBECCA**, 22, F, None listed, -, England, 291, 297, RICH. In HH of Aaron N. Cohen, M, 74, born England.

**COHEN, SAMUEL**, 33, M, Merchant, -, England, 291, 297, RICH. In HH of Aaron N. Cohen, M, 74, born England.

**COHEN, SOLOMON A.**, 27, M, Merchant, -, England, 259, 264, RICH. In HH of Henry S. Cohen, M, 34, born England.

**COLCHETT, GEORGE**, 52, M, Merchant., -, England, 525, 484, CHAS+.

**COLE, ANNA**, 30, F, None listed, -, England, 676, 656, CHAS-. In HH of Geo. F. Cole, M, 45, born MD.

**COLE, MARTHA L.**, 30, F, None listed, -, England, 676, 656, CHAS-. In HH of Geo F. Cole, M, 45, born MD.

**COLSON, CHARLES**, 48, M, Shopkeeper, -, England, 731, 689, CHAS+. In HH of Charles Colson, M, 48, born England.

**COMBS, JOHN**, 33, M, Bricklayer, -, England, 421, 421, EDGE.

**COMBS, SARAH**, 42, F, None listed, -, England, 421, 421, EDGE. In HH of John Combs, M, 33 bricklayer/planter, born England.

**CONNOR, CATHERINE**, 13, F, None listed, -, England, 91, 92, RICH. Note: apparently out of dwelling and family order. pg. 3 In HH of James Connor, M, 32, born Ireland.

COPPS, AMELIA, 38, F, None listed, -, England, 216, 193, CHAS*. In HH of John Copps, M, 44, born SC.
CORLY, ELIZABETH, 26, F, None, -, England, 75, 75, LEX. In HH of Jno. Corly, M, 25, born England. Census states that Elizabeth Corly, born New Castle, England.
CORLY, JNO., 24, M, None, -, England, 75, 75, LEX. Census states that Jno. Corly, born New Castle, England.
CORLY, JOSEPH, 22, M, None, -, England, 75, 75, LEX. In HH of Jno. Corly, M, 25, born England. Census states that Joseph Corly, born New Castle, England.
CORLY, MARGARET C., 24, F, None listed, -, England, 76, 76, LEX. In HH of Reubin Corly, M, 38, born England. Census states that Margaret Corly, born New Castle, England.
CORLY, MARY L., 5, F, None listed, -, England, 76, 76, LEX. In HH of Reubin Corly, M, 38, born England. Census states that Mary L.Corly, born New Castle, England.
CORLY, REUBIN, 38, M, Farmer, -, England, 76, 76, LEX. Census states that Reubin Corly, born New Castle, England.
CORLY, RUFUS, 1, M, None listed, -, England, 76, 76, LEX. In HH of Reubin Corly, M, 38, born England. Census states that Rufus Corly, born New Castle, England.
CORNELL, ANN, 9, F, None listed, -, England, 706, 697, CHAS%. In HH of John Cornell, M, 38, born England.
CORNELL, JOHN, 38, M, Engineer, -, England, 706, 697, CHAS%.
CORNELL, JOHN J., 12, M, None listed, -, England, 706, 697, CHAS%. In HH of John Cornell, M, 38, born England.
CORNELL, ROSE, 32, F, None listed, -, England, 706, 697, CHAS%. In HH of John Cornell, M, 38, born England.
CORRANCE, SUSAN, 70, F, None listed, -, England, 512, 470, CHAS+. In HH of John Burkley, M, 36, born England.
COURT, C.M., 33, M, Priv. U.S.A., -, England, 47, 43, CHAS$. In HH of John Ewing, M, 50, born MA.
CRAWFORD, TIMY, 22, M, Slater, -, England, 337, 311, CHAS. In HH of William H. Fowler, M, 38 running Boarding House, born England.
CRAWLEY, JAMES, 39, M, Taylor, -, England, 337, 311, CHAS. In HH of William H. Fowler, M, 38 running boarding house, born England.
CRAWLEY, MICHAEL, 27, M, Taylor, -, England, 337, 311, CHAS. In HH of William H. Fowler, M, 38 running Boarding House, born England.
CREBER, WILLIAM B., 49, M, Waggon maker, -, England, 30, 30, RICH+.
CREIGHTON, SARAH J., 29, F, None listed, -, England, 2398, 2405, EDGE. In HH of William J. Wightman, M, 57, born Scotland.

7

**CREWD, MARY**, 27, F, None listed, -, England, 10, 11, CHAS. In HH of William Crewd, M, 36, sailmaker, born Germany. Mary Crewd, born Liverpool, England.

**CREWS, ABRAHAM**, 37, M, Merchant, -, England, 543, 526, CHAS-.

**CREWS, REBECCA**, 30, F, None listed, -, England, 543, 526, CHAS-. In HH of Abraham Crews, M, 37, born England.

**CROPPER, JOSEPH**, 38, M, Baker, -, England, 18, 17, CHAS$.

**CROPPER, MARY A.**, 30, F, None listed, -, England, 18, 17, CHAS$. In HH of Joseph Cropper, M, 38, born England.

**CROWLY, JNO. S.**, 28, M, Farmer, -, England, 1146, 1146, DARL.

**CROWLY, SUSANNAH**, 25, F, None listed, -, England, 1146, 1146, DARL. In HH of Jno. S. Crowly, M, 28, born England.

**CROWTHER, HANNAH**, 30, F, None listed, -, England, 1285, 1285, ABB. In HH of James Crowther, M, 63, born England.

**CROWTHER, JAMES**, 63, M, None listed, -, England, 1285, 1285, ABB.

**CROWTHER, MARY**, 62, F, None listed, -, England, 1285, 1285, ABB. In HH of James Crowther, M, 63, born England.

**CROWTHER, WILLIAM.**, 36, M, Farmer, -, England, 960, 960, ABB.

**CRUISE, A.M.**, 25, F, None listed, -, England, 14, 14, LANC.

**CULPEPPER, MARTHA E.**, 7, F, None listed, -, England, 1146, 1146, DARL. In HH of Jno. S. Crowly, M, 28, born England.

**CUMMING, JOSEPH**, 35, M, Tailor, -, England, 541, 541, FAIR.

**CUMPSTY, WILLIAM**, 51, M, Machinist, -, England, 1642, 1642, EDGE.

**CUNNING, THOMAS**, 35, M, Rigger, -, England, 153, 136, CHAS. In HH of Edward Candler, M, 50, born MA.

**CURLESS, THOMAS**, 63, M, Baptist Minister, -, England, 2364, 2364, SPART.

**CURLESS, WILLIAM**, 33, M, Baptist Minister, -, England, 2364, 2364, SPART. In HH of Thomas Curless, M, 63, born England.

**CURRY, J.**, 23, M, Priv. U.S.A., -, England, 47, 43, CHAS$. In HH of John Ewing, M, 50, born MA.

**CURTIS, HENRY R.**, 23, M, Physician, -, England, 1, 1, FAIR. In HH of George Leitner, M, 48, born SC.

**CURTIS, MARIA B.**, 30, F, None listed, -, England, 365, 374, RICH. In HH of Franklin Curtis, M, 33, born CT.

# D

**DALLISON, JOS. B.**, 27, M, Baker, -, England, 751, 731, CHAS-.

**DANGERFIELD, RICHARD**, 40, M, Carpenter, -, England, 906, 883, CHAS%.

DARBY, FREDERICK, 36, M, Coppersmith, -, England, 420, 392, CHAS*. In HH of Emma Rogers, F, 22, born England.

DARCY, ROBERT, 45, M, Coach maker, -, England, 294, 278, CHAS-.

DAVENPORT, JOHN, 48, M, Carpenter, -, England, 10, 10, CHAS+.

DAVIES, O., 45, M, Clerk, -, England, 829, 809, CHAS-. In HH of Fisher Day, M, 56, born MA.

DAVIS, CAROLINE, 42, F, None listed, -, England, 563, 579, RICH. In HH of Thomas Davis, M, 40, born England.

DAVIS, CHAS. H., 47, M, None, -, England, 759, 759, KERS.

DAVIS, CHRISTIANNA, 60, F, None listed, -, England, 533, 569, RICH. In HH of John Davis, M, 33, born England.

DAVIS, HARRIET, 35, F, None listed, -, England, 563, 579, RICH. In HH of Thomas Davis, M, 40, born England.

DAVIS, HENRY, 61, M, Merchant, -, England, 28, 23, CHAS+.

DAVIS, JOHN, 34, M, Servant, -, England, 882, 840, CHAS+. In Charleston Hotel.

DAVIS, JOHN, 33, M, Bricklayer, -, England, 533, 569, RICH.

DAVIS, MARY A., 31, F, None listed, -, England, 682, 640, CHAS+. In HH of Thomas Bowman, M, 27, born SC.

DAVIS, THOMAS, 45, M, Shopkeeper, -, England, 21, 21, YORK+.

DAVIS, THOMAS, 40, M, Planter, -, England, 563, 579, RICH.

DAVIS, WILLIAM S., 40, M, Physician, -, England, 403, 403, WILL. In HH of William H. Johnson, M, 30, born SC.

DAWKINS, MARY, 27, F, None listed, -, England, 546, 546, UNION. In HH of Thomas Dawkins, M, 43, born SC.

DAWSON, CAROLINE, 46, F, None listed, -, England, 402, 404, AND. In HH of Joseph Dawson, M, 58, born England.

DAWSON, ELIZABETH, 12, F, None listed, -, England, 402, 404, AND. In HH of Joseph Dawson, M, 58, born England.

DAWSON, FRANKLIN, 7, M, None listed, -, England, 402, 404, AND. In HH of Joseph Dawson, M, 58, born England.

DAWSON, JOSEPH, 58, M, Farmer, -, England, 402, 404, And.

DEAN, MARY, 27, F, None listed, -, England, 1, 1, SPART., born London, England. In HH of H.F. Dean, M, 44, born SC.

DEARSON, JOHN, 49, M, Carpenter, -, England, 278, 278, COLL*.

DECURLE, WILLIAM, 35, M, Painter, -, England, 66, 67, ORNG+. In HH of Daniel Larey - in Hotel.

DELAVAULN, FRANCIS P., 71, M, Clergyman, -, England, 166, 166, COLL.

DELAVAUX, ELIZABETH, 70, F, None listed, -, England, 166, 166, COLL. In HH of Francis P. Delavaux, M, 71, born England.

DELAVAUX, FRANCIS P., 71, M, Clergyman, -, England, 166, 166, COLL.

9

**DENTON, RICHARD**, 48, M, Merchant Tailor, -, England, 447, 447, LAU.

**DEVINE, JAMES**, 25, M, Dragman, -, England, 47, 47, GEOR.

**DICURLE, WILLIAM**, 35, M, Painter, -, England, 66, 67, ORNG+. In HH of Daniel Larey - Hotel.

**DISTAND, ROBERT**, 45, M, Teacher, -, England, 470, 470, WILL. In HH of Willis J. Godwin, M, 47, born NC.

**DOBBINS, HARRIOT**, 5, F, None listed, -, England, 180, 170, CHAS-. In HH of John Dobbins, M, 30, born England.

**DOBBINS, JANE**, 25, F, None listed, -, England, 180, 170, CHAS-. In HH of John Dobbins, M, 30, born England.

**DOBBINS, JOHN**, 30, M, Nail maker, -, England, 180, 170, CHAS-.

**DOBBINS, MARY ANN**, 3, F, None listed, -, England, 180, 170, CHAS-. In HH of John Dobbins, M, 30, born England.

**DOLLARD, R.C.**, 26, M, Merchant, -, England, 562, 562, SUMT.

**DOUGHERTY, ANN**, 42, F, None listed, -, England, 226, 212, CHAS-. In HH of William M. Dougherty, M, 45, born NY.

**DOWNING, PHOEBE**, 30, F, Servant, -, England, 882, 840, CHAS+. In Charleston Hotel.

**DRURY, JOHN**, 44, M, Mariner, -, England, 334, 308, CHAS. In HH of William Bennett, M, 40, born NY.

**DUNJU, HENRY**, 29, M, Stable keeper, -, England, 37, 32, CHAS+.

**DYKES, SAMUEL**, 40, M, Restorature, -, England, 841, 821, CHAS-.

# E

**EARLY, JOHN**, 25, M, None listed, -, England, 254, 228, CHAS*. In HH of James L. Petigrw {sic}, M, 60, born SC.

**EASTON, MARTHA**, 35, F, None listed, -, England, 314, 288, CHAS*. In HH of Geo. L. Easton, M, 41, born RI.

**ELIAS, ELEANOR**, 23, F, None listed, -, England, 249, 254, RICH. In HH of David Elias, M, 35, born Germany.

**ELLWELL, HY, REVD.**, 45, M, Teacher, -, England, 427, 427, DARL.

**ELLWELL, MARY**, 42, F, None listed, -, England, 427, 427, DARL. In HH of Rev. Hy Ellwell, M, 45, born England.

**EMANUEL, N.**, 56, M, Merchant, -, England, 390, 373, CHAS-.

**ENSLOW, ALFRED**, 28, M, Cabinetmaker, -, England, 535, 501, CHAS*.

**ENSLOW, HARRIET**, 20, F, None listed, -, England, 535, 501, CHAS*. In HH of Alfred Enslow, M, 28, born England.

**ENSLOW, J.L.**, 58, M, Cooper, -, England, 278, 252, CHAS*.

**ENSTON, A.**, 27, M, Cabinetmaker, -, England, 80, 74, CHAS-. In HH of Wm. Enston, M, 42, born England.

ENSTON, HANNAH, 41, F, None listed, -, England, 80, 74, CHAS-. In HH of Wm. Enston, M, 42, born England.

ENSTON, WM., 42, M, Cabinetmaker, -, England, 80, 74, CHAS-.

EVANS, JOHN, 24, M, Plasterer, -, England, 312, 296, CHAS-. In HH of Bernard Connely, M, 26, born Ireland.

# F

FANCY, JOHN, 22, M, Baker, -, England, 219, 197, CHAS. In HH of A. Fink, M, 30, born Hanover.

FARBRIDGE, ROBERT, 56, M, Carpenter, -, England, 1220, 1221, FAIR.

FARRAR, ALFRED, 6, M, None listed, -, England, 134, 134, LEX. In HH of Jno. Farrar, M, 35 Mich. Spinner, born England.

FARRAR, JNO., 35, M, Mich. Spinner, -, England, 136, 136, LEX.

FARRAR, SARAH M., 5, F, None listed, -, England, 134, 134, LEX. In HH of Jno. Farrar, M, 35 Mich. Spinner, born England.

FARRAR, SIBLA, 32, F, None listed, -, England, 134, 134, LEX. In HH of Jno. Farrar, M, 35 Mich. Spinner, born England.

FARRAR, WILLIAM, 11, M, None listed, -, England, 134, 134, LEX. In HH of Jno. Farrar, M, 35 Mich. Spinner, born England.

FERGUSON, MARY, 37, F, None listed, -, England, 451, 408, CHAS. In HH of William Ferguson, M, 44, born England.

FERGUSON, MATILDA, 16, F, None listed, -, England, 451, 408, CHAS. In HH of William Ferguson, M, 44, born England.

FERGUSON, WILLIAM, 44, M, Taylor, -, England, 451, 408, CHAS.

FISHER, SAMUEL, 60, M, Shopkeeper, -, England, 832, 812, CHAS-.

FISHER, SAMUEL, 57, M, Planter, -, England, 300, 300, CHAS3.

FISHER, SARAH, 50, F, None listed, -, England, 832, 812, CHAS-. In HH of Samuel Fisher, M, 60, born England.

FITZER, THOMAS, 38, M, Laborer, -, England, 165, 168, Rick+.

FLEMING, JANE, 28, F, None listed, -, England, 79, 71, CHAS+. In HH of Thomas Roberts, M, 44, born England.

FOSTER, ELIZA, 34, F, None listed, -, England, 173, 159, CHAS*. In HH of John P. Bee, M, 40, born SC.

FOSTER, WILLIAM, 60, M, None, -, England, 173, 159, CHAS*. In HH of John P. Bee, M, 40, born SC.

FOWLER, JOSEPH, 28, M, None listed, -, England, 332, 298, CHAS+.

FOWLER, WILLIAM H., 38, M, Boarding House, -, England, 337, 311, CHAS.

FOY, ESTHER, 52, F, None listed, -, England, 150, 150, BEAU.

FRANCES, CAROLINE ANN, 39, F, None listed, -, England, 347, 309,

11

CHAS+. In HH of John Francis, M, 44, born England.

FRANCES, JOHN, 44, M, Sadler, -, England, 347, 309, CHAS+.

FRANCES, JOHN, 25, M, Tailor, -, England, 347, 309, CHAS+. In HH of John Francis, M, 44, born England.

FRANKLIN, JOHN H., 50, M, Planter, -, England, 542, 557, RICH. Date 1850 by name. In Lunatic Asylum.

FRASBROOK, HENRY, 65, M, Tailor, -, England, 477, 477, ABB.

FREEMAN, WILLIAM, 65, M, Master mariner, -, England, 83, 93, CHAS.

FRILLINGS, EDWARD, 31, M, Merchant, -, England, 232, 237, RICH.

FRYER, BLANCOUIE, 14, M, Student of law, -, England, 224, 202, CHAS. In HH of Helena Fryer, F, 40, born England.

FRYER, GREVILLE, 16, M, Student of law, -, England, 224, 202, CHAS. In HH of Helena Fryer, F, 40, born England.

FRYER, HELEN A., 7, F, None listed, -, England, 224, 202, CHAS. In HH of Helena Fryer, F, 40, born England.

FRYER, HELENA, 40, F, None listed, -, England, 224, 202, CHAS.

FRYER, JOHN L., 13, M, None listed, -, England, 224, 202, CHAS. In HH of Helena Fryer, F, 40, born England.

FRYER, OTHO, 9, M, None listed, -, England, 224, 202, CHAS. In HH of Helena Fryer, F, 40, born England.

FRYER, WILLIAM, 18, M, Student of law, -, England, 224, 202, CHAS. In HH of Helena Fryer, F, 40, born England.

FURSE, JAMES SENR., 76, M, Plant., -, England, 472, 472, BARN.

## G

GAGE, HENRY, 29, M, Mariner, -, England, 62, 56, CHAS-. In HH of James Gage, M, 32, born England.

GAGE, JAMES, 32, M, Master Mariner, -, England, 62, 56, CHAS-.

GAMBLE, R., 48, M, None listed, -, England, 29, 25, CHAS$. In HH of Lucien Perouonet, M, 35, born France.

GAMBLETON, JAMES, 27, M, Steward, -, England, 326, 301, CHAS. In HH of William Rollins, M, 40, born {-}.

GARCIDE, K., 21, M, Boot maker, -, England, 47, 47, KERS. In HH of Thos. Wilson, M, 28 born Ireland.

GARRETT, GEORGE, 41, M, Shoemaker, -, England, 57, 52, CHAS-.

GARRETT, PHILADELPHIA, 35, F, None listed, -, England, 57, 52, CHAS-. In HH of George Garrett, M, 41, born England.

GARRISON, FRANCES, 45, F, None listed, -, England, 837, 841, AND. In HH of Henry Garrison, M, 26, born SC.

GATES, THOMAS, 51, M, Butcher, -, England, 1139, 1118, CHAS%.

GIBSON, HENRY, 33, M, Farmer, -, England, 888, 888, GREE.
GIBSON, SAML., 67, M, Baptist Clergyman, -, England, 548, 548, GREE.
GIBSON, WILLIAM, 39, M, Blacksmith, -, England, 853, 853, GREE.
GILES, CHARLES, 33, M, Planter, -, England, 290, 291, ORNG+.
GILL, GEO., 27, M, Teacher, -, England, 721, 701, CHAS-. In Boarding
House.
GLEAVE, THOMAS, 32, M, Tavern Keeper, -, England, 115, 107, CHAS+.
GOLDSMITH, HENRY, 45, M, Clerk, -, England, 243, 218, CHAS*. In HH of
Morris Goldsmith, M, 64, born England.
GOLDSMITH, JOHN, 40, M, None, -, England, 237, 222, CHAS-. Poor
House.
GOLDSMITH, MORRIS, 64, M, U.S. Deputy Marshall, -, England, 243, 218,
CHAS*.
GOODWIN, GEO. M., 30, M, Clerk, -, England, 1288, 1288, DARL.
GOTHAM, THOMAS, 40, M, Laborer, -, England, 1154, 1133, CHAS%. In
HH of Andrew Gray, M, 50, born Scotland.
GOULDSMITH, RICHARD, 60, M, Cabinetmaker, -, England, 855, 813,
CHAS+.
GRAHAM, ELIZABETH, 10, F, None listed, -, England, 332, 298, CHAS+. In
HH of Joseph Fowler, M, 28, born England.
GRAHAM, JOSEPH, 4, M, None listed, -, England, 332, 298, CHAS+. In HH
of Joseph Fowler, M, 28, born England.
GRAHAM, MARY, 24, F, None listed, -, England, 332, 298, CHAS+. In HH
of Joseph Fowler, M, 28, born England.
GRAHAM, WILLIAM, 8, M, None listed, -, England, 332, 298, CHAS+. In
HH of Joseph Fowler, M, 28, born England.
GRAMHILL, JOHN, 52, M, Farmer, -, England, 632, 632, KERS.
GRAVELY, CURAM, 24, M, Clerk, -, England, 294, 271, CHAS. In HH of
John Gravely, M, 45, born England.
GRAVELY, JOHN, 45, M, Merchant, -, England, 294, 271, CHAS.
GREEN, JOHN C., 31, M, Merchant, -, England, 403, 414, RICH.
GREEN, RACHEL L., 23, F, None listed, -, England, 403, 414, RICH. In HH
of John C. Green, M, 31, born England.
GRIFFETH, A., 44, F, None listed, -, England, 438, 421, CHAS-. In Pavillion
Hotel.
GRIMKE, EMMA, 25, F, None listed, -, England, 12, 12, CHAS*. In HH of
Sarah Grimke, F, 48, born SC.
GRIMLINTON, MARY, 47, F, None listed, -, England, 484, 480, CHAS%.
GUTHREY, ELIZABETH, 10, F, None listed, -, England, 445, 404, CHAS+.
In HH of Mary Manson, F, 65, born SC.
GUTHREY, MARGARET, 12, F, None listed, -, England, 445, 404, CHAS+.

In HH of Mary Manson, F, 65, born SC.

**GYLES, MARY R.**, 70, F, None listed, -, England, 297, 274, CHAS. In HH of John A. Gyles, M, 36, born SC.

# H

**HADEN, JOSEPH**, 76, M, None listed, -, England, 2337, 2337, GREE. In HH of O.H. Wells, M, 46, born MA.

**HALE, FRANCES**, 60, F, None listed, -, England, 233, 220, CHAS+. In HH of W. Blamyer Hale, M, 60, born SC.

**HALL, GEORGE**, 35, M, Overseer, -, England, 342, 348, RICH.

**HALLIDAY, DUNCAN**, 10, M, None listed, -, England, 641, 600, CHAS+. In HH of William Halliday, M, 30, born Scotland.

**HALLIDAY, JANE**, 8, F, None listed, -, England, 641, 600, CHAS+. In HH of William Halliday, M, 30, born Scotland.

**HALLIDAY, SUSAN**, 28, F, None listed, -, England, 641, 600, CHAS+. In HH of William Halliday, M, 30, born Scotland.

**HAMASON{?}, E.T.**, 28, M, Schoolmaster, -, England, 558, 558, Horr.

**HAMBLETON, ANN**, 30, F, None listed, -, England, 476, 442, CHAS*. In HH of William N. Hambleton, M, 30, born Ireland.

**HAMILTON, JANE**, 49, F, None listed, -, England, 341, 305, CHAS+.

**HAMSON, ROBERT**, 22, M, Machinest, -, England, 346, 308, CHAS+. In Boarding House.

**HARLEY, J.**, 22, M, Blacksmith, -, England, 23, 23, NEWB. In HH of J. Wilson 33, M, Hotel Keeper, born SC.

**HARLY, FRED**, 35, M, Cabinetmaker, -, England, 2625, 2625, SPART.

**HARPY, ELIZABETH**, 53, F, None listed, -, England, 220, 198, CHAS. In HH of Taba. Scott, F, 45, born MA.

**HARRIS, ELIZABETH**, 60, F, None listed, -, England, 275, 252, CHAS. In HH of Nathan A. Cohen, M, 45, born England.

**HARRIS, JANE**, 31, F, None listed, -, England, 62, 63, RICH. In HH of Zachariah Harris, M, 35, born SC.

**HARRISON, BARTHOLOMEW**, 27, M, Shoemaker, -, England, 167, 171, RICH.

**HARRISON, ELLEN**, 27, F, None listed, -, England, 167, 171, RICH. In HH of Bartholonew Harrison, M, 27, born England.

**HART, ANN S.**, 28, F, None listed, -, England, 373, 382, RICH. In HH of James Hart, M, 34, born England.

**HART, BELLA**, 87, F, None listed, -, England, 724, 715, CHAS%. In HH of Samuel Hart, Sr., M, 45, born SC.

**HART, JAMES**, 34, M, Merchant, -, England, 373, 382, RICH.

HART, MARY, 54, F, None listed, -, England, 1902, 1902, SUMT.
HEMMINGWAY, ANN, 26, F, None listed, -, England, 948, 948, YORK. In HH of William Hemmingway, M, 54, born England.
HEMMINGWAY, HELEN, 23, F, None listed, -, England, 948, 948, YORK. In HH of William Hemmingway, M, 54, born England.
HEMMINGWAY, HENRIETTA, 51, F, None listed, -, England, 948, 948, YORK. In HH of William Hemmingway, M, 54, born England.
HEMMINGWAY, WILLIAM, 54, M, Plasterer, -, England, 948, 948, YORK.
HENSON, HENRY, 29, M, Laborer, -, England, 184, 167, CHAS. In Boarding House.
HERIOT, BATHESIME, 70, F, None listed, -, England, 41, 41, CHAS*. In HH of Octavis B. Heriot, M, 35, born SC.
HERRIOTT, JOHN R., 47, M, Treasurer of Gas Co., -, England, 232, 207, CHAS*.
HIGMAN, JOHN W., 32, M, Shoemaker, -, England, 165, 169, RICH.
HIGMAN, MARY B., 26, F, None listed, -, England, 165, 169, RICH. In HH of John W. Higman, M, 32, born England.
HILL, EDMOND, 26, M, Merchant, -, England, 2215, 2218, EDGE. In HH of Samuel C. Scott, M, 43, born SC.
HILL, EDWIN, 21, M, Carpenter, -, England, 2195, 2202, EDGE. In HH of James Hill, M, 44, born England.
HILL, ELIZABETH, 44, F, None listed, -, England, 2195, 2202, EDGE. In HH of James Hill, M, 44, born England.
HILL, JAMES, 45, M, Carpenter, -, England, 2195, 2202, EDGE.
HOBBS, MARY ANN, 30, F, None listed, -, England, 409, 392, CHAS-. In HH of William Hobbs, M, 45, born England.
HOBBS, WILLIAM, 45, M, Seedsman & Gardner, -, England, 409, 392, CHAS-.:
HOBBS, WILLIAM, 13, M, None listed, -, England, 409, 392, CHAS-. In HH of William Hobbs, M, 45, born England.
HODGES, WILLIAM, 43, M, Baker, -, England, 490, 448, CHAS+.
HODGESON, ELIZ, 30, F, None listed, -, England, 481, 439, CHAS+. In HH of Elizabeth Hodgeson, F, 55, born England.
HODGESON, ELIZABETH, 55, F, None listed, -, England, 481, 439, CHAS+.
HODGESON, MARY, 28, F, None listed, -, England, 481, 439, CHAS+. In HH of Elizabeth Hodgeson, F, 55, born England.
HOLT, MARY, 34, F, None listed, -, England, 143, 134, CHAS+. In HH of Thomas Holt, M, 32, born England.
HOLT, RACHEL, 8, F, None listed, -, England, 143, 134, CHAS+. In HH of Thomas Holt, M, 32, born England.
HOLT, SARAH, 6, F, None listed, -, England, 143, 134, CHAS+. In HH of

15

Thomas Holt, M, 32, born England.

HOLT, THOMAS, 32, M, Gass fitter, -, England, 143, 134, CHAS+.

HOPE, EDWARD, 25, M, Merchant, -, England, 393, 403, RICH. In Hotel.

HOPKINS, ANN, 49, F, None listed, -, England, 1752, 1757, EDGE. In HH of Edward Hopkins, M, 56, born England.

HOPKINS, EDWARD, 56, M, Taylor, -, England, 1752, 1757, EDGE.

HOPKINS, EDWIN, 26, M, Clerk in store, -, England, 1752, 1757, EDGE. In HH of Edward Hopkins, M, 56, born England.

HOPKINS, EMMA, 21, F, None listed, -, England, 247, 225, CHAS. In HH of James Hopkins, M, 28, born England.

HOPKINS, JAMES, 28, M, Sadler, -, England, 247, 225, CHAS.

HOPKINS, MARY ANN, 24, F, None listed, -, England, 247, 225, CHAS. In HH of James Hopkins, M, 28, born England.

HOPKINSON, EDWARD, 27, M, Baker, -, England, 211, 197, CHAS-. In HH of Jacob Small, M, 30, born Germany.

HOPLEY, GEO. A., 38, M, Merchant, -, England, 126, 118, CHAS*.

HORSEY, EMILIE, 26, F, None listed, -, England, 434, 393, CHAS+.

HUGHES, SARAH, 45, F, None listed, -, England, 856, 814, CHAS+. In HH of Thomas Hughes, M, 50, born England.

HUGHES, THOMAS, 50, M, Cabinetmaker, -, England, 856, 814, CHAS+.

HUGHES, WILLIAM, 22, M, Laborer, -, England, 1197, 1176, CHAS%. In Boarding House.

HYAMS, LOUISA, 17, F, None listed, -, England, 791, 771, CHAS-.

HYMAN, ELIZA, 62, F, None listed, -, England, 642, 660, RICH. In HH of Lipman T. Levin, M, 32, born SC.


I

INGRAHAM, JOHN, 64, M, Farmer, -, England, 1593, 1593, YORK.

IVES, FREDERICK, 42, M, Tailor, -, England, 4, 4, ABB.


J

JACKS, ANN, 47, F, None listed, -, England, 314, 289, CHAS. In HH of Frederick A. Jacks, M, 54, born England.

JACKS, FREDERICK A., 54, M, Ship wright, -, England, 314, 289, CHAS.

JACKS, GEORGE, 34, M, Carpenter, -, England, 314, 289, CHAS. In HH of Frederick A. Jacks, M, 54, born England.

JACKSON, E.H., 46, M, Merchant, -, England, 882, 840, CHAS+. In Charleston Hotel.

JACKSON, JOHN, 21, M, Labourer, -, England, 34, 34, COLL. In HH of E.W.C. Snipes, M, 50, Planter, born SC.

JACKSON, JOHN B., 26, M, Engineer, -, England, 393, 403, RICH. In Hotel.

JACKSON, THOMAS, 50, M, Coach maker, -, England, 778, 778, ABB.

JACOBI, NATHANIEL, 22, M, Merchant, -, England, 694, 674, CHAS-. In HH of W.J. Jacobi, M, 53, born Prussia.

JACOBS, D., 27, M, Jeweler, -, England, 798, 778, CHAS-.

JACOBS, D., 25, M, Shopkeeper, -, England, 404, 377, CHAS*. In HH of Sarah A. Motte, F, 63, born SC.

JAMISON, DAVID, 40, M, Farmer, -, England, 368, 369, ORNG+.

JEFFREYS, JAMES C., 49, M, Merchant, -, England, 13, 13, YORK+.

JENKINS, JOHN, 25, M, Laborer, -, England, 166, 148, CHAS.

JENKINSON, CHARLES, 28, M, Mariner, -, England, 249, 234, CHAS+. In HH of John Brown, M, 36, born Ireland.

JLEFFE, CHARLES, 30, M, Ladies shoemaker, -, England, 422, 394, CHAS*.

JOBLIN, JOSEPH, 38, M, Tanner, -, England, 74, 74, LEX. In HH of Thos. Wilson, M, 40, born SC. Census states that Joseph Joblin, born New Castle, England.

JOHNSON, BENJN., 52, M, Umbrella maker, -, England, 760, 740, CHAS-.

JOHNSON, CHS. W., 44, M, Mariner, -, England, 362, 333, CHAS. In Boarding House.

JOHNSON, ELIZABETH, 22, F, None listed, -, England, 760, 740, CHAS-. In HH of Benj. Johnson, M, 52, born England.

JOHNSON, HANNAH, 58, F, None listed, -, England, 760, 740, CHAS-. In HH of Benj. Johnson, M, 52, born England.

JOHNSON, JOHN, 15, M, Clerk, -, England, 760, 740, CHAS-. In HH of Benj. Johnson, M, 52, born England.

JOHNSON, THOMAS, 22, M, Plasterer, -, England, 223, 199, CHAS*. In HH of Elizabeth Lawrence, F, 42, born SC.

JOHNSON, W.C., 34, M, Painter, -, England, 13, 13, NEWB.

JONES, ANN, 29, F, None listed, -, England, 700, 700, WILL. In HH of Daniel Jones, M, 45, born England.

JONES, DANIEL, 45, M, Taylor, -, England, 700, 700, WILL.

JONES, EDWARD, 50, M, None listed, -, England, 466, 424, CHAS+.

JONES, J.W., 29, M, Gardner, -, England, 1113, 1091, CHAS%.

JONES, JAMES, 40, M, Tailor, -, England, 57, 58, ORNG+.

JONES, JAMES W., 30, M, Gardner, -, England, 1219, 1198, CHAS%.

JONES, JOHN, 54, M, Shoemaker, -, England, 73, 65, CHAS+.

JONES, JOHN, 50, M, Teacher, -, England, 299, 299, BEAU*. In HH of Benjamin Godley, M, 58, born SC.

JONES, JOHN, 30, M, Tailor, -, England, 487, 445, CHAS+.

JONES, MARY, 48, F, None listed, -, England, 73, 65, CHAS+. In HH of

John Jones, M, 54, born England.

**JONES, MARY**, 40, F, Stewardess, -, England, 326, 301, CHAS. On Steam Ship Southerner.

**JONES, MARY J.**, 8, F, None listed, -, England, 1113, 1091, CHAS%. In HH of J.W. Jones, M, 29, born England.

**JONES, PHOEBE**, 26, F, None listed, -, England, 487, 445, CHAS+. In HH of John Jones, M, 30, born England.

**JONES, REBECCA**, 29, F, None listed, -, England, 1219, 1198, CHAS%. In HH of James W. Jones, M, 30, born England.

**JONES, REBECCA**, 26, F, None listed, -, England, 1113, 1091, CHAS%. In HH of J.W. Jones, M, 29, born England.

**JONES, SUSAN**, 50, F, None listed, -, England, 237, 222, CHAS-. Poor House.

**JONES, THOMAS**, 56, M, Farmer, -, England, 1026, 1026, NEWB.

**JONES, THOMAS G.**, 20, M, Mariner, -, England, 341, 305, CHAS+. In HH of Jane Hamilton, F, 49, born England.

**JONES, THOMAS L.**, 50, M, Laborer, -, England, 1255, 1255, YORK.

**JORDAN, EDWARD**, 34, M, Cooper, -, England, 1197, 1176, CHAS%. In Boarding House.

**JORDAN, JAMES**, 50, M, Miller, -, England, 1197, 1176, CHAS%. In Boarding House.

**JORDAN, W. MEYER**, 32, M, Cooper, -, England, 1197, 1176, CHAS%. In Boarding House.

**JUDD, CECELIA**, 28, F, None listed, -, England, 469, 435, CHAS*. In HH of Samuel Judd, M, 25, born England.

**JUDD, SAMUEL**, 24, M, Clerk, -, England, 469, 435, CHAS*.

**JUDGEE, PETER**, 14, M, Cutler, -, England, 318, 292, CHAS+. In HH of Charles Judgee, M, 39, born Italy.

# K

**KAIN, ROBT.**, 43, M, Mariner, -, England, 217, 195, CHAS.

**KEEFE, ALICE**, 16, F, None listed, -, England, 403, 414, RICH. In HH of John C. Green, M, 31, born England.

**KEMP, ROBERT**, 28, M, Moulder, -, England, 1032, 1010, CHAS%.

**KENNEDY, FLORANCE**, 26, F, Servant, -, England, 310, 286, CHAS. In HH of James Anderson, M, 36, born England.

**KERRISON, CHARLES**, 35, M, Merchant, -, England, 336, 310, CHAS*.

**KERRISON, MARY**, 40, F, None listed, -, England, 336, 310, CHAS*. In HH of Charles Kerrison, M, 35, born England.

**KILGORE, HARRIET E.**, 21, F, None listed, -, England, 1147, 1147, DARL.

In HH of James Kilgore, M, 44, born England.
KILGORE, JAMES, 44, M, Farmer, -, England, 1147, 1147, DARL.
KILGORE, JNO. W., 17, M, None listed, -, England, 1147, 1147, DARL. In HH of James Kilgore, M, 44, born England.
KILGORE, REBECCA, 41, F, None listed, -, England, 1147, 1147, DARL. In HH of James Kilgore, M, 44, born England.
KILGORE, SAML. H., 20, M, None listed, -, England, 1147, 1147, DARL. In HH of James Kilgore, M, 44, born England.
KING, J., JR., 58, M, Rail Road Dept., -, England, 913, 893, CHAS-.
KINGDOM, THOMAS, 52, M, Tailor, -, England, 237, 222, CHAS-. Works in Poor House.
KINGLEY, MARTHA, 55, F, None listed, -, England, 132, 123, CHAS-.
KINGSMORE, AGNESS M., 56, F, None listed, -, England, 766, 766, ABB.
KINLOCH, CHARLOTTE, 50, F, None listed, -, England, 161, 152, CHAS+. In HH of George Kinloch, M, 65, born England.
KINLOCH, GEORGE, 65, M, Merchant, -, England, 161, 152, CHAS+.
KITTERSON, ELIZABETH, 28, F, None listed, -, England, 98, 99, RICH+. In HH of Richard Kitterson, M, 31, born England.
KITTERSON, RICHARD, 31, M, Carpenter, -, England, 98, 99, RICH+.
KNOWLES, E., 30, F, None listed, -, England, 851, 831, CHAS-.
KRAFT, HESTER, 32, F, None listed, -, England, 9, 9, NEWB. In HH of J.M. Kraft 40, M, born Germany.

## L

LAMBERT, CHARLES, 40, M, None listed, -, England, 882, 840, CHAS+. In Charleston Hotel.
LAMBERT, MARY, 3, F, None listed, -, England, 882, 840, CHAS+. In Charleston Hotel.
LAMLPIER, CHARLES, 33, M, Carriage maker, -, England, 303, 287, CHAS-. In HH of Austides Bristol, M, 32, born CT.
LANGFORD, H., 26, M, Seaman, -, England, 326, 301, CHAS. On Steam Ship Southerner.
LAWTON, HAGUE, 62, M, None listed, -, England, 317, 317, ABB.
LAZARUS, P.Y., 54, F, None listed, -, England, 879, 837, CHAS+. In HH of Joshua Lazarus, M, 54, born SC.
LEA, WILLIAM P., 55, M, Pilot, -, England, 34, 42, CHAS., born London, England.
LEAMAN, DAVID, 12, M, None listed, -, England, 411, 370, CHAS+. In HH of Jeannet Leaman, F, 40, born England.
LEAMAN, JEANNET, 40, F, None listed, -, England, 411, 370, CHAS+.

19

LEAMAN, LEONARD, 16, M, Carpenter, -, England, 411, 370, CHAS+. In HH of Jeannet Leaman, F, 40, born England.

LEBLEARY, ANN, 45, F, None listed, -, England, 84, 78, CHAS-. In HH of Eleanor Dubois, F, 60, born Ireland.

LEE, ANN, 60, F, None listed, -, England, 38, 38, CHAS*. In HH of W.W. Smith, M, 40, born SC.

LEE, ANN, 39, F, None listed, -, England, 143, 131, CHAS*.

LEONARD, JANE, 21, F, None listed, -, England, 210, 284, CHAS*. In HH of Susan H. Service, F, 63, born England.

LEVIN, EMANUEL, 50, M, Auctioneer, -, England, 542, 557, RICH. Date 1839 by name. In Lunatic Asylum.

LEVIN, JACOB, 45, M, Merchant, -, England, 302, 308, RICH.

LEVINE, MAURICE, 34, M, Clerk, -, England, 26, 31, CHAS. In HH of Moses Levy, M, 45 tavern keeper, born SC. Maurice Levine born London, England.

LEVY, L.L., 45, M, Merchant, -, England, 869, 827, CHAS+.

LEVY, LEWIS, 45, M, Merchant, -, England, 205, 209, RICH.

LEVY, POLLY, 66, F, None listed, -, England, 27, 22, CHAS+. In HH of Isaac Woolfe, M, 68, born England.

LEWIS, ISAAC, 76, M, Merchant, -, England, 580, 538, CHAS+.

LIMEHOUSE, ROBERT, 75, M, None listed, -, England, 263, 237, CHAS*.

LINDSAY, ANN, 29, F, None listed, -, England, 337, 302, CHAS+. In HH of John Lindsay, M, 30, born England.

LINDSAY, JOHN, 30, M, Painter, -, England, 337, 302, CHAS+.

LIPMAN, ABRAHAM, 72, M, Merchant, -, England, 404, 377, CHAS*. In HH of Sarah A. Motte, F, 63, born SC.

LOCKER, THOMAS, 50, M, Mariner, -, England, 341, 305, CHAS+. In HH of Jane Hamilton, F, 49, born England.

LOCKWOOD, WILLIAM, 42, M, Tailor, -, England, 11, 11, SPART.

LOGAN, WILLIAM, 75, M, Librarian, -, England, 827, 810, CHAS%.

LOMAS, JOHN, 50, M, Engineer, -, England, 886, 896, RICH+.

LOMAS, MARGARET, 35, F, None listed, -, England, 886, 896, RICH+. In HH of John Lomas, M, 50, born England.

LONG, BENJAMIN, 21, M, Laborer, -, England, 457, 415, CHAS+. In HH of James Karvin, M, 30, born Ireland.

LONG, JOSHUA, 32, M, None listed, -, England, 557, 557, HORR.

LORYEA, ABRAHAM, 11, M, None listed, -, England, 263, 248, CHAS-. In HH of Aaron Loryea, M, 29, born Russia.

LORYEA, GODFREY, 13, M, None listed, -, England, 263, 248, CHAS-. In HH of Aaron Loryea, M, 29, born Russia.

LUCAS, BENJAMIN, 33, M, Bricklayer, -, England, 438, 407, CHAS*. In HH of John Lucas, M, 35, born England.

**LUCAS, ELLEN**, 60, F, None listed, -, England, 1106, 1083, CHAS-. In Charleston Orphan House.

**LUCAS, JOHN**, 35, M, Bricklayer, -, England, 438, 407, CHAS*.

# M

**MACK, JOHN**, 25, M, Merchant, -, England, 376, 359, CHAS-.

**MAGUIRE, MARGARET**, 35, F, None listed, -, England, 192, 176, CHAS*. In HH of Laura F. DeCamp, F, 66, born St. Domingo.

**MAIDLEY, ELIZABETH**, 20, F, None listed, -, England, 1213, 1192, CHAS%. In HH of George A. Trenholm, M, 44, born SC.

**MALONE, THOMAS W.**, 43, M, Atty at Law, -, England, 127, 118, CHAS-.

**MANIFOLD, EDWARD M.**, 22, M, Merchant, -, England, 39, 47, CHAS. In Boarding House.

**MARCHANT, JOHN**, 31, M, Saddler, -, England, 58, 59, ORNG+.

**MARSHAL, JOHN**, 48, M, Brick maker, -, England, 223, 223, CHAS%.

**MARSHAL, RUTH**, 36, F, None listed, -, England, 253, 231, CHAS. In HH of John T. Marshal, M, 48, born Scotland.

**MARSHALL, CHARLOTTE**, 80, F, None listed, -, England, 620, 638, RICH.

**MARSHALL, JOHN F.**, 60, M, Merchant, -, England, 433, 444, RICH.

**MARSHALL, MELLEN**, 45, M, Laborer, -, England, 237, 222, CHAS-. Poor House.

**MARTIN, ELIZA**, 54, F, None listed, -, England, 97, 95, CHAS*.

**MARTIN, J.**, 32, M, Cooper, -, England, 379, 344, CHAS. In HH of N.R. Schineder, M, 32, born Germany.

**MARTIN, THOMAS**, 19, M, Clerk, -, England, 261, 246, CHAS-. In HH of Isaac Martin, M, 27, born Ireland.

**MARTIN, WILLIAM**, 14, M, Clerk, -, England, 261, 246, CHAS-. In HH of Isaac Martin, M, 27, born Ireland.

**MASTERMAN, WILLIAM**, 46, M, Watchmaker, -, England, 303, 287, CHAS-. In HH of Austides Bristol, M, 32, born CT.

**MATHESEN, MARY**, 50, F, None listed, -, England, 323, 297, CHAS*. In HH of William S. Palmer, M, 30, born SC.

**MATHEWS, W.**, 32, M, Farmer, -, England, 708, 708, Horr.

**MATTHEWS, JOSEPH**, 46, M, Superintendent State Arsenal Academy, -, England, 595, 612, RICH.

**MAYFOUSE, LUCRETIA**, 50, F, None listed, -, England, 658, 617, CHAS+. In HH of William C. Mann, M, 30, born SC.

**MAYS, JAMES**, 70, M, Farmer, -, England, 848, 848, GREE.

**MCCARY, WILLIAM**, 22, M, Carpenter, -, England, 333, 333, GREE. In HH of John W. Hodges, M, 39, born SC.

**MCCLAIN, MARY,** 50, F, None listed, -, England, 1021, 998, CHAS%. In HH of William McClain, M, 50, born England.

**MCCLAIN, WILLIAM,** 50, M, Farmer, -, England, 1021, 998, CHAS%.

**MCCOHEN, LAZARUS,** 26, M, Student, -, England, 1, 1, FAIR. In HH of George Leitner, M, 48, born SC.

**MCCONNELL, SAMUEL,** 35, M, Laborer, -, England, 92, 93, RICH. Note: Apparently out of order, pg. 3.

**MCCRADY, MARY ANN,** 70, F, None listed, -, England, 993, 972, CHAS-.

**MCDANALA, A.E.,** 41, M, School Teacher, -, England, 91, 91, AND*.

**MCDONALD, ANN J.,** 50, F, None listed, -, England, 2394, 2398, EDGE. In HH of John E. McDonald, M, 60, born CT.

**MCFRE, CATHERINE,** 42, F, None listed, -, England, 540, 555, RICH.

**MCGINNIS, HUGH,** 65, M, None listed, -, England, 1501, 1501, YORK.

**MCGINNIS, NANCY,** 60, F, None listed, -, England, 1501, 1501, YORK. In HH of Hugh McGinnis, M, 65, born England.

**MCGREGOR, PETER G.,** 36, M, Druggist, -, England, 362, 371, RICH.

**MCKUON, PETER,** 7, M, None listed, -, England, 38, 34, CHAS$. In HH of Mary McKuon, F, 40, born Ireland.

**MCNEILL, ROBERT,** 23, M, Clerk, -, England, 236, 211, CHAS*.

**MCNELLY, GEORGE,** 17, M, Clerk, -, England, 228, 214, CHAS-. In HH of Mary Roddy, F, 60, born Ireland.

**MEALES, EDWARD,** 30, F, Mariner, -, England, 219, 197, CHAS. In HH of A. Fink, M, 30, born Hanover.

**MEALES, GEORGE,** 40, M, Mariner, -, England, 219, 197, CHAS. In HH of A. Fink, M, 30, born Hanover.

**MEANEY, JOHN,** 45, M, Mariner, -, England, 357, 329, CHAS. In HH of E. Groves, F, 50, runs boarding house, born SC.

**MERRIMAN, CATHARINE,** 20, F, None listed, -, England, 105, 105, GEOR. In HH of J.M. Merriman, M, 28, born SC.

**MESDORFF, MARY,** 40, F, None listed, -, England, 449, 416, CHAS*. In HH of Jacob Mesdorff, M, 50, born Denmark.

**METZLER, CAROLINE,** 28, F, None listed, -, England, 481, 438, CHAS. In HH of George Belton, M, 50, born England.

**METZLER, LOUISA,** 18, F, None listed, -, England, 481, 438, CHAS. In HH of George Belton, M, 50, born England.

**MEYER, HANNAH,** 48, F, None listed, -, England, 419, 378, CHAS+. In HH of Frederick C. Meyer, M, 54, born Germany.

**MEYER, JACOB,** 21, M, Merchant, -, England, 419, 378, CHAS+. In HH of Frederick C. Meyer, M, 54, born Germany.

**MEYER, JANE,** 24, F, None listed, -, England, 419, 378, CHAS+. In HH of

Frederick C. Meyer, M, 54, born Germany.
**MEYER, REBECCA**, 31, F, None listed, -, England, 419, 378, CHAS+. In HH of Frederick C. Meyer, M, 54, born Germany.
**MEYRS, J.J.**, 27, M, Clerk, -, England, 396, 358, CHAS+.
**MIDDLETON, ANN**, 25, F, None listed, -, England, 195, 178, CHAS. In HH of F. Middleton, M, 30, born England.
**MIDDLETON, F.**, 30, M, Master mariner, -, England, 195, 178, CHAS.
**MIDDLETON, L.**, 51, M, Overseer, -, England, 37, 33, CHAS$.
**MIDDLETON, PHOEBE**, 60, F, None listed, -, England, 37, 33, CHAS$. In HH of L. Middleton, M, 51, born England.
**MILLER, E.R.**, 55, F, None listed, -, England, 52, 52, EDGE. In HH of H.A. Kenrick, M, 33, born MA.
**MILLER, ESTHER**, 23, F, None listed, -, England, 473, 488, RICH. In HH of Daniel B. Miller, M, 24, born SC.
**MILLER, WILLIAM**, 37, M, Cabinetmaker, -, England, 564, 530, CHAS*.
**MILNER, AGNESS**, 30, F, None listed, -, England, 478, 444, CHAS*. In HH of J.G. Milner, M, 32, born GA.
**MONRNEY, ANNA**, 28, F, Servant, -, England, 882, 840, CHAS+. In Charleston Hotel.
**MOORE, ANN**, 32, F, None listed, -, England, 751, 751, ABB. Note: Age is difficult to read.
**MOORE, ANNA**, 28, F, Servant, -, England, 882, 840, CHAS+. In Charleston Hotel.
**MORGAN, CHARLES**, 37, M, Tailor, -, England, 23, 23, BEAU.
**MORGAN, HENRY**, 4, M, None listed, -, England, 23, 23, BEAU. In HH of Charles Morgan, M, 37, born England.
**MORGAN, MATILDA**, 30, F, None listed, -, England, 23, 23, BEAU. In HH of Charles Morgan, M, 37, born England.
**MORGAN, THOMAS**, 10, M, None listed, -, England, 986, 963, CHAS%. In HH of Benjn. Morgan, M, 48, born SC.
**MORRISON, ELIZABETH**, 55, F, None listed, -, England, 14, 14, CHAS*. In HH of Robert Bee, M, 51, born SC.
**MORRISON, ROBERT**, 29, M, Merchant, -, England, 224, 229, RICH. { Page out of order, follow HH 177/181.}
**MORTON, SARAH**, 25, F, None listed, -, England, 813, 793, CHAS-. In HH of Isaac Seckendorffe, M, 40, born Germany.
**MOSES, SOL.**, 65, M, Dept. Sheriff, -, England, 769, 749, CHAS-.
**MOSS, HUGH**, 27, M, Engineer, -, England, 219, 197, CHAS. In HH of A. Fink, M, 30, born Hanover.
**MUDD, WILLIAM**, 23, M, Farmer, -, England, 779, 779, MARL.
**MURRAY, ELIZABETH**, 43, F, None listed, -, England, 23, 23, CHAS*. In

HH of James L. Murray, M, 50, born GA.

MURRAY, JOHN, 50, M, None listed, -, England, 53, 53, BEAU.

MURRAY, W.C., 40, M, Merchant, -, England, 74, 84, CHAS.

MURTAUGH, JAMES, 34, M, Tailor, -, England, 1475, 1475, NEWB. In HH of John W. Folk, M, 35, born SC.

MYERS, GEO., 38, M, Overseer, -, England, 1222, 1222, DARL.

MYERS, JOHN, 39, M, Coach maker, -, England, 697, 655, CHAS+.

MYERS, MARY, 54, F, Shopkeeper, -, England, 601, 559, CHAS+.

# N

NATHAN, RACHAEL, 44, F, None listed, -, England, 217, 194, CHAS*. In HH of Nathan Myer, M, 50, born Poland.

NATHANS, MEYER, 40, M, Merchant, -, England, 250, 255, RICH.

NATHANS, NATHAN, 66, M, Merchant, -, England, 87, 87, CHAS%.

NAYLOR, WILLIAM, 40, M, Merchant, -, England, 333, 316, CHAS-. In HH of Maria Horlbeck, F, 60, born SC.

NEAL, JEANETTA, 20, F, None listed, -, England, 183, 183, EDGE*. In HH of Peter Neal, M, 75, born Scotland.

NEELAND, ROBERT, 62, M, Farmer, -, England, 967, 967, YORK.

NEVELLE, ELIZABETH, 76, F, None listed, -, England, 277, 261, CHAS-. In HH of Alexander Hamilton, M, 52, born SC.

NEVILLE, JOSHUA, 85, M, Cabinetmaker, -, England, 484, 499, RICH.

NEWBOLD, CHARLES, 40, M, Mariner, -, England, 399, 363, CHAS.

NICHOLS, R.H., 47, M, Teacher, -, England, 86, 86, EDGE.

NIGHTING, LOUISA, 16, F, None listed, -, England, 427, 396, CHAS*. In HH of Elizabeth Hood, F, 45, born NY.

NORRIS, HENRY, 32, M, Clerk, -, England, 136, 126, CHAS-. In HH of Rosa Stien, F, 22, born Germany.

NORTHY, FRANCES, 28, M, None listed, -, England, 1040, 1040, YORK.

NORTHY, JOSEPH, 30, M, Miner, -, England, 1038, 1038, YORK.

NORTHY, WILLIAM, 32, M, Miner, -, England, 1039, 1039, YORK.

# O

OATES, EDWARD, 24, M, Clerk, -, England, 837, 817, CHAS-. In HH of George Oates, M, 55, born England.

OATES, FRANCES, 54, F, None listed, -, England, 837, 817, CHAS-. In HH of George Oates, M, 55, born England.

OATES, GEORGE, 55, M, Book seller, -, England, 837, 817, CHAS-.

OATES, HENRY T., 26, M, Clerk, -, England, 837, 817, CHAS-. In HH of George Oates, M, 55, born England.

OHEAR, JAMES F., 65, M, Planter, -, England, 1198, 1177, CHAS%.
OLIPHANT, ELIZA J., 45, F, None listed, -, England, 474, 457, CHAS-.
OLIVER, JOSEPH H., 50, M, Carver/Gilder, -, England, 74, 72, CHAS*.
OLIVER, SARAH, 22, F, None listed, -, England, 300, 306, RICH. In
Boarding House.
OLLANGUE, ABRAHAM, 60, M, Merchant, -, England, 561, 519, CHAS+.
ONEALE, RICHARD, 58, M, Merchant, -, England, 316, 322, RICH.
ORCHARD, JOHN, 21, M, Mariner, -, England, 125, 116, CHAS-. In HH of
John Hill, M, 60, born SC.
ORCHARD, WILLIAM H., 39, M, Professor of Music at the Female
Institute, -, England, 867, 877, RICH+.
ORLANDO, THOMAS, 63, M, Painter, -, England, 104, 96, CHAS+.
OSGOOD, GEORGE, 35, M, Mariner, -, England, 161, 144, CHAS.

P
PAGE, JAMES H., 60, M, Hotel keeper, -, England, 285, 262, CHAS. In
Planters Hotel.
PAINE, R.W., 32, M, Mariner, -, England, 317, 291, CHAS+. In HH of Tim
Kennedy, M, 71, born Ireland.
PARK, CATHERINE, 60, F, None listed, -, England, 84, 82, CHAS*. In HH
of Julia Coutrier, F, 32, born GA.
PARKERSON, JOHN, 66, M, Bell hanger, -, England, 374, 340, CHAS.
PARKERSON, MARY, 42, F, None listed, -, England, 374, 340, CHAS. In
HH of John Parkerson, M, 66, born England.
PATEY, ANN, 31, F, None listed, -, England, 82, 92, CHAS. In HH of James
Patey, M, 40, born Scotland.
PEARMAN, ISABELLA, 72, F, None listed, -, England, 354, 327, CHAS*. In
HH of Paul Dunbar, M, 60, born Scotland.
PEERS, ALICE H., 45, M, None listed, -, England, 520, 535, RICH.
PELERS, GERARD, 56, M, Laborer, -, England, 94, 106, CHAS. In HH of
Michael Bolger, M, 29, born Ireland.
PENNINGTON, JOHN, 22, M, Saddler, -, England, 89, 90, RICH. Note:
dwelling 89/family 90 followed 43/44, apparently copied out oforder.
PETCH, JANE H., 63, F, None listed, -, England, 137, 137, CHAS%. In HH
of Julius D. Petch, M, 42, born SC.
PETERS, C., 45, F, None listed, -, England, 659, 617, CHAS+.
PIERCE, MARY ANN, 25, F, None listed, -, England, 204, 191, CHAS-. In
HH of W.H. Smith, M, 21, born SC.
PIKE, DANIEL, 50, M, Farmer, -, England, 873, 873, PICK+.
PIKE, ELLEN, 19, F, None listed, -, England, 873, 873, PICK+. In HH of

25

Daniel Pike, M, 50, born England.

**PIKE, JOHN**, 23, M, Carriage maker, -, England, 873, 873, PICK+. In HH of Daniel Pike, M, 50, born England.

**PIKE, MARY**, 52, F, None listed, -, England, 873, 873, PICK+. In HH of Daniel Pike, M, 50, born England.

**PLANE, LOUISA**, 50, F, None listed, -, England, 427, 396, CHAS*. In HH of Elizabeth Hood, F, 45, born NY.

**PLANE, WILLIAM**, 48, M, Customs Inspector, -, England, 43, 51, CHAS.

**PLATT, ABLE**, 24, M, Covering Rolls, -, England, 1730, 1733, EDGE.

**PLATT, ELIZABETH**, 21, F, None listed, -, England, 119, 119, LEX. In HH of Sarah Platt, F, 49, born England.

**PLATT, GEORGE**, 9, M, None listed, -, England, 119, 119, LEX. In HH of Sarah Platt, F, 49, born England.

**PLATT, NOAH**, 26, M, Spinner, -, England, 1730, 1733, EDGE. In HH of Able Platt, M, 24, born England.

**PLATT, SARAH**, 49, F, None listed, -, England, 119, 119, LEX.

**PLATT, WILLIAM**, 17, M, None listed, -, England, 119, 119, LEX. In HH of Sarah Platt, F, 49, born England.

**PLATT, WILLIAM**, 17, M, Oiling/frames, -, England, 1730, 1733, EDGE. In HH of Able Platt, M, 24, born England.

**POLOCK, ELIAS**, 43, M, Clerk, -, England, 257, 262, RICH.

**POLOCK, FRANCES**, 48, F, None listed, -, England, 203, 207, RICH.

**PORCHER, ELIZA**, 38, F, None listed, -, England, 16, 16, CHAS*. In HH of Middleton Smith, F,{sic} 70, born England.

**PORCHER, HARRIOT**, 60, F, None listed, -, England, 16, 16, CHAS*. In HH of Middleton Smith, F,{sic} 70, born England.

**POULSON, CATHARINE**, 20, F, None listed, -, England, 546, 546, UNION. In HH of Thomas Dawkins, M, 43, born SC.

**POWELL, MARY**, 60, F, None listed, -, England, 2239, 2239, GREE. In HH of Thomas Powell, M, 60, born England.

**POWELL, THOMAS**, 60, M, Painter, -, England, 2239, 2239, GREE.

**POWELL, THOMAS**, 23, M, Port Painter, -, England, 2239, 2239, GREE. In HH of Thomas Powell, M, 60, born England.

**POWERS, ANN**, 17, F, None listed, -, England, 82, 92, CHAS. In HH of James Patey, M, 40, born Scotland.

**PREGNAL, HENRY**, 48, M, Carpenter, -, England, 650, 630, CHAS-.

**PREGNAL, SARAH**, 42, F, None listed, -, England, 650, 630, CHAS-. In HH of Henry Pregnal, M, 48, born England

**PRICE, JAMES**, 34, M, Stone mason, -, England, 352, 314, CHAS+.

**PRICE, MARIA**, 30, F, None listed, -, England, 352, 314, CHAS+. In HH of James Price, M, 34, born England.

PRINCE, HENRY, 21, M, Clerk, -, England, 154, 145, CHAS+. In HH of Sarah Prince, F, 36, born Poland.
PRINCE, REBECCA, 16, F, None listed, -, England, 154, 145, CHAS+. In HH of Sarah Prince, F, 36, born Poland.
PRINCE, SAMUEL, 14, M, None listed, -, England, 154, 145, CHAS+. In HH of Sarah Prince, F, 36, born Poland.
PRITCHARD, EDWARD, 58, M, Merchant, -, England, 157, 148, CHAS+.
PRITCHARD, THOMAS, 43, M, None listed, -, England, 237, 222, CHAS-. Poor House.
PRITCHARD, WM., 26, M, Gardener, -, England, 1220, 1220, DARL.
PROUTING, CHARLES, 57, M, Pilot, -, England, 91, 103, CHAS.

**Q**
QUAIL, MARGARET, 24, F, None listed, -, England, 749, 729, CHAS-.
QUAIL, MARGARET, 23, F, None listed, -, England, 174, 164, CHAS+. In HH of Richard Hogan, M, 36, born Ireland.
QUINN, MICHAEL, 23, M, Boarding house keeper, -, England, 322, 297, CHAS. Michael Quinn, born Liverpool, England.
QUINTIN, SUSAN, 40, F, Teacher, -, England, 173, 159, CHAS*. In HH of John P. Bee, M, 40, born SC.

**R**
RAINE, B., 40, F, None listed, -, England, 414, 373, CHAS.
RAINE, MARY JANE, 13, F, None listed, -, England, 414, 373, CHAS. In HH of B. Raine, F, 40, born England.
RAINSFORD, JAMES, 50, M, Planter, -, England, 1311, 1311, EDGE.
RANDAL, ELIZABETH, 27, F, Servant, -, England, 882, 840, CHAS+. In Charleston Hotel.
RED, FRANCIS, 51, F, None listed, -, England, 45, 45, CHES. In HH of Thos. Brown 43, M, born SC.
REDFERN, ELIZA., 33, F, None listed, -, England, 256, 234, CHAS. In HH of Robert James, M, 37, born SC.
REDFERN, ELIZABETH, 57, F, None listed, -, England, 256, 234, CHAS. In HH of Robert James, M, 37, born SC.
REDMOND, W.S., 35, M, Merchant, -, England, 126, 118, CHAS*. In HH of Geo. A. Hopley, M, 38, born England.
REES, WILLIAM, 27, M, Well digger, -, England, 1737, 1737, ABB.
REEVES, GEO., 29, M, Mariner, -, England, 362, 333, CHAS. In Boarding House.
RHODES, WILLIAM, 38, M, Barber, -, England, 542, 557, RICH. Date 1845

by name. In Lunatic Asylum.

**RICHARDS, ANN**, 30, F, None listed, -, England, 839, 819, CHAS-. In HH of John S. Richards, M, 45, born GA.

**RICHARDSON, C.Y.**, 35, M, Locksmith, -, England, 318, 302, CHAS-.

**RICHARDSON, J.E.**, 14, F, None listed, -, England, 230, 230, BEAU+. In HH of Mrs. A. Hugerwin?, F, 60, born SC.

**RICHARDSON, JOHN**, 58, M, Saddler, -, England, 89, 90, RICH. Note: dwelling 89/family 90 followed 43/44, apparently copied out of order.

**RICHARDSON, MARY**, 55, F, None listed, -, England, 318, 302, CHAS-. In HH of C.Y. Richardson, M, 35, born England.

**RIDDELL, JOHN H.**, 35, M, Shoemaker, -, England, 663, 643, CHAS-.

**ROBERTS, ANN**, 28, F, None listed, -, England, 368, 338, CHAS. In HH of William Roberts, M, 31, born England.

**ROBERTS, ELIZA**, 3, F, None listed, -, England, 368, 338, CHAS. In HH of William Roberts, M, 31, born England.

**ROBERTS, ELIZABETH**, 45, F, None listed, -, England, 753, 733, CHAS-. In HH of John McAllister, M, 37, born Ireland. In American Hotel.

**ROBERTS, GEORGE**, 8, M, None listed, -, England, 368, 338, CHAS. In HH of William Roberts, M, 31, born England.

**ROBERTS, MARIA**, 25, F, None listed, -, England, 676, 656, CHAS-. In HH of Geo F. Cole, M, 45, born MD.

**ROBERTS, MARY**, 37, F, None listed, -, England, 79, 71, CHAS+. In HH of Thomas Roberts, M, 44, born England.

**ROBERTS, THOMAS**, 44, M, Tailor, -, England, 79, 71, CHAS+.

**ROBERTS, WILLIAM**, 31, M, Shoemaker, -, England, 368, 338, CHAS.

**ROBERTS, WILLIAM**, 6, M, None listed, -, England, 368, 338, CHAS. In HH of William Roberts, M, 31, born England.

**ROBSON, SARAH A.**, 48, F, None listed, -, England, 472, 455, CHAS-. In HH of Mary Cooper, F, 50, born SC.

**RODDY, MARTIN**, 23, M, Grocer, -, England, 117, 112, CHAS*.

**RODDY, ROSANA**, 22, F, None listed, -, England, 117, 112, CHAS*. In HH of Martin Roddy, M, 23, born England.

**ROGERS, EMMA**, 22, F, None listed, -, England, 420, 392, CHAS*.

**ROSA, MARGARAET**, 25, F, None listed, -, England, 189, 178, CHAS+. In HH of Jose Rosa, M, 35, born Cuba.

**ROSE, WILLIAM P.**, 31, M, Master mariner, -, England, 109, 121, CHAS. In HH of Richard Bringlow, M, 59, born England.

# S

**SALAMANS, H.**, 23, M, Acct., -, England, 24, 24, KERS. In HH of Moses

Drucker, M, 45, born Germany.
SAMPSON, JANE, 57, F, None listed, -, England, 525, 508, CHAS-.
SAMPSON, L.W., 37, M, Merchant, -, England, 14, 14, COLL.
SAMSON, JOSEPH, 35, M, Deputy Sheriff, -, England, 243, 218, CHAS*. In
HH of Morris Goldsmith, M, 64, born England.
SAMSON, SAMPSON, 24, M, Mariner, -, England, 243, 218, CHAS*. In HH
of Morris Goldsmith, M, 64, born England.
SAMSON, SAMUEL, 32, M, Jeweler, -, England, 243, 218, CHAS*. In HH of
Morris Goldsmith, M, 64, born England.
SAMUEL, ELIZA, 25, F, None listed, -, England, 93, 93, CHAS%. In HH of
R. Berlin, M, 30, born MD.
SANDRY, JOHN, 23, M, Miner, -, England, 827, 827, LANC*.
SANDRY, S., 23, F, None listed, -, England, 827, 827, LANC*. In HH of
John Sandry, M, 23, born England.
SAVAGE, JOSEPH C., 12, M, None listed, -, England, 765, 750, CHAS%. In
HH of Sarah Barcley, F, 39, born SC.
SAVAGE, T.P., 24, M, Engineer, -, England, 765, 750, CHAS%. In HH of
Sarah Barcley, F, 39, born SC.
SCOTT, JOHN, 24, M, Servant, -, England, 882, 840, CHAS+. In Charleston
Hotel.
SCOTT, ROBERT R., 30, M, Servant, -, England, 882, 840, CHAS+. In
Charleston Hotel.
SEALES, JENNY, 21, F, None listed, -, England, 856, 836, CHAS-. In HH of
Otes J. Chaffe, M, 35, born RI.
SEALES, MARY, 45, F, None listed, -, England, 856, 836, CHAS-. In HH of
Otes J. Chaffe, M, 35, born RI.
SEARLE, WILLIAM, 36, M, Teacher, -, England, 886, 866, CHAS-.
SEDDONS, JOSEPH, 54, M, Cabinetmaker, -, England, 419, 391, CHAS*.
SERVICE, SUSAN H., 63, F, None listed, -, England, 210, 284, CHAS*.
SHAW, CHARLES, 28, M, Engineer, -, England, 874, 851, CHAS%. In HH
of Thomas Barnes, M, 40, born Ireland.
SHAW, MARGARET, 28, F, None listed, -, England, 874, 851, CHAS%. In
HH of Thomas Barnes, M, 40, born Ireland.
SILCORE, DANIEL H., 36, M, Cabinetmaker, -, England, 75, 69, CHAS-.
SILCORE, JAMES, 34, M, Cabinetmaker, -, England, 75, 69, CHAS-. In HH
of Daniel H. Silcore, M, 36, born England.
SILDA, WILHAM, 22, M, Stone mason, -, England, 328, 328, YORK. In HH
of Owen Matthews, M, 41, born Lancester Dist., SC.
SIMMONS, HENRY, 34, M, Baker, -, England, 268, 273, RICH.
SIMMONS, JOHN, 35, M, Ditcher, -, England, 1883, 1883, SUMT. In Hotel.
SIMMONS, LEWIS, 31, M, Merchant, -, England, 266, 271, RICH.

SIMONS, ELLEN, 32, F, None listed, -, England, 328, 302, CHAS*. In HH of George Wm. Simons, M, 36, born England.
SIMONS, GEORGE WM., 36, M, Gardner, -, England, 328, 302, CHAS*.
SIMONS, JOHN, 35, M, Ditcher, -, England, 727, 727, SUMT.
SIMONS, JOHN Y., 40, M, Mariner, -, England, 191, 174, CHAS.
SIMONS, MARGERY, 18, F, None listed, -, England, 328, 302, CHAS*. In HH of George Wm. Simons, M, 36, born England.
SIMONS, MARY ANN, 30, F, None listed, -, England, 191, 174, CHAS. In HH of John Y. Simons, M, 40, born England.
SINCLAIR, MARTHA, 22, F, None listed, -, England, 1135, 1135, CHES. In HH of James Loury, M, 69, born SC.
SLAVICK, MARY ANN, 18, F, None listed, -, England, 212, 190, CHAS*. In HH of J.L. Slavick, M, 27, born Italy.
SLOWMAN, ANN, 20, F, None listed, -, England, 879, 859, CHAS-. In HH of John Slowman, M, 50, born England.
SLOWMAN, ELIZABETH, 40, F, None listed, -, England, 879, 859, CHAS-. In HH of John Slowman, M, 50, born England.
SLOWMAN, ELIZABETH, 21, F, None listed, -, England, 879, 859, CHAS-. In HH of John Slowman, M, 50, born England.
SLOWMAN, JOHN, 50, M, Professor of Music, -, England, 879, 859, CHAS-.
SMITH, A.P., 38, M, Soda water mfg., -, England, 93, 86, CHAS-.
SMITH, AMELIA R., 33, F, None listed, -, England, 159, 149, CHAS-. In HH of Stephen Watson, M, 53, born England.
SMITH, CAROLINE, 22, F, None listed, -, England, 1221, 1221, DARL.
SMITH, E., 31, F, None listed, -, England, 828, 828, LANC*. In HH of Robt. Smith, M, 30, born England.
SMITH, E., 12, F, None listed, -, England, 828, 828, LANC*. In HH of Robt. Smith, M, 30, born England.
SMITH, ELI., 2, F, None listed, -, England, 828, 828, LANC*. In HH of Robt. Smith, M, 30, born England.
SMITH, HARRIET, 28, F, None listed, -, England, 543, 502, CHAS+.
SMITH, J., 39, M, Merchant, -, England, 882, 840, CHAS+. In Charleston Hotel.
SMITH, JOSHUA, 35, M, Engineer, -, England, 326, 301, CHAS. In HH of William Rollins, M, 40, born {-}.
SMITH, M.A., 4, M, None listed, -, England, 828, 828, LANC*. In HH of Robt. Smith, M, 30, born England.
SMITH, MIDDLETON, 70, F, None listed, -, England, 16, 16, CHAS*.
SMITH, R., 8, M, None listed, -, England, 828, 828, LANC*. In HH of Robt. Smith, M, 30, born England.

SMITH, ROBT., 30, M, Miner, -, England, 828, 828, LANC*.
SMITH, S., 30, M, Merchant, -, England, 882, 840, CHAS+. In Charleston
Hotel.
SMITH, T., 6, M, None listed, -, England, 828, 828, LANC*. In HH of Robt.
Smith, M, 30, born England.
SMITH, THOS. A., 38, M, Schoolteacher, -, England, 531, 531, SUMT.
SMITH, THOS. M.D., 56, M, Farmer, -, England, 857, 857, DARL.
SMITH, W., 10, M, None listed, -, England, 828, 828, LANC*. In HH of
Robt. Smith, M, 30, born England.
SMITH, WILLIAM, 42, M, Shoemaker, -, England, 447, 444, CHAS%.
SMITH, WILLIAM, 36, M, Engineer, -, England, 543, 502, CHAS+. In HH of
Harriet Smith, F, 28, born England.
SORBER, GEORGE, 26, M, Servant, -, England, 882, 840, CHAS+. In
Charleston Hotel.
SORBER, WILLIAM, 30, M, Servant, -, England, 882, 840, CHAS+. In
Charleston Hotel.
SPEARS, CAROLINE P., 57, F, None listed, -, England, 1113, 1090, CHAS-.
In HH of John M. Righton, M, 56, born SC.
SPELLMAN, SUSAN, 44, F, None listed, -, England, 57, 51, CHAS+. In HH
of A. Spellman, M, 37, born Bavaria.
SPENCER, AGNES, 33, F, None listed, -, England, 909, 909, DARL. In HH
of Ambrose Spencer, M, 39, born NY.
SPENCER, MARIA, 63, F, None listed, -, England, 728, 708, CHAS-.
STACY, OLIVER, 22, M, Shoemaker, -, England, 850, 850, MARL.
STEEN, THOMAS, 27, M, Tavern keeper, -, England, 540, 523, CHAS-.
STEIN, JAMES N., 30, M, Merchant, -, England, 246, 251, RICH.
STRADLEY, JOHN, 25, M, Student, -, England, 290, 290, GREE. In HH of
Thomas Roe, M, 30, born SC.
STREIT, JOSEPH, 52, M, Wheelwright, -, England, 351, 351, SUMT.
STRONG, FARNES, 60, M, House carpenter, -, England, 25, 25, BEAU+.
STUART, MARY ANN, 50, F, None listed, -, England, 25, 23, CHAS$.
STUBS, JOHN, 43, M, Painter, -, England, 1188, 1188, LEX.
STYLES, C.W., 28, M, Painter, -, England, 163, 146, CHAS.
STYLES, MARGARET, 27, F, None listed, -, England, 163, 146, CHAS. In
HH of C.W. Styles, M, 28, born England.
SWAFFIELD, EDWIN R., 19, M, Merchant, -, England, 427, 438, RICH.

T
TALMAN, THOMAS W., 60, M, None listed, -, England, 47, 47, ABB.
TARBER, WM., 23, M, Cabinetmaker, -, England, 56, 56, KERS. In HH of

31

C.L. Chartan, M, 30, born NJ.

**TAYLOR, JAMES**, 30, M, Mariner, -, England, 819, 777, CHAS+.

**TAYLOR, JOHN F.**, 24, M, Engineer, -, England, 326, 301, CHAS. In HH of William Rollins, M, 40, born {blank}.

**TAYLOR, LOUISA**, 50, F, None listed, -, England, 494, 460, CHAS*.

**TAYLOR, ROSA**, 27, F, None listed, -, England, 819, 777, CHAS+. In HH of James Taylor, M, 30, born England.

**TEAPE, ELIZABETH**, 23, F, Hatter, -, England, 991, 970, CHAS-.

**TEMPLE, FANNY**, 50, F, None listed, -, England, 2343, 2343, GREE. In HH of William Chrico, M, 54, born SC.

**TENNENT, ISABELLA**, 55, F, None listed, -, England, 725, 683, CHAS+.

**TERRY, MARY**, 44, F, None listed, -, England, 1715, 1715, GREE. In HH of Gastin Terry, M, 46, born SC.

**THOMAS, WILLIAM**, 27, M, Stone cutter, -, England, 235, 210, CHAS*.

**THOMLINSON, ROBERT**, 32, M, Merchant, -, England, 1062, 1039, CHAS-.

**THOMPSON, HENRY**, 32, M, Boarding house keeper, -, England, 351, 324, CHAS.

**THOMPSON, JANE**, 43, F, None listed, -, England, 215, 192, CHAS*. In HH of John Thompson, M, 54, born England.

**THOMPSON, JANE**, 42, F, None listed, -, England, 632, 590, CHAS+. In HH of William Thompson, M, 48, born England.

**THOMPSON, JOHN**, 54, M, Cabinetmaker, -, England, 215, 192, CHAS*.

**THOMPSON, JOHN EDWARD**, 30, M, Ship joiner, -, England, 215, 192, CHAS*. In HH of John Thompson, M, 54, born England.

**THOMPSON, MARY**, 22, F, None listed, -, England, 215, 192, CHAS*. In HH of John Thompson, M, 54, born England.

**THOMPSON, WILLIAM**, 50, M, Peddler, -, England, 324, 299, CHAS.

**THOMPSON, WILLIAM**, 48, M, Blacksmith, -, England, 632, 590, CHAS+.

**THOMPSON, WILLIAM B.**, 40, M, Tavern keeper, -, England, 251, 236, CHAS-.

**THORN, HENRY**, 28, M, Physician, -, England, 717, 717, WILL. In HH of J. Nelson, M, 50, born SC.

**TOMLINSON, JOSEPH**, 40, M, Merchant, -, England, 967, 947, CHAS-.

**TOPHEN, JOHN**, 21, M, Plasterer, -, England, 223, 199, CHAS*. In HH of Elizabeth Lawrence, F, 42, born SC.

**TORRENT, JOHN**, 40, M, Rigger, -, England, 539, 498, CHAS+.

**TRESONTHICK?, AGNES**, 29, F, None listed, -, England, 1188, 1188, EDGE. In HH of George Fresonthick, M, 35, born England.

**TRESONTHICK?, GEORGE**, 35, M, Carpenter, -, England, 1188, 1188, EDGE.

**TRESONTHICK?, JAMES**, 18, M, Carpenter, -, England, 1188, 1188, EDGE.

In HH of George Fresonthick, M, 35, born England.
TRESONTHICK?, JAMES, 11, M, None listed, -, England, 1188, 1188, EDGE. In HH of George Fresonthick, M, 35, born England.
TRESONTHICK?, JOHN, 20, M, Carpenter, -, England, 1188, 1188, EDGE. In HH of George Fresonthick, M, 35, born England.
TRUSEN, J., 25, F, None listed, -, England, 827, 827, LANC*. In HH of John Sandry, M, 23, born England.
TRUSEN, JAMES, 26, M, Miner, -, England, 827, 827, LANC*. In HH of John Sandry, M, 23, born England.
TUFFNEL, JAMES, 103, M, Farmer, -, England, 1028, 1029, AND*.
TURNER, GEORGE, 34, M, Painter, -, England, 465, 473, RICH+.

U
USHER, JOHN, 26, M, Clerk, -, England, 337, 302, CHAS+. In HH of John Lindsay, M, 30, born England.

V
VERDIER, MARY A., 72, F, None listed, -, England, 166, 166, COLL. In HH of Francis P. Delavaux, M, 71, born England.
VINCENT, HUGH E., 42, M, Ship chandler, -, England, 154, 137, CHAS.

W
WAGSTAFF, MARY, 36, F, None listed, -, England, 683, 687, AND. In HH of William Wagstaff, M, 56, born England.
WAGSTAFF, WILLIAM, 56, M, Musician, -, England, 683, 687, AND.
WALKER, DOROTHY M., 30, F, None listed, -, England, 280, 257, CHAS. In HH of H.P. Walker, M, 34, born England.
WALKER, GEORGE, 28, M, Mariner, -, England, 788, 746, CHAS+. In HH of William Norris, M, 28, born Ireland.
WALKER, H.P., 34, M, Attorney at law, -, England, 280, 257, CHAS.
WALKER, RICHARD, 30, M, Merchant, -, England, 231, 218, CHAS+. In HH of Harriot Howard, F, 60, born SC.
WALKINSHAND, MARY, 45, F, None listed, -, England, 104, 97, CHAS-. In HH of William Walkinshand, M, 57, born Ireland.
WARD, RICHARD, 47, M, Mail Contractor, -, England, 1441, 1441, EDGE.
WATER, CATHERINE, 27, F, Servant, -, England, 882, 840, CHAS+. In Charleston Hotel.
WATER, MARY, 25, F, Servant, -, England, 882, 840, CHAS+. In Charleston Hotel.
WATSON, ELIZA T., 36, F, None listed, -, England, 159, 149, CHAS-. In HH

of Stephen Watson, M, 53, born England.

**WATSON, MARIAH**, 51, F, None listed, -, England, 1020, 1021, AND*.

**WATSON, STEPHEN**, 53, M, Merchant, -, England, 159, 149, CHAS-.

**WATTS, L.**, 32, F, None listed, -, England, 1003, 981, CHAS-.

**WEAR, JOHN**, 78, M, Shoemaker, -, England, 508, 474, CHAS*.

**WEAR, JOHN S.**, 34, M, Clerk, -, England, 412, 423, RICH.

**WEARN, RICHARD**, 23, M, Coach maker, -, England, 504, 508, AND. In HH of W.B. Gibson, M, 31, born SC.

**WEBB, CATHARN**, 5, F, None listed, -, England, 1145, 1145, DARL. In HH of Evan Webb, M, 24, born England.

**WEBB, EVAN**, 24, M, Miller, -, England, 1145, 1145, DARL.

**WEBB, MARY**, 55, F, None listed, -, England, 105, 117, CHAS. In HH of Michael Webb, M, 58, born ME. Mary Webb, born Liverpool, England.

**WEBB, MARY E.**, 3, F, None listed, -, England, 1145, 1145, DARL. In HH of Evan Webb, M, 24, born England.

**WEBB, R.**, 30, M, Baptist clergyman, -, England, 1156, 1156, GREE. In HH of Thomas T. Hopkins, M, 31, born SC.

**WEBB, SARAH**, 27, F, None listed, -, England, 1145, 1145, DARL. In HH of Evan Webb, M, 24, born England.

**WEBB, SARAH M.**, 1, F, None listed, -, England, 1145, 1145, DARL. In HH of Evan Webb, M, 24, born England.

**WELCH, HARRIS**, 25, M, Mariner, -, England, 337, 311, CHAS. In HH of William H. Fowler, M, 38 running Boarding House, born England.

**WELLS, AMELIA**, 46, F, None listed, -, England, 2337, 2337, GREE. In HH of O.H. Wells, M, 46, born MA.

**WERNER, HANNAH**, 65, F, None listed, -, England, 175, 165, CHAS+. In HH of C. Werner, M, 45, born Prussia.

**WERNER, ISABELLA**, 23, F, None listed, -, England, 175, 165, CHAS+. In HH of C. Werner, M, 45, born Prussia.

**WHEELER, CHARLOTTE**, 43, F, None listed, -, England, 412, 423, RICH. In HH of John S. Wear, M, 34, born England.

**WHEELER, PHILIS**, 86, F, None listed, -, England, 1733, 1733, GREE. In HH of William Wheeler, M, 43, born England.

**WHEELER, WILLIAM**, 43, M, Carpenter, -, England, 1733, 1733, GREE.

**WHITE, MARY**, 27, F, Stewardess, -, England, 326, 301, CHAS. On Steam Ship Southerner.

**WHITEHEAD, THOMAS**, 22, M, Mariner, -, England, 237, 222, CHAS-. Poor House.

**WHITING, JAS.**, 40, M, Carpenter, -, England, 259, 243, CHAS+. In HH of T.L. Quackenbush, M, 35, born NY.

**WIGHTMAN, ANN**, 62, F, None listed, -, England, 2398, 2405, EDGE. In HH of William J. Wightman, M, 57, born Scotland.

**WILCOX, LOUISA**, 40, F, None listed, -, England, 672, 652, CHAS-.

**WILKENSON, THOMAS**, 41, M, Mariner, -, England, 362, 333, CHAS. In Boarding House.

**WILLIAMS, CATHERINE**, 72, F, None listed, -, England, 302, 302, WILL. In HH of James Graham, M, 75, born SC.

**WILLIAMS, HARRIET**, 19, F, None listed, -, England, 839, 819, CHAS-. In HH of John S. Richards, M, 45, born GA.

**WILLIAMS, JOHN**, 69, M, Planter, -, England, 681, 681, SUMT.

**WILLIAMS, SARAH**, 22, F, None listed, -, England, 839, 819, CHAS-. In HH of John S. Richards, M, 45, born GA.

**WILLIAMS, WILLIAM**, 32, M, Mariner, -, England, 334, 308, CHAS. In HH of William Bennett, M, 40, born NY.

**WILSMAN, AMELIA**, 65, F, None listed, -, England, 52, 62, CHAS. In HH of James Wilsman, M, 65, born England.

**WILSMAN, JAMES**, 65, M, Merchant, -, England, 52, 62, CHAS.

**WILSON, ANN**, 23, F, None listed, -, England, 2364, 2364, SPART. At Limestone High School.

**WILSON, W.A.**, 27, M, Watch maker, -, England, 160, 143, CHAS. In HH of John H. Ostendosff, M, 38, born Germany.

**WILSON, WILLIAM**, 49, M, Mechanic, -, England, 220, 220, BEAU*. In HH of Wyley Peeples, M, 53, born SC. William Wilson listed as, born in London, England.

**WILSON, WILLIAM**, 35, M, Artist, -, England, 690, 670, CHAS-.

**WINDSOR, ELIZABETH**, 34, F, None listed, -, England, 134, 138, RICH. In HH of James Windsor, M, 36, born England.

**WINDSOR, GEORGE E.**, 8, M, None listed, -, England, 134, 138, RICH. In HH of James Windsor, M, 36, born England.

**WINDSOR, JAMES**, 36, M, Laborer, -, England, 134, 138, RICH.

**WINDSOR, MARY J.**, 11, F, None listed, -, England, 134, 138, RICH. In HH of James Windsor, M, 36, born England.

**WING, ROBERT**, 22, M, Whitesmith, -, England, 414, 386, CHAS*.

**WISH, ELIZABETH**, 50, F, None listed, -, England, 70, 68, CHAS*. In HH of Peter Rottereau, M, 50, born SC.

**WOLSTON, GEORGE**, 27, M, Tailor, -, England, 57, 58, ORNG+. In HH of James Jones, M, 40, born England.

**WOLSTON, GEORGE**, 27, M, Tailor, -, England, 57, 58, ORNG+. In HH of James Jones, M, 40, born England.

**WOOD, DANIEL**, 45, M, Laborer, -, England, 956, 933, CHAS%.

**WOOD, HENRY**, 54, M, Baptist Clergyman, -, England, 509, 509, GREE.

**WOODHURST, ANDREW**, 16, M, None listed, -, England, 421, 421, EDGE.

In HH of John Combs, M, 33 bricklayer/planter, born England.
**WOODHURST, ELIZABETH**, 11, F, None listed, -, England, 421, 421, EDGE.
In HH of John Combs, M, 33 bricklayer/planter, born England.
**WOODHURST, GEORGE W.**, 13, M, None listed, -, England, 421, 421,
EDGE. In HH of John Combs, M, 33 bricklayer/planter, born England.
**WOODHURST, M.A.**, 15, F, None listed, -, England, 421, 421, EDGE. In HH
of John Combs, M, 33 bricklayer/planter, born England.
**WOODHURST, ROBT. B.**, 19, M, None listed, -, England, 421, 421, EDGE.
In HH of John Combs, M, 33 bricklayer/planter, born England.
**WOODHURST, ROBT. W.**, 20, M, Shoe/bootmaker, -, England, 1015, 1015,
EDGE. In HH of W.J. Winn, M, 38, born SC.
**WOODHURST, SUSANNAH**, 21, F, None listed, -, England, 421, 421, EDGE.
In HH of John Combs, M, 33 bricklayer/planter, born England.
**WOODWORTH, CAROLINE**, 20, F, None listed, -, England, 720, 700,
CHAS-. In HH of L. Schackmand, M, 45, born Germany.
**WOOLEY, JOHN**, 27, M, Hatter, -, England, 1751, 1756, EDGE. In HH of
Joseph Wooley, M, 52, born England.
**WOOLEY, JOSEPH**, 52, M, Bos? Weaver, -, England, 1751, 1756, EDGE.
**WOOLEY, MARGARET**, 50, F, None listed, -, England, 1751, 1756, EDGE.
In HH of Joseph Wooley, M, 52, born England.
**WOOLEY, WILLIAM**, 35, M, Ostler, -, England, 303, 309, RICH.
**WOOLFE, ANN**, 37, F, None listed, -, England, 507, 473, CHAS*.
**WOOLFE, ISAAC**, 68, M, None, -, England, 27, 22, CHAS+.
**WOOLFE, SARAH**, 68, F, None listed, -, England, 27, 22, CHAS+. In HH of
Isaac Woolfe, M, 68, born England.
**WOTHERSPOON, SARAH**, 52, F, None listed, -, England, 238, 213,
CHAS*. In HH of Robert Wotherspoon, M, 55, born Scotland.
**WRIGHT, GEORGE W.**, 43, M, Blacksmith, -, England, 358, 367, RICH.
**WRIGHT, HARRIOT**, 60, F, None listed, -, England, 996, 975, CHAS-.
**WRIGHT, J.D.**, 30, M, Painter, -, England, 815, 795, CHAS-.
**WRIGHT, MARGARET**, 39, F, None listed, -, England, 358, 367, RICH. In
HH of George W. Wright, M, 43, born England.
**WYLER, VINCENT**, 47, M, Boiler maker, -, England, 671, 629, CHAS+.

**Y**
**YATES, ANN**, 60, F, None listed, -, England, 191, 174, CHAS. In HH of John
Y. Simons, M, 40, born England.
**YOUNG, BRIDGET**, 40, F, None listed, -, England, 509, 459, CHAS. In HH
of William Young, M, 52, born Scotland.
**YOUNG, JAMES**, 60, M, Mariner, -, England, 499, 453, CHAS. In HH of

Eliza O. Hanlin, F, 58, born SC.

YOUNG, PHILIP, 24, M, Engineer, -, England, 244, 229, CHAS+. In Boarding House run by Ellen Pratt.

## Z

ZACHARIAH, AMELIA, 53, F, None listed, -, England, 668, 648, CHAS-. In HH of Jonathan Zachariah, M, 58, born Poland.

❖

## BORN IN SCOTLAND - (579)

## A

ADAMS, JANE, 55, F, None listed, -, Scotland, 1630, 1630, GREE. In HH of Robert Adams, M, 55, born Scotland.

ADAMS, JENNETTE, 23, F, None listed, -, Scotland, 1630, 1630, GREE. In HH of Robert Adams, M, 55, born Scotland.

ADAMS, JOHN, 40, M, Machinist, -, Scotland, 1620, 1620, GREE.

ADAMS, MARY, 40, F, None listed, -, Scotland, 1620, 1620, GREE. In HH of John Adams, M, 40, born Scotland.

ADAMS, ROBERT, 55, M, Farmer, -, Scotland, 1630, 1630, GREE.

AENOT, ALEXANDER, 18, M, Clerk, , Scotland, 225, 203, CHAS. In HH of William Aenot, M, 35, born Scotland.

AENOT, WILLIAM, 35, M, Painter, -, Scotland, 225, 203, CHAS.

ALLAN, ALEXANDER, 50, M, Carpenter, -, Scotland, 1226, 1205, CHAS%.

ALLAN, ISABELLA, 50, F, None listed, -, Scotland, 1226, 1205, CHAS%. In HH of Alexander Allan, M, 50, born Scotland.

ALLAN, JAMES, 18, M, Watch maker, -, Scotland, 1226, 1205, CHAS%. In HH of Alexander Allan, M, 50, born Scotland.

ANDERSON, ALEXANDER, 57, M, Laborer, -, Scotland, 801, 801, YORK.

ANDERSON, CATEY, 12, F, None listed, -, Scotland, 329, 303, CHAS*. In HH of William Anderson, M, 34, born Scotland.

ANDERSON, ELIZABETH, 51, F, None listed, -, Scotland, 801, 801, YORK. In HH of Alexander Anderson, M, 57, born Scotland.

ANDERSON, ELIZABETH, 28, F, None listed, -, Scotland, 329, 303, CHAS*. In HH of William Anderson, M, 34, born Scotland.

ANDERSON, G., 77, M, Methodist Minister, -, Scotland, 83, 83, CHAS2.

ANDERSON, JANE, 49, F, None listed, -, Scotland, 324, 298, CHAS*. In HH of Robert Anderson, M, 56, born Scotland.

ANDERSON, JOHN, 23, M, Sergt. U.S.A., -, Scotland, 47, 43, CHAS$. In HH of John Ewing, M, 50, born MA.

ANDERSON, ROBERT, 56, M, Block maker, -, Scotland, 324, 298, CHAS*.

ANDERSON, WILLIAM, 45, M, Stone cutter, -, Scotland, 346, 346, YORK. In HH of James Ballou, M, 37, born RI.

ANDERSON, WILLIAM, 34, M, Clerk, -, Scotland, 329, 303, CHAS*.

ANDERSON, WM., 43, M, Merchant, -, Scotland, 815, 815, KERS.

ASHFORD, ROSS, 27, M, Mariner, -, Scotland, 362, 333, CHAS. In Boarding House.

# B

BANKS, SAML. SR., 87, M, Planter, -, Scotland, 791, 792, FAIR. In HH of Saml. Banks, M, 38, born SC.

BARCLAY, AGNES, 64, F, None listed, -, Scotland, 360, 369, RICH. In HH of William Barcley, M, 68, born Scotland.

BARCLAY, WILLIAM, 68, M, Mattress maker, -, Scotland, 360, 369, RICH.

BEHAN, AGNES, 32, F, None listed, -, Scotland, 1158, 1137, CHAS%. In HH of Thomas Behan, M, 40, born Ireland.

BELMAIN, WILLIAM, 36, M, Baker, -, Scotland, 6, 6, CHAS$.

BELMONT, D.R., 30, M, Music Teacher, -, Scotland, 35, 35, EDGE. In HH of Charles J. Glover, M, 41, born SC.

BIRNIE, WILLIAM, 68, M, Merchant, -, Scotland, 625, 606, CHAS-.

BISHOP, JOHN, 39, M, Farmer, -, Scotland, 1914, 1914, GREE.

BLACK, EDWARD J., 26, M, Clerk, -, Scotland, 457, 424, CHAS*. In HH of Alexander W. Black, M, 45, born MA.

BLAKE, ANN, 18, F, None listed, -, Scotland, 116, 118, RICH. In HH of Dempey Blake, M, 27, born SC.

BLAKE, MARGARET, 20, F, None listed, -, Scotland, 116, 117, RICH. In HH of Joseph Blake, M, 36, born SC.

BLYTHE, ALEXANDER A., 39, M, Carpenter, -, Scotland, 1575, 1575, EDGE.

BOYNE, THOMAS, 30, M, Stone cutter, -, Scotland, 357, 366, RICH.

BRAND, JOHN, 16, M, Laborer, -, Scotland, 1273, 1273, GREE. In HH of Janius Smith, M, 50, born CT.

BROWN, ALEXANDER, 58, M, Stone Cutter, -, Scotland, 280, 286, RICH.

BROWN, ELIZABETH E., 36, F, None listed, -, Scotland, 234, 212, CHAS. In HH of Geo. Brown, M, 45, born Scotland.

BROWN, GEO., 45, M, Wine merchant, -, Scotland, 234, 212, CHAS.

BROWN, JOHN, 29, M, Hotel keeper, -, Scotland, 72, 72, CHAS!.

BROWN, ROBERT, 75, M, Factor, -, Scotland, 524, 474, CHAS.

BRYCE, JANE C., 49, F, Teacher, -, Scotland, 11, 11, LEX. Census stated

38

Jane C. Bryce, born Glasgow, Scotland.
**BRYCE, JOHN**, 60, M, None, -, Scotland, 301, 307, RICH.
**BRYCE, PETER**, 57, M, Merchant, -, Scotland, 465, 479, RICH.
**BRYCE, ROBERT**, 52, M, Merchant, -, Scotland, 361, 370, RICH.
**BURNS, MARY**, 60, F, None listed, -, Scotland, 269, 269, COLL*. In HH of
P. Burns, M, 32, born Scotland.
**BURNS, P.**, 32, M, Store keeper, -, Scotland, 269, 269, COLL*.
**BURNSIDE, JAMES**, 27, M, Packer, -, Scotland, 113, 105, CHAS+. In HH
of Peter Hanschild, M, 59, born Germany.
**BUZZELS, DAVID**, 20, M, Merchant, -, Scotland, 253, 231, CHAS. In HH of
John T. Marshal, M, 48, born Scotland.

**C**

**CAIN, JAMES**, 54, M, None listed, -, Scotland, 237, 222, CHAS-. Poor
House.
**CALDER, JAMES**, 60, M, Hotel Keeper, -, Scotland, 1, 1, CHAS$.
**CALDER, JAMES**, 60, M, Cabinetmaker, -, Scotland, 7, 7, CHAS+.
**CALDER, WILLIAM**, 50, M, Merchant, -, Scotland, 1074, 1051, CHAS-.
**CALDWELL, JAMES**, 29, M, Upholsterer, -, Scotland, 811, 791, CHAS-. In
HH of John Caldwell, M, 53, born Scotland.
**CALDWELL, JANE**, 56, F, None listed, -, Scotland, 811, 791, CHAS-. In HH
of John Caldwell, M, 53, born Scotland.
**CALDWELL, JOHN**, 53, M, Upholsterer, -, Scotland, 811, 791, CHAS-.
**CALDWELL, JOHN JR.**, 24, M, Clerk, -, Scotland, 811, 791, CHAS-. In HH
of John Caldwell, M, 53, born Scotland.
**CALDWELL, JOHN W.**, 55, M, Wheelwright, -, Scotland, 60, 60, COLL. In
HH of Jesse Dubois, M, 37, born SC.
**CALDWELL, SARAH**, 23, F, None listed, -, Scotland, 811, 791, CHAS-. In
HH of John Caldwell, M, 53, born Scotland.
**CALDWELL, WM.**, 34, M, Clerk, -, Scotland, 401, 361, CHAS+. In HH of
Catherine Brady, F, 40, born Ireland.
**CAMBELL, JOHN**, 58, M, Shoemaker, -, Scotland, 178, 178, PICK+.
**CAMERON, ANN**, 8, F, None listed, -, Scotland, 721, 679, CHAS+. In HH of
Archibald Cameron, M, 27, born Scotland.
**CAMERON, ARCHEBALD**, 27, M, Blacksmith, -, Scotland, 721, 679,
CHAS+.
**CAMERON, DUNCAN**, 24, M, Blacksmith, -, Scotland, 317, 301, CHAS-. In
HH of Henry Carmanade, M, 42, born Jamaica.
**CAMERON, GEO. S.**, 40, M, Merchant, -, Scotland, 371, 354, CHAS-.
**CAMERON, H.P.**, 35, M, Merchant, -, Scotland, 371, 354, CHAS-. In HH of

Geo. S. Cameron, M, 40, born Scotland.
CAMERON, JANE, 11, F, None listed, -, Scotland, 721, 679, CHAS+. In HH of Archibald Cameron, M, 27, born Scotland.
CAMERON, MARY ANN, 17, F, None listed, -, Scotland, 721, 679, CHAS+. In HH of Archibald Cameron, M, 27, born Scotland.
CAMERON, ROBERT, 45, M, Blacksmith, -, Scotland, 721, 679, CHAS+. In HH of Archibald Cameron, M, 27, born Scotland.
CAMMERON, R., 44, M, Overseer, -, Scotland, 846, 846, KERS.
CAMPBELL, CHRISTAIN, 48, F, None listed, -, Scotland, 498, 498, MARL. In HH of Duncan Campbell, M, 20, born SC.
CAMPBELL, DANIEL, 43, M, Tailor, -, Scotland, 1884, 1884, ABB. In HH of James W. Child, M, 45, Inn keeper, born VA.
CAMPBELL, H., 51, M, Commissioner in Equity, -, Scotland, 108, 108, COLL.
CAMPBELL, JAMES, 38, M, None listed, -, Scotland, 48, 48, CHAS!. In HH of Peter Campbell, M, 66, born Scotland.
CAMPBELL, JOHN, 24, M, Clerk, -, Scotland, 325, 300, CHAS. In HH of Nathaniel McManes, M, 29, born MD.
CAMPBELL, MARGARET, 61, F, None listed, -, Scotland, 1632, 1638, MAR.
CAMPBELL, MARGARET, 60, F, None listed, -, Scotland, 178, 178, PICK+. In HH of John Cambell, M, 58, born Scotland.
CAMPBELL, NANCY, 75, F, None listed, -, Scotland, 597, 597, MARL.
CAMPBELL, PETER, 66, M, Planter, -, Scotland, 48, 48, CHAS!.
CARMICHAEL, DOUGAL, 65, M, Farmer, -, Scotland, 1000, 1065, MAR.
CHALMERS, ALEXANDER, 21, M, Blacksmith, -, Scotland, 599, 557, CHAS+. In HH of James Chalmers, M, 50, born Scotland.
CHALMERS, BARBARA, 42, F, None listed, -, Scotland, 599, 557, CHAS+. In HH of James Chalmers, M, 50, born Scotland.
CHALMERS, BARBARA, 20, F, None listed, -, Scotland, 599, 557, CHAS+. In HH of James Chalmers, M, 50, born Scotland.
CHALMERS, JAMES, 50, M, Blacksmith, -, Scotland, 599, 557, CHAS+.
CHALMERS, JAMES, 30, M, Baker, -, Scotland, 173, 173, BEAU+.
CHAMBERS, WM. H., 15, M, Saddler, -, Scotland, 233, 211, CHAS. In HH of Charles Love, M, 40, born Scotland.
CHISHOLM, MARY MISS, 40, F, None listed, -, Scotland, 7, 7, MARL. In HH of R.A. McRae, M, 54, born NC.
CHISLOM, ANN, 58, F, None listed, -, Scotland, 1603, 1609, MAR. In HH with Catherine Kelly, 63 born Scotland.
CHRISTIE, ELIZABETH, 29, F, None listed, -, Scotland, 588, 588, EDGE. In HH of John Christie, M, 56, born Scotland.
CHRISTIE, JOHN, 56, M, Farmer, -, Scotland, 588, 588, EDGE.

CLARK, A.Q., 35, M, Blacksmith, -, Scotland, 11, 11, NEWB. In HH of James Cranford 38, M, Stone mason born SC.

CLARK, ALEX, 41, M, Paper maker, -, Scotland, 1626, 1626, GREE.

CLARK, ELIZABETH, 41, F, None listed, -, Scotland, 1626, 1626, GREE. In HH of Alex Clark, M, 41, born Scotland.

CLARK, ELLEN, 16, F, None listed, -, Scotland, 1626, 1626, GREE. In HH of Alex Clark, M, 41, born Scotland.

CLARK, JAMES, 55, M, None listed, -, Scotland, 999, 999, YORK.

CLARK, JENNETTE, 22, F, None listed, -, Scotland, 1626, 1626, GREE. In HH of Alex Clark, M, 41, born Scotland.

CLARKE, JOSEPH, 51, M, Agent of Dipo, -, Scotland, 1765, 1769, EDGE.

CLATWORTHY, JANETTE, 38, F, None listed, -, Scotland, 547, 547, ABB. In HH of James Clatworthy, M, 45, born Ireland.

CLYDE, THOS. M., 55, M, Tanner, -, Scotland, 939, 939, PICK+.

COCKREN, JOHN W., 50, M, Planter, -, Scotland, 403, 403, SUMT.

COLE, ANNA, 23, F, None listed, -, Scotland, 202, 189, CHAS-. In HH of Grace Piexolla, F , 30, born SC.

COLLINGWOOD, JOHN, 40, M, Goaler Charleston District, -, Scotland, 40, 37, CHAS-.

COLSON, GEORGIANA, 42, F, None listed, -, Scotland, 731, 689, CHAS+. In HH of Charles Colson, M, 48, born England.

COOK, MARIA, 50, F, Midwife, -, Scotland, 141, 141, BEAU.

COOK, ROBT. D., 52, M, Miller, -, Scotland, 356, 356, EDGE.

COOPER, CHRISTIANA, 35, F, None listed, -, Scotland, 26, 26, GEOR.

COOPER, J.R., 28, F, None listed, -, Scotland, 32, 32, KERS. In HH of J.M. Cooper, M, 35, born Ireland.

CRAMMER, JAMES, 27, M, Gardner, -, Scotland, 479, 494, RICH.

CRAWFORD, ELIZABETH, 48, F, None listed, -, Scotland, 331, 331, ABB. In HH of Robert Crawford, M, 50, born Scotland.

CRAWFORD, ROBERT, 50, M, Miller, -, Scotland, 331, 331, ABB.

CREIGHTON, W. J., 28, M, Physician, -, Scotland, 2398, 2405, EDGE. In HH of William J. Wightman, M, 57, born Scotland.

CROOKS, A., 22, M, Clerk, -, Scotland, 317, 291, CHAS+. In HH of Tim Kennedy, M, 71, born Ireland.

CRUCKSHANKS, D., 69, M, None, -, Scotland, 204, 192, CHAS+. In HH of Mary M. Maher, F, 52, born Ireland.

CUNNINGHAM, ANDREW, 38, M, Carpenter, -, Scotland, 114, 106, CHAS-.

# D

DAVIDSON, WILLIAM, 53, M, Planter, -, Scotland, 443, 401, CHAS.

DAWSON, JANE, 29, F, None listed, -, Scotland, 255, 233, CHAS. In HH of J.L. Dawson, M, 34, born Scotland.
DEWER, ELIZABELLA, 45, F, None listed, -, Scotland, 507, 457, CHAS.
DICK, JAMES, 50, M, Industrial Engineer, -, Scotland, 425, 425, HORR. In HH of Thos. W. Beatey, M, 24, born SC.
DOUGLAS, ANTHONY, 42, M, Merchant, -, Scotland, 27, 27, KERS. In HH of G.S. Douglas, M, 33, born Scotland.
DOUGLAS, CAMPBELL, 69, M, Accountant, -, Scotland, 355, 328, CHAS*.
DOUGLAS, G.S., 33, M, Merchant, -, Scotland, 27, 27, KERS.
DOUGLAS, J.K., 70, M, Merchant, -, Scotland, 161, 161, KERS.
DOUGLAS, JENNY, 59, F, None listed, -, Scotland, 778, 778, KERS. In HH of Robt. Douglas, M, 59, born Scotland.
DOUGLAS, ROBT., 59, M, Weaver, -, Scotland, 778, 778, KERS.
DOUGLASS, JOHN, 60, M, Carpenter, -, Scotland, 1512, 1518, MAR.
DOUGLASS, JOHN, 50, M, Coach maker, -, Scotland, 1426, 1432, MAR.
DOUGLASS, ROBERT, 40, M, Mail contractor, -, Scotland, 2263, 2263, GREE.
DOVE, CATHARINE, 74, F, None listed, -, Scotland, 291, 291, DARL. In HH of James W. Hill, M, 51, born SC.
DOWNIE, ROBERT, 60, M, Merchant, -, Scotland, 444, 402, CHAS.
DRUMMOND, JOHN, 50, M, Shoemaker, -, Scotland, 239, 217, CHAS.
DUNKIN, ALEXANDER, 9, M, None listed, -, Scotland, 364, 326, CHAS+. In HH of Archibald Dunkin, M, 37, born Scotland.
DUNKIN, ARCHIBALD, 37, M, Blacksmith, -, Scotland, 364, 326, CHAS+.
DUNKIN, ARCHIBALD, 4, M, None listed, -, Scotland, 364, 326, CHAS+. In HH of Archibald Dunkin, M, 37, born Scotland.
DUNKIN, JAMES, 7, M, None listed, -, Scotland, 364, 326, CHAS+. In HH of Archibald Dunkin, M, 37, born Scotland.
DUNKIN, JOHN, 16, M, Blacksmith, -, Scotland, 364, 326, CHAS+. In HH of Archibald Dunkin, M, 37, born Scotland.
DUNKIN, MARY, 35, F, None listed, -, Scotland, 364, 326, CHAS+. In HH of Archibald Dunkin, M, 37, born Scotland.
DUNKIN, WILLIAM, 13, M, None listed, -, Scotland, 364, 326, CHAS+. In HH of Archibald Dunkin, M, 37, born Scotland.
DUNN, JOHN, 74, M, Farmer, -, Scotland, 688, 688, HORR.

E
EASTERLING, JANE, 42, F, None listed, -, Scotland, 58, 58, GEOR.
EDGAR, ADAM, 80, M, None, -, Scotland, 177, 181, RICH.
EDMONSTON, CHARLES, 68, M, Merchant, -, Scotland, 43, 43, CHAS*.

EDWARDS, JOHN, 34, M, Shoemaker, -, Scotland, 473, 473, FAIR. In HH of William Gordon, M, 25, born Ireland.

EWING, ANDREW, 26, M, Clerk, -, Scotland, 727, 707, CHAS-. In HH of Mary Ewing, F, 25, born Canada.

# F

FENTON, JAMES, 56, M, Merchant, -, Scotland, 296, 302, RICH.

FERGUSON, CHARLY, 49, M, Mechanic, -, Scotland, 42, 42, BARN.

FERGUSON, JENNEY, 36, F, None listed, -, Scotland, 828, 811, CHAS%. In HH of John Ferguson, M, 40, born Scotland.

FERGUSON, JOHN, 40, M, Laborer, -, Scotland, 828, 811, CHAS%.

FERGUSON, THO., 25, M, Saddler, -, Scotland, 325, 300, CHAS. In HH of Nathaniel McManes, M, 29, born MD.

FIGAN, THOMAS, 24, M, Painter, -, Scotland, 495, 449, CHAS. In HH of Joseph Douglas, M, 44, born NY.

FINLASON, ALEXR., 27, M, Clerk, -, Scotland, 167, 149, CHAS. In Boarding house.

FLEMING, W., 28, M, Clerk, -, Scotland, 721, 701, CHAS-. In Boarding House.

FORREST, JOHN, REV., 51, M, Minister, D.D. Presbyterian, -, Scotland, 565, 531, CHAS*.

FRASER, JOHN, 70, M, Merchant, -, Scotland, 459, 426, CHAS*.

FRAZIER, JOHN, 40, M, Cabinetmaker, -, Scotland, 513, 513, FAIR. In HH of J.M. Cranford, M, 27, born Ireland. At the Fairfield Hotel.

FRAZIER, JOHN, 30, M, Post Clerk, -, Scotland, 1005, 982, CHAS%. Under command of Major P. Hagnes, Commanding Officer U.S. Arsenal.

FREELING, CAROLINE, 70, F, None listed, -, Scotland, 784, 764, CHAS-. In HH of D. O'Conner, M, 22, born Ireland.

# G

GANDY, LIDDEY, 73, F, Farmer, -, Scotland, 459, 459, DARL.

GARDNAR, ISABELLA, 50, F, None listed, -, Scotland, 924, 924, KERS. In HH of Wm. Gardnar, M, 57, born Scotland.

GARDNAR, WM., 57, M, Mechanic, -, Scotland, 924, 924, KERS.

GARDNER, JAINY M., 29, M, Watch maker, -, Scotland, 221, 199, CHAS.

GARLEY, JAMES, 15, M, Saddler, -, Scotland, 233, 211, CHAS. In HH of Charles Love, M, 40, born Scotland.

GIBSON, ALEXANDER, 68, M, Merchant, -, Scotland, 210, 210, CHAS%.

GIBSON, ALEXANDER, 39, M, Shopkeeper, -, Scotland, 478, 436, CHAS+.

GIBSON, ALEXANDER, 16, M, Carpenter, -, Scotland, 478, 436, CHAS+. In

HH of Alexander Gibson, M, 39, born Scotland.

**GIBSON, DAVID,** 57, M, Farmer, -, Scotland, 627, 630, MAR.

**GIBSON, MARY,** 26, F, None listed, -, Scotland, 478, 436, CHAS+. In HH of Alexander Gibson, M, 39, born Scotland.

**GIBSON, THOMAS,** 14, M, None listed, -, Scotland, 478, 436, CHAS+. In HH of Alexander Gibson, M, 39, born Scotland.

**GORDON, ALEXR.,** 50, M, Merchant, -, Scotland, 221, 199, CHAS.

**GORDON, ELIZABETH,** 3, F, None listed, -, Scotland, 473, 456, CHAS-. In HH of Margaret M. McKenzie, F, 35, born SC.

**GORDON, GRACE,** 20, F, None listed, -, Scotland, 473, 456, CHAS-. In HH of Margaret M. McKenzie, F, 35, born SC.

**GORDON, JAMES,** 25, M, Plumber, -, Scotland, 473, 456, CHAS-. In HH of Margaret M. McKenzie, F, 35, born SC.

**GORDON, JAMES,** 2, M, None listed, -, Scotland, 473, 456, CHAS-. In HH of Margaret M. McKenzie, F, 35, born SC.

**GOWEN, PETER,** 58, M, Watch maker, -, Scotland, 389, 353, CHAS.

**GRAHAM, DONALD,** 35, M, Shoemaker, -, Scotland, 78, 76, CHAS*.

**GRAHAM, GEORGE,** 9, M, None listed, -, Scotland, 853, 833, CHAS-. In HH of John Graham, M, 30, born Scotland.

**GRAHAM, JOHN,** 30, M, Clerk, -, Scotland, 853, 833, CHAS-.

**GRAHAM, MARGARET,** 32, F, None listed, -, Scotland, 78, 76, CHAS*. In HH of Donald Graham, M, 35, born Scotland.

**GRAHAM, SUSAN,** 30, F, None listed, -, Scotland, 853, 833, CHAS-. In HH of John Graham, M, 30, born Scotland.

**GRANT, CATHERINE,** 16, F, None listed, -, Scotland, 771, 754, CHAS%. In HH of Thomas Grant, M, 37, born Scotland.

**GRANT, COLLIN M.,** 10, M, None listed, -, Scotland, 771, 754, CHAS%. In HH of Thomas Grant, M, 37, born Scotland.

**GRANT, DONALD,** 14, M, None listed, -, Scotland, 771, 754, CHAS%. In HH of Thomas Grant, M, 37, born Scotland.

**GRANT, ELIZABETH,** 8, F, None listed, -, Scotland, 771, 754, CHAS%. In HH of Thomas Grant, M, 37, born Scotland.

**GRANT, MARGARET,** 35, F, None listed, -, Scotland, 771, 754, CHAS%. In HH of Thomas Grant, M, 37, born Scotland.

**GRANT, MARGARET,** 12, F, None listed, -, Scotland, 771, 754, CHAS%. In HH of Thomas Grant, M, 37, born Scotland.

**GRANT, THOMAS,** 37, M, Engineer, -, Scotland, 771, 754, CHAS%.

**GRANT, THOMAS,** 6, M, None listed, -, Scotland, 771, 754, CHAS%. In HH of Thomas Grant, M, 37, born Scotland.

**GRANT, WM.,** 25, M, Carpenter, -, Scotland, 995, 974, CHAS-. In HH of James Shaw, M, 28, born Scotland.

GRAVES, CHRISTINA, 18, F, None listed, -, Scotland, 253, 231, CHAS. In HH of John T. Marshal, M, 48, born Scotland.

GRAY, ANDREW, 50, M, Florist, -, Scotland, 1154, 1133, CHAS%.

GRAY, ISABELLA, 45, F, None listed, -, Scotland, 1154, 1133, CHAS%. In HH of Andrew Gray, M, 50, born Scotland.

GREER, MARY, 20, F, None listed, -, Scotland, 459, 416, CHAS. In HH of Wm. McClush, M, 39, born Scotland.

# H

HABERHAUSEN, ISABELLA, 32, F, None listed, -, Scotland, 273, 253, CHAS+. In HH of John Haberhausen, M, 47, born Germany.

HADDEN, JOSEPH, 35, M, Engineer, -, Scotland, 471, 468, CHAS%. In HH of Herman Meyer, M, 33, born Germany.

HALLFORD, ELY, 18, F, None listed, -, Scotland, 33, 33, KERS. In Boarding house.

HALLIDAY, WILLIAM, 30, M, Engineer, -, Scotland, 641, 600, CHAS+.

HARRINGTON, GEORGE, 29, M, Laborer, -, Scotland, 237, 222, CHAS-. Poor House

HASELL, ANDREW, 47, M, MD, -, Scotland, 33, 33, GEOR.

HASELL, JOANA, 47, F, None listed, -, Scotland, 33, 33, GEOR. In HH of Andrew Hasell, M, 47, born Scotland.

HAY, JOHN, 28, M, Carpenter, -, Scotland, 805, 805, UNION. In HH of John Rodgers, F, 30, born Scotland.

HAY, MARG., 30, F, None listed, -, Scotland, 348, 348, UNION. In HH of James Hay, M, 47, born SC.

HECTOR, ELIZABETH, 17, F, None listed, -, Scotland, 752, 732, CHAS-. In HH of John McAllister, M, 37, born Ireland.

HENDERSON, ALEXANDER, 35, M, Blacksmith, -, Scotland, 709, 667, CHAS+.

HENDERSON, R., 27, M, Priv. U.S.A., -, Scotland, 47, 43, CHAS$. In HH of John Ewing, M, 50, born MA.

HERVEY, ELIZABETH, 54, F, None listed, -, Scotland, 520, 470, CHAS. In HH of George Hervey, M, 62, born Scotland.

HERVEY, GEORGE, 62, M, Merchant, -, Scotland, 520, 470, CHAS.

HILE, WILLIAM, 40, M, Laborer, -, Scotland, 410, 369, CHAS+.

HUCKABY, NANCY, 79, F, None listed, -, Scotland, 297, 297, MARL. In HH of Thomas W. Huckaby, M, 38 Schoolmaster, born SC.

HUNTER, WILLIAM, 48, M, Brick mason, -, Scotland, 936, 936, SPART. In HH of William White, M, 50, born SC.

HYNES, JAMES, 73, M, Custom H{house}Boatman, -, Scotland, 150, 138,

CHAS*. In HH of Samuel McGivley, M, 64, born PA.

## J

JACKSON, GEORGE, 60, M, Merchant, -, Scotland, 729, 709, CHAS-.
JACKSON, MARY M.V., 34, F, None listed, -, Scotland, 1622, 1622, YORK.
In HH of William B. Jackson, M, 35, born York Dist., SC.
JENKINS, JAMES, 45, M, Carpenter, -, Scotland, 322, 322, FAIR. In HH of
Robert Boyd, M, 50, born SC.
JOHNSTON, RICHARD, 23, M, Painter, -, Scotland, 495, 449, CHAS. In HH
of Joseph Douglas, M, 44, born NY.
JONES, ANDREW, 29, M, Blacksmith, -, Scotland, 497, 463, CHAS*. In HH
of William Jones, M, 64, born Scotland.
JONES, JOHN, 25, M, Painter, -, Scotland, 495, 449, CHAS. In HH of
Joseph Douglas, M, 44, born NY.
JONES, MARY, 55, F, None listed, -, Scotland, 497, 463, CHAS*. In HH of
William Jones, M, 64, born Scotland.
JONES, ROBERT, 25, M, Blacksmith, -, Scotland, 497, 463, CHAS*. In HH
of William Jones, M, 64, born Scotland.
JONES, WILLIAM, 64, M, Carpenter, -, Scotland, 497, 463, CHAS*.

## K

KAY, ANN, 97, F, None listed, -, Scotland, 532, 515, CHAS-. In HH of James
Smith, M, 59, born SC.
KELLY, CATHERINE, 63, F, None listed, -, Scotland, 1603, 1609, MAR.
KEMP, ARCHIBALD, 50, M, Farmer, -, Scotland, 187, 187, EDGE.
KENNEDY, A.M., 33, M, Merchant, -, Scotland, 13, 13, KERS.
KENNEDY, R.W., 29, M, Merchant, -, Scotland, 14, 14, KERS.
KENNEDY, WM., 46, M, Farmer, -, Scotland, 825, 825, KERS.
KENZIE, KATHERINE, 43, F, None listed, -, Scotland, 146, 134, CHAS*.
KETCHIN, THOMAS, 56, M, Preacher, -, Scotland, 397, 397, FAIR.
KIDD, ISABELLA, 30, F, None listed, -, Scotland, 15, 15, CHAS%. In HH of
Robert Adger, M, 36, born SC.
KING, A., 40, M, Store Keeper, -, Scotland, 283, 262, CHAS+. In HH of
Emily Goodrich, F, 35, born SC.
KING, GEORGE, 28, M, Clerk, -, Scotland, 325, 300, CHAS. In HH of
Nathaniel McManes, M, 29, born MD.
KING, M., THE HONBLE, 66, M, Attorney at Law, -, Scotland, 571, 554,
CHAS-.
KIRKPATRICK, JOHN, 48, M, Merchant, -, Scotland, 37, 45, CHAS.

# L

**LAMONT, DAVID**, 30, M, Taylor, -, Scotland, 35, 35, EDGE. In HH of Charles J. Glover, M, 41, born SC.

**LANG, CHARLES**, 27, M, Blacksmith, -, Scotland, 1680, 1680, EDGE. In HH of William Lang, M, 39, born Scotland.

**LANG, DAVID**, 14, M, None listed, -, Scotland, 1680, 1680, EDGE. In HH of William Lang, M, 39, born Scotland.

**LANG, JANE**, 23, F, None listed, -, Scotland, 1680, 1680, EDGE. In HH of William Lang, M, 39, born Scotland.

**LANG, SUSAN**, 35, F, None listed, -, Scotland, 1680, 1680, EDGE. In HH of William Lang, M, 39, born Scotland.

**LANG, WILLIAM**, 39, M, Millwright, -, Scotland, 1680, 1680, EDGE.

**LANG, WILLIAM**, 15, M, None listed, -, Scotland, 1680, 1680, EDGE. In HH of William Lang, M, 39, born Scotland.

**LAWTON, A. J.**, 50, M, Merchant, -, Scotland, 286, 263, CHAS. In Carolina Hotel .

**LECKIE, DAVID**, 35, M, None listed, -, Scotland, 298, 282, CHAS-.

**LESLIE, ISABELLA**, 30, F, None listed, -, Scotland, 785, 743, CHAS+. In HH of James Leslie, M, 35, born Scotland.

**LESLIE, JAMES**, 35, M, Boiler maker, -, Scotland, 785, 743, CHAS+.

**LINSEY, WILLIAM**, 31, M, Tailor, -, Scotland, 398, 398, LAU.

**LITTLE, ELIZA**, 25, F, None listed, -, Scotland, 643, 643, UNION. In HH of Thomas Little, M, 30, born Scotland.

**LITTLE, THOMAS**, 30, M, Machinist, -, Scotland, 643, 643, UNION.

**LIVINGSTON, ALEXR.**, 40, M, Saddler, -, Scotland, 59, 59, MARL.

**LIVINGSTON, MARY**, 30, F, None listed, -, Scotland, 59, 59, MARL. In HH of Alexr. Livingston, M, 40, born Scotland.

**LOCKHART, JOHN**, 38, M, Miner, -, Scotland, 1618, 1618, YORK. In HH of John B. Hunter, M, 47, born Ireland.

**LOGAN, J.C.**, 38, M, Taylor, -, Scotland, 172, 172, GEOR.

**LOVE, CHARLES**, 40, M, Saddler, -, Scotland, 233, 211, CHAS.

**LUDLEY, ROBERT**, 50, M, Planter, -, Scotland, 820, 820, BARN.

**LUNGBALLE, ELIZABETH**, 48, F, None listed, -, Scotland, 102, 102, BEAU. In HH of D.M. Lungballe, M, 52, born Denmark.

# M

**MACKEY, JAMES**, 30, M, Machinist, -, Scotland, 471, 429, CHAS. In HH of John McKenzie, M, 58, born Scotland.

**MACKEY, MARY**, 28, F, None listed, -, Scotland, 471, 429, CHAS. In HH of John McKenzie, M, 58, born Scotland.

47

MANNING, SABINA, 37, F, None listed, -, Scotland, 845, 849, AND. In HH of Mauldin Manning, M, 41, born SC.

MARSHAL, JOHN T., 48, M, Baker, -, Scotland, 253, 231, CHAS.

MARSHALL, ANDREW, 35, M, Bootmaker, -, Scotland, 424, 394, CHAS*.

MARSHALL, CHRISTINA, 35, F, None listed, -, Scotland, 424, 394, CHAS*. In HH of Andrew Marshall, M, 35, born Scotland.

MARSHALL, CHRISTINA, 16, F, None listed, -, Scotland, 424, 394, CHAS*. In HH of Andrew Marshall, M, 35, born Scotland.

MARSHALL, JESSE, 5, M, None listed, -, Scotland, 424, 394, CHAS*. In HH of Andrew Marshall, M, 35, born Scotland.

MARSHALL, JOHN, 12, M, None listed, -, Scotland, 424, 394, CHAS*. In HH of Andrew Marshall, M, 35, born Scotland.

MARSHALL, MARY, 3, F, None listed, -, Scotland, 424, 394, CHAS*. In HH of Andrew Marshall, M, 35, born Scotland.

MARSHALL, WM., 26, M, Boot maker, -, Scotland, 47, 47, KERS. In HH of Thos. Wilson, M, 28, born Ireland.

MARTIN, MARGARET, 43, F, None listed, -, Scotland, 545, 560, RICH. In HH of William Martin, M, 43, born NC.

MATHERSON, C., 54, M, Merchant, -, Scotland, 59, 59, KERS.

MATHISON, D., 40, M, Attorney at Law, -, Scotland, 608, 608, MARL.

MAULE, C.S., 45, M, Store keeper, -, Scotland, 733, 713, CHAS-.

MAULE, CLEMENTINA, 33, F, None listed, -, Scotland, 733, 713, CHAS-. In HH of C.S. Maule, M, 45, born Scotland.

MAXWELL, THOMAS, 60, M, Saddler, -, Scotland, 513, 513, FAIR. In HH of J.M. Cranford, M, 27, born Ireland. At the Fairfield Hotel.

MCALLISTER, BARBARA, 27, F, None listed, -, Scotland, 752, 732, CHAS-. In HH of John McAllister, M, 37, born Ireland.

MCARN, MARGARET, 51, F, None listed, -, Scotland, 6, 6, MARL. In HH of John McArn, M, 44, born SC.

MCBRYDE, MARY, 48, F, None listed, -, Scotland, 1986, 1992, EDGE. {Note: out of order, after fam. 1988.} In HH of E.C. West, F, 50, born GA.

MCCALL, CATHERINE, 79, F, None listed, -, Scotland, 151, 151, MARL. In HH of Dugald McCall, M, 53, born SC.

MCCALL, DOLLY, 72, F, None listed, -, Scotland, 1589, 1595, MAR. In HH of John McCall, 73 born Scotland.

MCCALL, EFFY, 50, F, None listed, -, Scotland, 151, 151, MARL. In HH of Dugald McCall, M, 53, born SC.

MCCALL, JOHN, 73, M, Farmer, -, Scotland, 1589, 1595, MAR.

MCCALL, NANCY, 51, F, None listed, -, Scotland, 151, 151, MARL. In HH of Dugald McCall, M, 53, born SC.

MCCALLEEM, DUNCAN, 66, M, Farmer, -, Scotland, 428, 428, YORK*.

MCCALLUM, PETER, 42, M, Farmer, -, Scotland, 592, 592, YORK.
MCCASKELL, ANGUS, 47, M, Farmer, -, Scotland, 426, 426, KERS.
MCCASKELL, KENNETH, 51, M, Farmer, -, Scotland, 623, 623, KERS.
MCCASKELL, NANCY, 76, F, None listed, -, Scotland, 426, 426, KERS. In
HH of Angus McClaskell, M, 47, born Scotland.
MCCASKELL, NANCY, 45, F, None listed, -, Scotland, 623, 623, KERS. In
HH of Kenneth McCaskell, M, 51, born Scotland.
MCCASKELL, PETER, 80, M, Farmer, -, Scotland, 567, 567, KERS.
MCCLARIN, PETER, 43, M, Mariner, -, Scotland, 139, 123, CHAS. In HH
of Barthohs Costwick, M, 50, born Austria.
MCCLEISH, AGNESS, 28, F, None listed, -, Scotland, 672, 630, CHAS+. In
HH of James McCleish, M, 40, born Scotland.
MCCLEISH, JAMES, 40, M, Engineer, -, Scotland, 672, 630, CHAS+.
MCCLUSH, MARGARET C., 20, F, None listed, -, Scotland, 459, 416, CHAS.
In HH of Wm. McClush, M, 39, born Scotland.
MCCLUSH, W., 39, M, Store Keeper, -, Scotland, 459, 416, CHAS.
MCCOLL, CATHARINE, 79, F, None listed, -, Scotland, 230, 230, MARL.
In HH of Duncan N. McColl, M, 76, born Scotland.
MCCOLL, CHRISTIAN, 35, F, None listed, -, Scotland, 230, 230, MARL. In
HH of Duncan N. McColl, M, 76, born Scotland.
MCCOLL, DUGALD, T., 48, M, Farmer, -, Scotland, 640, 640, MARL.
MCCOLL, DUNCAN N., 76, M, Farmer, -, Scotland, 230, 230, MARL.
MCCOLL, JOHN, 77, M, None listed, -, Scotland, 19, 19, MARL. In HH of
John L. McColl, M, 38; Merchant, born SC.
MCCOLL, JOHN, 60, M, Farmer, -, Scotland, 225, 225, MARL.
MCCORMICK, DAVID, 38, M, Clerk, -, Scotland, 401, 361, CHAS+. In HH
of Catherine Brady, F, 40, born Ireland.
MCCREDY, ROBERT, 33, M, Manager, -, Scotland, 236, 236, BEAU-.
MCCULLEY, ALEXANDER, 74, M, Laborermaster, -, Scotland, 1232, 1232,
GREE.
MCCULLEY, ELIZABETH, 68, F, None listed, -, Scotland, 1232, 1232, GREE.
In HH of Alexander McCulley, M, 74, born Scotland.
MCCULLEY, HENRY, 30, M, Carpenter, -, Scotland, 1232, 1232, GREE. In
HH of Alexander McCulley, M, 74, born Scotland.
MCCULLOCH, CHARLES, 63, M, Planter, -, Scotland, 857, 867, RICH+.
MCCULLOCH, SARAH, 39, F, None listed, -, Scotland, 857, 867, RICH+. In
HH of Charles McCulloch, M, 63, born Scotland.
MCDANIEL, DUNCAN, 80, M, None, -, Scotland, 1462, 1468, MAR.
MCDANIEL, MALCOM, 65, M, Farmer, -, Scotland, 1607, 1613, MAR.
MCDANIEL, MARY, 75, F, None listed, -, Scotland, 1462, 1468, MAR. In
HH of Duncan McDaniel 80 born Scotland.

**MCDERWARD, DUNCAN**, 34, M, Engineer, -, Scotland, 793, 751, CHAS+.
**MCDERWARD, MALCOLM**, 7, M, None listed, -, Scotland, 793, 751, CHAS+. In HH of Duncan McDerward, M, 34, born Scotland.
**MCDERWARD, MARGARET**, 29, F, None listed, -, Scotland, 793, 751, CHAS+. In HH of Duncan McDerward, M, 34, born Scotland.
**MCDONALD, ALEXANDER**, 22, M, Clerk, -, Scotland, 439, 408, CHAS*. In HH of Duncan McDonald, M, 25, born Scotland.
**MCDONALD, DANL.**, 85, M, Farmer, -, Scotland, 654, 654, KERS.
**MCDONALD, DONALD**, 12, M, None listed, -, Scotland, 1096, 1074, CHAS%. In HH of J.T. McDonald, M, 39, born Scotland.
**MCDONALD, DUNCAN**, 25, M, Accountant, -, Scotland, 439, 408, CHAS*.
**MCDONALD, FLORA**, 65, F, None listed, -, Scotland, 654, 654, KERS. In HH of Danl. McDonald, M, 85, born Scotland.
**MCDONALD, HUGH**, 9, M, None listed, -, Scotland, 1096, 1074, CHAS%. In HH of J.T. McDonald, M, 39, born Scotland.
**MCDONALD, J.T.**, 39, M, Laborer, -, Scotland, 1096, 1074, CHAS%.
**MCDONALD, JESSIE**, 32, F, None listed, -, Scotland, 1096, 1074, CHAS%. In HH of J.T. McDonald, M, 39, born Scotland.
**MCDONALD, JOHN**, 30, M, Cabinetmaker, -, Scotland, 667, 647, CHAS-. In Boarding House.
**MCDONALD, MARGARET**, 70, F, None listed, -, Scotland, 667, 647, CHAS-. In Boarding House.
**MCDONALD, ROBERT**, 50, M, Genl Agency, -, Scotland, 1987, 1990, EDGE. In HH of William Kitcham, M, 38, born NJ.
**MCDOUGAL, AGNESS**, 10, F, None listed, -, Scotland, 568, 534, CHAS*. In HH of David McDugal, M, 30, born Scotland.
**MCDOUGAL, EFFA**, 82, F, None listed, -, Scotland, 1398, 1404, MAR.
**MCDOWAL, SAMUEL**, 61, M, Farmer, -, Scotland, 11, 11, YORK.
**MCDOWALL, ANDREW**, 60, M, Merchant, -, Scotland, 76, 86, CHAS.
**MCDOWALL, W. D.**, 43, M, Merchant, -, Scotland, 84, 84, KERS.
**MCDUGAL, ANN LEITCH**, 27, F, None listed, -, Scotland, 568, 534, CHAS*. In HH of David McDugal, M, 30, born Scotland.
**MCDUGAL, DAVID**, 30, M, Engineer, -, Scotland, 568, 534, CHAS*.
**MCDUGAL, JANE**, 30, F, None listed, -, Scotland, 568, 534, CHAS*. In HH of David McDugal, M, 30, born Scotland.
**MCEACHIN, DUNCAN**, 38, M, Farmer, -, Scotland, 232, 232, MARL.
**MCEACHIN, EFFY**, 60, F, None listed, -, Scotland, 231, 231, MARL. In HH of John McEachin, M, 26, born NC.
**MCEVAN, DINAH**, 61, F, None listed, -, Scotland, 85, 85, KERS. In HH of Jas. McEvan, M, 71, born Scotland.
**MCEVAN, DINAH**, 35, F, None listed, -, Scotland, 85, 85, KERS. In HH of

Jas. McEvan, M, 71, born Scotland.
MCEVAN, JAS., 71, M, Merchant, -, Scotland, 85, 85, KERS.
MCFEELY, ELIZA, 46, F, None listed, -, Scotland, 1034, 1011, CHAS-. In HH
of James McFeely, M, 52, born Scotland.
MCFEELY, JAMES, 52, M, Planter, -, Scotland, 1034, 1011, CHAS-.
MCGEE, JEHU, 60, M, Master mariner, -, Scotland, 147, 131, CHAS.
MCGILL, A.C., 49, M, Farmer, -, Scotland, 29, 29, MARL.
MCGILVERY, A.B., 48, M, Methodist Clergyman, -, Scotland, 1248, 1248,
GREE.
MCGINNIS, CHS., 20, M, Painter, -, Scotland, 124, 115, CHAS+. In
Boarding House.
MCGINNIS, ELIZA J., 11, F, None listed, -, Scotland, 716, 707, CHAS%. In
HH of James McGinnis, M, 35, born Scotland.
MCGINNIS, JAMES, 35, M, Baker, -, Scotland, 716, 707, CHAS%.
MCGINNIS, JOSEPH, 87, M, None listed, -, Scotland, 211, 211, CHAS%.
MCGINNIS, NANCY, 30, F, None listed, -, Scotland, 716, 707, CHAS%. In
HH of James McGinnis, M, 35, born Scotland.
MCGREGGER, CHARLES, 35, M, Coach Painter, -, Scotland, 11, 11, EDGE.
In HH of J.L. Doby, M, 32, Landlord, born in SC.
MCGUGGAN, JOHN, 67, M, Farmer, -, Scotland, 569, 569, KERS.
MCGUGGAN, MARY, 55, F, None listed, -, Scotland, 569, 569, KERS. In HH
of John McGuggan, M, 67, born Scotland.
MCHARLING, MARY, 89, F, None listed, -, Scotland, 1806, 1806, ABB. In
HH of Mary McKellar, F, 49, born Scotland.
MCINNIS, A., 65, M, Land Surveyor, -, Scotland, 359, 360, ORNG+. In HH
of W. Riley, M, 68, born SC.
MCINNIS, B., 38, M, Blacksmith, -, Scotland, 210, 196, CHAS-.
MCINTISE, JANE, 55, F, None listed, -, Scotland, 445, 404, CHAS+. In HH
of Mary Manson, F, 65, born SC.
MCINTISE, JOHN, 67, M, Collector, -, Scotland, 445, 404, CHAS+. In HH
of Mary Manson, F, 65, born SC.
MCINTOCH, WILLIAM, 65, M, Carpenter, -, Scotland, 1069, 1047, CHAS%.
MCINTYER, C. MRS., 70, F, None listed, -, Scotland, 219, 219, MARL.
MCKAY, JOHN, 36, M, Clerk, -, Scotland, 2301, 2301, GREE.
MCKEEN, JAMES, 50, M, Clerk, -, Scotland, 2, 2, CHAS-. In HH of
James Moorhead, M, 50, born Ireland.
MCKELLAR, MARY, 40, F, None listed, -, Scotland, 1806, 1806, ABB.
MCKELLAR, PETER, 40, M, Farmer, -, Scotland, 1836, 1836, ABB.
MCKENZIE, ALEXR., 22, M, Wharfinger, -, Scotland, 473, 456, CHAS-. In
HH of Margaret M. McKenzie, F, 35, born SC.
MCKENZIE, DAVID, 36, M, Boot maker, -, Scotland, 226, 204, CHAS.

MCKENZIE, JOHN, 58, M, Cabinetmaker, -, Scotland, 471, 429, CHAS.
MCKENZIE, JOHN, 40, M, Confectioner, -, Scotland, 402, 413, RICH.
MCKENZIE, JOHN, 32, M, Clerk, -, Scotland, 471, 429, CHAS. In HH of
John McKenzie, M, 58, born Scotland.
MCKENZIE, MARGARET, 34, F, None listed, -, Scotland, 226, 204, CHAS.
In HH of David McKenzie, M, 36, born Scotland.
MCKENZIE, MARY, 58, F, None listed, -, Scotland, 471, 429, CHAS. In HH
of John McKenzie, M, 58, born Scotland.
MCKENZIE, MARY ANN, 60, F, None listed, -, Scotland, 354, 327, CHAS*.
In HH of Paul Dunbar, M, 60, born Scotland.
MCKENZIR, JAMES, 76, M, Farmer, -, Scotland, 124, 124, DARL.
MCKINZIE, DANIEL, 54, M, Farmer, -, Scotland, 130, 130, MARL.
MCKINZIE, MARY, 48, F, None listed, -, Scotland, 130, 130, MARL. In HH
of Daniel McKinzie, M, 54, born Scotland.
MCLAREN, AVES (?), 73, F, None listed, -, Scotland, 788, 788, ABB.
MCLAREN, JANNET, 46, F, None listed, -, Scotland, 788, 788, ABB. In HH
of Aves (?) McLaren 73, F,born Ireland.
MCLAREN, JOHN, 26, M, Post Master, -, Scotland, 788, 788, ABB. In HH
of Aves (?) McLaren 73, F,born Ireland.
MCLAURIN, JAMES, 63, M, Miller, -, Scotland, 1053, 1030, CHAS-.
MCLAURIN, SARAH M., 47, F, None listed, -, Scotland, 1053, 1030, CHAS-.
In HH of James McLaurin, M, 63, born Scotland.
MCLEAN, SARAH, 55, F, None listed, -, Scotland, 985, 985, SUMT. In HH
of Charles McLean, M, 55, born NC.
MCLELLAND, ANDREW, 47, M, Planter, -, Scotland, 668, 677, RICH+.
MCLELLAND, SARAH, 46, F, None listed, -, Scotland, 668, 677, RICH+. In
HH of Andrew McLelland, M, 47, born Scotland.
MCLENNAN, JOHN, 47, M, Farmer, -, Scotland, 1896, 1896, ABB.
MCLUCAS, MARY, 80, F, None listed, -, Scotland, 37, 37, MARL. In HH
of Mary McLucas, F, 42, born SC.
MCMASTER, JANE, 68, F, None listed, -, Scotland, 302, 279, CHAS. In HH
of Peter Porcher, M, 48, born SC.
MCMELLAN, THOMAS, 46, M, Tailor, -, Scotland, 78, 70, CHAS+.
MCMILLAN, AGNES, 50, F, None listed, -, Scotland, 143, 143, BEAU. In
HH of Thomas McMillan, M, 50, born Scotland.
MCMILLAN, DOUGLAS, 14, M, None listed, -, Scotland, 929, 909, CHAS-.
In HH of Mary McMillan, F, 59, born Scotland.
MCMILLAN, JAMES, 30, M, Painter, -, Scotland, 235, 222, CHAS+.
MCMILLAN, JOHN, 33, M, Laborer, -, Scotland, 1197, 1176, CHAS%. In
Boarding House.
MCMILLAN, JOHN J., 21, M, Clerk, -, Scotland, 929, 909, CHAS-. In HH of

Mary McMillan, F, 59, born Scotland.

MCMILLAN, MARY, 59, F, None listed, -, Scotland, 929, 909, CHAS-.

MCMILLAN, THOMAS, 50, M, Baker, -, Scotland, 143, 143, BEAU.

MCMILLAN, THOS., 44, M, Mechanic/Farm, -, Scotland, 50, 50, CHAS!.

MCMILLIAN, MARY, 43, F, None listed, -, Scotland, 103, 103, UNION.

MCMULLAN, JOHN, 65, M, Merchant, -, Scotland, 378, 343, CHAS.

MCMULLAN, MARGARET E., 55, F, None listed, -, Scotland, 378, 343, CHAS. In HH of John McMullan, M, 65, born Scotland.

MCNEIL, DONALD, 5, M, None listed, -, Scotland, 779, 762, CHAS%. In HH of Richard McNeil, M, 34, born Scotland.

MCNEIL, MARGARET, 30, F, None listed, -, Scotland, 779, 762, CHAS%. In HH of Richard McNeil, M, 34, born Scotland.

MCNEIL, NEIL, 70, M, Custom House In, -, Scotland, 240, 218, CHAS. Custom House Inspector.

MCNEIL, RICHARD, 34, M, Engineer, -, Scotland, 779, 762, CHAS%.

MCNEILL, SUSAN, 58, F, None listed, -, Scotland, 732, 690, CHAS+.

MCPHAIL, JOHN, 62, M, Farmer, -, Scotland, 704, 708, AND.

MCPHAIL, MARARETTA, 56, F, None listed, -, Scotland, 704, 708, AND. In HH of John McPhail, M, 62, born Scotland.

MCPHAIL, PETER, 38, M, Farmer, -, Scotland, 245, 247, AND.

MCPHERSON, ALEX., 50, M, Farmer, -, Scotland, 2435, 2435, SPART.

MCPHERSON, DUGALD, 60, M, Farmer, -, Scotland, 32, 32, MARL.

MCPHERSON, JAMES, 37, M, Baker, -, Scotland, 2299, 2299, GREE.

MCQUEEN, DANIEL, 30, M, Clerk, -, Scotland, 570, 528, CHAS+.

MCRAE, CHRISTIAN, 82, F, None listed, -, Scotland, 523, 523, MARL.

MCRAE, CHRISTIAN, 55, F, None listed, -, Scotland, 7, 7, MARL. In HH of R.A. McRae, M, 54, born NC.

MCSWEEN, ANGUS, 65, M, Farmer, -, Scotland, 663, 663, KERS.

MCSWEEN, CHRISTIAN, 55, F, None listed, -, Scotland, 663, 663, KERS. In HH of Angus McSween, M, 65, born Scotland.

MCVEIN, JOHN, 35, M, Engineer, -, Scotland, 346, 308, CHAS+. In Boarding House.

MILLS, JANNETTE, 32, F, None listed, -, Scotland, 371, 371, ABB. In HH of William S. Mills, M, 33, born GA.

MILNE, ANDREW, 55, M, Planter, -, Scotland, 641, 622, CHAS-.

MILNE, JOHN, 55, M, Planter, -, Scotland, 87, 87, BEAU.

MOFFATT, JAMES, 76, M, None listed, -, Scotland, 15, 15, KERS. In HH of L.M. Barland, M, 40, born SC.

MOFFATT, KEITH S., 30, M, Acct., -, Scotland, 15, 15, KERS. In HH of L.M. Barland, M, 40, born SC.

MONROE, ALY, 54, M, Farmer, -, Scotland, 279, 279, KERS.

MONTGOMERY, AMOS, 84, M, Shoemaker, -, Scotland, 450, 407, CHAS.
MONTGOMERY, CAROLINE, 38, F, None listed, -, Scotland, 450, 407, CHAS. In HH of Amos Montgomery, M, 84, born Scotland.
MONTGOMERY, GEORGE, 44, M, Carpenter, -, Scotland, 450, 407, CHAS. In HH of Amos Montgomery, M, 84, born Scotland.
MONTGOMERY, JAMES, 50, M, Superintendent, -, Scotland, 1723, 1724, EDGE. In HH of Hiram Jordan, M, 36, Landlord, born SC.
MONTGOMERY, SUSANNAH, 63, F, None listed, -, Scotland, 450, 407, CHAS. In HH of Amos Montgomery, M, 84, born Scotland.
MORETON, THOMAS J., 60, M, Taylor, -, Scotland, 566, 570, AND. In HH of James H. Strange 29, M, Taylor, born SC.
MORGAN, SUSAN, 17, F, None listed, -, Scotland, 986, 963, CHAS%. In HH of Benjn. Morgan, M, 48, born SC.
MORRISON, EFFY, 57, F, None listed, -, Scotland, 532, 532, MARL.
MORTON, E., 24, M, Clerk, -, Scotland, 721, 701, CHAS-. In Boarding House.
MUIR, ROBERT, 40, M, Merchant, -, Scotland, 444, 402, CHAS.
MULLINGS, ANN, 50, F, None listed, -, Scotland, 438, 390, CHAS.
MUNHEAD ?, ROBT., 50, M, Overseer, -, Scotland, 783, 783, COLL.
MURDOCK, WILLIAM, 38, M, Bridge contractor, -, Scotland, 1193, 1193, YORK.
MURRY, JAMES, 45, M, Plasterer, -, Scotland, 202, 202, CHAS%. In HH of Thomas Swinton, M, 18, born SC.
MUSTARD, DAVID, 33, M, Engineer, -, Scotland, 619, 577, CHAS+.

N
NEAL, JOHN, 45, M, Farmer, -, Scotland, 99, 99, EDGE*.
NEAL, PETER, 75, M, Farmer, -, Scotland, 183, 183, EDGE*.
NELLES, JAMET, 54, F, Cooper, -, Scotland, 107, 100, CHAS-. In HH of P.D. Nelles, M, 30, born NY.
NEWELL, W.M., 28, M, Bank/clerk, -, Scotland, 1987, 1990, EDGE. In HH of William Kitcham, M, 38, born NJ.
NICHOLS, JOHN, 35, M, Farmer, -, Scotland, 1369, 1375, MAR.
NICHOLSON, JOHN, 54, M, Overseer, -, Scotland, 337, 337, MARL.
NICOL, ALEXANDER, 46, M, Merchant, -, Scotland, 2271, 2271, GREE. In Hotel.
NORTON, JAMES, 23, M, Clerk, -, Scotland, 312, 288, CHAS. In HH of Jane Norton, F, 50, born Scotland.
NORTON, JANE, 50, F, None listed, -, Scotland, 312, 288, CHAS.

# O

OGILVEY, MATHEW, 41, M, Merchant, -, Scotland, 332, 306, CHAS*.

OLIVER, ADAM, 45, M, Master Armourer, -, Scotland, 1005, 982, CHAS%. Under Command of Major P. Hagnes Comg. Off. U.S. Arsnel.

OLIVER, ALEXANDER, 32, M, Shoemaker, -, Scotland, 300, 306, RICH. In Boarding House.

OLIVER, JOHN, 39, M, Shoemaker, -, Scotland, 300, 306, RICH. In Boarding House.

ORR, JAMES, 63, M, Planter, -, Scotland, 1182, 1182, UNION.

ORR, MARTHA, 54, F, None listed, -, Scotland, 1182, 1182, UNION. In HH of James Orr, M, 53, born Scotland.

ORR, WILLIAM, 54, M, Gin maker, -, Scotland, 829, 829, UNION.

OWENS, MARY, 34, F, None listed, -, Scotland, 977, 957, CHAS-. In HH of Stephen Owens, M, 45, born Scotland.

OWENS, STEPHEN, 45, M, Clerk, -, Scotland, 977, 957, CHAS-.

# P

PARK, ERNEST, 38, M, Carpenter, -, Scotland, 806, 806, UNION.

PARK, HENRIETTA, 38, F, None listed, -, Scotland, 806, 806, UNION. In HH of Ernest Park, M, 38, born Scotland.

PARK, JANE, 10, F, None listed, -, Scotland, 806, 806, UNION. In HH of Ernest Park, M, 38, born Scotland.

PATEY, JAMES, 40, M, Master mariner, -, Scotland, 82, 92, CHAS.

PATTERSON, JOHN, 35, M, Boot maker, -, Scotland, 227, 205, CHAS.

PAUL, ALEXANDER, 21, M, Farmer, -, Scotland, 982, 959, CHAS%.

PAUL, DUNBAR, 60, M, Merchant, -, Scotland, 354, 327, CHAS*.

PAUL, JOHN, 17, M, Clerk, -, Scotland, 354, 327, CHAS*. In HH of Paul Dunbar, M, 60, born Scotland.

PEEBLES, WILLIAM, 22, M, Tailor, -, Scotland, 57, 58, ORNG+. In HH of James Jones, M, 40, born England.

PEEBLES, WILLIAM, 22, M, Tailor, -, Scotland, 57, 58, ORNG+. In HH of James Jones , M, 40, born England.

PHIN, A.C., 40, M, Farmer, -, Scotland, 983, 960, CHAS%.

POWELL, ELIZABETH, 21, F, None listed, -, Scotland, 426, 395, CHAS*. In HH of Thomas Powell, M, 35, born Scotland.

POWELL, ELIZABETH, 2, F, None listed, -, Scotland, 426, 395, CHAS*. In HH of Thomas Powell, M, 35, born Scotland.

POWELL, GEORGIANA, 0, F, None listed, -, Scotland, 426, 395, CHAS*. In HH of Thomas Powell, M, 35, born Scotland. Georgiana age 6/12 yr, twin.

POWELL, JANE, 0, F, None listed, -, Scotland, 426, 395, CHAS*. In HH

of Thomas Powell, M, 35, born Scotland. Jane age 6/12 yr, twin.
POWELL, THOMAS, 35, M, Clerk, -, Scotland, 426, 395, CHAS*.
PRICE, ISABELLA, 75, F, None listed, -, Scotland, 120, 120, EDGE*.

# R

RAMSEY, ANDREW, 30, M, Carriage maker, -, Scotland, 94, 94, EDGE.
ROBB, JAMES, 60, M, Grocer, -, Scotland, 637, 618, CHAS-.
ROBB, LOUISA, 25, F, None listed, -, Scotland, 637, 618, CHAS-. In HH of
James Robb, M, 60, born Scotland.
ROBB, MARTHA, 59, F, None listed, -, Scotland, 637, 618, CHAS-. In HH
of James Robb, M, 60, born Scotland.
ROBERTSON, ADAM, 25, M, Acct., -, Scotland, 1, 1, KERS. In HH of
Jesse S. Neales, M, 54, born SC.
ROBERTSON, ANDREW, 44, M, Mariner, -, Scotland, 362, 333, CHAS. In
Boarding House.
ROBERTSON, JAMES, 60, M, None listed, -, Scotland, 82, 74, CHAS+. In
HH of Joseph Pattena, M, 41, born Italy.
ROBERTSON, JAMES, 57, M, Laborer, -, Scotland, 237, 222, CHAS-. Poor
House
ROBERTSON, JAMES, 50, M, Merchant, -, Scotland, 508, 458, CHAS.
RODGER, ANN, 30, F, None listed, -, Scotland, 805, 805, UNION. In HH of
John Rodgers, M, 30, born Scotland.
RODGER, JAMES, 4, M, None listed, -, Scotland, 805, 805, UNION. In HH
of John Rodgers, M, 30, born Scotland.
RODGER, JOHN, 29, M, Carpenter, -, Scotland, 805, 805, UNION.
RODGER, JOHN, 6, M, None listed, -, Scotland, 805, 805, UNION. In HH
of John Rodgers, M, 30, born Scotland.
ROEMPKE, JESSE, 23, M, None listed, -, Scotland, 178, 164, CHAS*.
ROSS, JAMES, 60, M, Port Warden, -, Scotland, 167, 149, CHAS. In
Boarding house.
ROSS, WM., 66, M, Planter, -, Scotland, 1213, 1213, SUMT.
RUDDOCK, ARTHUR, 40, M, Cabinetmaker, -, Scotland, 184, 168, CHAS*.
RUDDOCK, BARBARA, 30, F, None listed, -, Scotland, 184, 168, CHAS*.
In HH of Arthur Ruddock, M, 40, born Scotland.

# S

SALMOND, THOS., 67, M, Bank officer, -, Scotland, 2, 2, KERS.
SCRIVEN, JAMES, 40, M, Refiner, -, Scotland, 401, 361, CHAS+. In HH of
Catherine Brady, F, 40, born Ireland.
SCRIVEN, MARY, 29, F, None listed, -, Scotland, 401, 361, CHAS+. In HH

of Catherine Brady, F, 40, born Ireland.

**SHAW, ELIZABETH**, 21, F, None listed, -, Scotland, 995, 974, CHAS-. In HH of James Shaw, M, 28, born Scotland.

**SHAW, JAMES**, 28, M, Shopkeeper, -, Scotland, 995, 974, CHAS-.

**SHEPPARD, JOHN**, 75, M, None, -, Scotland, 643, 661, RICH. InPoor House.

**SHERDON, JOHN**, 25, M, Miller, -, Scotland, 600, 558, CHAS+.

**SHERDON, MARY**, 22, F, None listed, -, Scotland, 600, 558, CHAS+. In HH of John Sherdon, M, 25, born Scotland.

**SHIELDS, DUNCAN**, 44, M, Engineer, -, Scotland, 446, 429, CHAS-.

**SHIELDS, MARY ANN**, 40, F, None listed, -, Scotland, 446, 429, CHAS-. In HH of Duncan Shields, M, 44, born Scotland.

**SHIELLS, ELIZABETH**, 52, F, None listed, -, Scotland, 612, 629, RICH.

**SHIELLS, JANE**, 45, F, None listed, -, Scotland, 612, 629, RICH. In HH of Elizabeath Shiells, F, 52, born Scotland.

**SHILLINGLAN, ANDREW**, 57, M, Farmer, -, Scotland, 112, 112, YORK.

**SINCLAIR, GEORGE**, 30, M, Mechanic, -, Scotland, 1135, 1135, CHES. In HH of James Loury, M, 69, born SC.

**SINCLAIR, JOHN**, 24, M, Mechanic, -, Scotland, 429, 429, KERS.

**SINCLAIR, JOHN C.**, 31, M, Farmer, -, Scotland, 3, 3, MARL.

**SINKLER, CATHERINE**, 42, F, None listed, -, Scotland, 1400, 1406, MAR.

**SINKLER, DANIEL**, 57, M, Farmer, -, Scotland, 1401, 1407, MAR.

**SINKLER, FLORA**, 53, F, None listed, -, Scotland, 1401, 1407, MAR. In HH of Daniel Sinkler 57, born Scotland.

**SMITH, AGNESS**, 24, F, None listed, -, Scotland, 423, 394, CHAS*. In HH of James Smith, M, 28, born Scotland.

**SMITH, AGNESS**, 2, F, None listed, -, Scotland, 423, 394, CHAS*. In HH of James Smith, M, 28, born Scotland.

**SMITH, ANGUS**, 23, M, Clerk, -, Scotland, 223, 199, CHAS*. In HH of Elizabeth Lawrence, F, 42, born SC.

**SMITH, J. BENA**, 55, F, None listed, -, Scotland, 184, 184, EDGE*.

**SMITH, JAMES**, 28, M, Engineer, -, Scotland, 423, 394, CHAS*.

**SMITH, JOHN**, 18, M, Blacksmith, -, Scotland, 223, 199, CHAS*. In HH of Elizabeth Lawrence, F, 42, born SC.

**SMITH, JOHN**, 3, M, None listed, -, Scotland, 423, 394, CHAS*. In HH of James Smith, M, 28, born Scotland.

**SMYTH, JOHN**, 35, M, Cabinetmaker, -, Scotland, 986, 965, CHAS-.

**SPARKS, JANE**, 68, F, None listed, -, Scotland, 1105, 1105, DARL. In HH of Alexr. Sparks, M, 70, born NC.

**SPENCE, H.**, 77, M, None listed, -, Scotland, 8, 8, NEWB. In HH of Isabella Welch 50 f, born SC.

STAY, GILBERT, 40, M, Mariner, -, Scotland, 784, 742, CHAS+.

STENHOUSE, EBENEZER, 16, M, Drayman, -, Scotland, 346, 346, CHAS%. In HH of Thomas Stenhouse, M, 29, born Scotland.

STENHOUSE, JANE, 19, F, None listed, -, Scotland, 346, 346, CHAS%. In HH of Thomas Stenhouse, M, 29, born Scotland.

STENHOUSE, THOMAS, 29, M, None listed, -, Scotland, 346, 346, CHAS%.

STENNIP, ADAM, 53, M, Farmer, -, Scotland, 1701, 1701, GREE.

STENNIP, ELIZABETH, 55, F, None listed, -, Scotland, 1701, 1701, GREE. In HH of Adam Stennip, M, 53 for Scotland.

STENNIP, ISABELLA, 25, F, None listed, -, Scotland, 1701, 1701, GREE. In HH of Adam Stennip, M, 53 for Scotland.

STEWARD, JAMES, 40, M, Merchant, -, Scotland, 522, 488, CHAS*. In HH of Pricilla Steward, F, 35, born Scotland.

STEWARD, PRISCILLA, 35, F, None listed, -, Scotland, 522, 488, CHAS*.

STEWART, DUNCAN, 61, M, Farmer, -, Scotland, 290, 290, COLL.

STUART, DONALD, 30, M, Painter, -, Scotland, 81, 75, CHAS-.

STUART, JANE, 30, F, None listed, -, Scotland, 81, 75, CHAS-. In HH of Donald Stuart, M, 30, born Scotland.

STUART, W., 24, M, Priv. U.S.A., -, Scotland, 47, 43, CHAS$. In HH of John Ewing, M, 50, born MA.

SUTHERLAND, WILLIAM, 34, M, Laborer, -, Scotland, 239, 225, CHAS+.

## T

TEPLADY, JAMES, 44, M, Mariner, -, Scotland, 26, 31, CHAS. In HH of Moses Levy, M, 45 tavern keeper, born SC.

THOMPSON, MARION, 39, F, None listed, -, Scotland, 251, 236, CHAS-. In HH of William B. Thompson, M, 40, born England.

THOMPSON, MARY, 51, F, None listed, -, Scotland, 546, 546, ABB. In HH of Ninion Thompson, M, 50, born Scotland.

THOMPSON, NINION, 60, M, Farmer, -, Scotland, 546, 546, ABB.

THOMPSON, THEODORE, 34, M, Mariner, -, Scotland, 362, 333, CHAS. In Boarding House.

THOMSON, DAVID L., 45, M, Farmer, -, Scotland, 93, 93, BEAU.

THOMSON, GEORGE, 21, M, Wheelwright, -, Scotland, 39, 40, ORNG+. In HH of Daniel Kitterell, M, 44, born SC.

THOMSON, GEORGE, 21, M, Wheelwright, -, Scotland, 39, 40, ORNG+.

THOMSON, JOHN, 40, M, Shopkeeper, -, Scotland, 357, 319, CHAS+.

THOMSON, JOHN, 38, M, Seedsman, -, Scotland, 828, 808, CHAS-.

THOMSON, N., 27, M, Painter/Glazer, -, Scotland, 479, 445, CHAS*.

THOMSON, THOMAS, 35, M, Lawyer, -, Scotland, 784, 784, ABB.

TUNIS, MARY, 40, F, None listed, -, Scotland, 146, 130, CHAS.
TURNBALL, JAMES, 65, M, None, -, Scotland, 266, 234, CHAS.
TURPUN ?, LOUISA, 27, F, None listed, -, Scotland, 2341, 2341, GREE. In
HH of W.P.Turpun ?, M, 29, born SC.
TWEED, SUSANAH, 30, F, None listed, -, Scotland, 86, 86, KERS. In HH of
R.L. Tweed, M, 34, born Ireland.

## V

VEREE, ROBERT, 55, M, Merchant, -, Scotland, 265, 233, CHAS. In HH of
Eliza Trouchet, F, 45, born SC.

## W

WALLACE, ANDREW, 70, M, Clerk, -, Scotland, 261, 246, CHAS-. In HH
of Isaac Martin, M, 27, born Ireland.
WALLACE, ANDREW, 67, M, None, -, Scotland, 876, 886, RICH+.
WALLACE, THOMAS, 47, M, Merchant, -, Scotland, 780, 760, CHAS-.
WARRINGTON, ELIZABETH, 50, F, None listed, -, Scotland, 558, 541,
CHAS-. In HH of Amelia Cornwell, F, 35 mulatto, born SC.
WATSON, JAMES, 50, M, Merchant, -, Scotland, 286, 263, CHAS. In
Carolina Hotel.
WATSON, THOMAS, 40, M, Master mariner, -, Scotland, 114, 129, CHAS.
WEST, MARIA, 35, F, None listed, -, Scotland, 313, 288, CHAS. In HH of
W. Norton West, M, 44, born Scotland.
WEST, W. NORTON, 44, M, None listed, -, Scotland, 313, 288, CHAS.
WHITE, JOHN, 59, M, Stone cutter, -, Scotland, 273, 257, CHAS-.
WHITE, JOSEPH, 35, M, Merchant, -, Scotland, 392, 356, CHAS. In HH of
F. W. Theus, M, 28, born Germany.
WHITE, MARGARET, 39, F, None listed, -, Scotland, 976, 956, CHAS-. In
HH of McCauley White, M, 43, born Scotland.
WHITE, MASSOLIN, 35, M, Blacksmith, -, Scotland, 219, 197, CHAS. In HH
of A. Fink, M, 30, born Hanover.
WHITE, MCCAULEY, 43, M, Moulder, -, Scotland, 976, 956, CHAS-.
WHITEMAN, JAMES, 32, M, Painter, -, Scotland, 179, 164, CHAS*.
WHITEMAN, MARGERY, 23, F, None listed, -, Scotland, 179, 164, CHAS*.
In HH of James Whiteman, M, 32, born Scotland.
WHITESIDES, MARY, 65, F, None listed, -, Scotland, 1088, 1088, YORK. In
HH of Mayer Whitsides, M, 24, born York Dist., SC.
WIGHTMAN, WILLIAM J., 57, M, Merchant, -, Scotland, 2398, 2405, EDGE.
WILDON, JANE, 37, F, None listed, -, Scotland, 1155, 1155, SUMT. In HH
of Saml. Weldon, M, 37, born SC.

WILLIAMS, JANETTE, 37, F, None listed, -, Scotland, 428, 428, YORK*. In HH of Duncan McCallum, M, 66, born Scotland.

WILSON, ADAM, 40, M, Shopkeeper, -, Scotland, 421, 380, CHAS+.

WILSON, AGNES, 22, F, None listed, -, Scotland, 52, 52, KERS. In HH of Jas. Wilson, M, 29, born Scotland.

WILSON, DAVID, 58, M, Teacher, -, Scotland, 116, 116, BEAU.

WILSON, ELIZABETH, 45, F, None listed, -, Scotland, 864, 844, CHAS-. In HH of Angus Wilson, M, 27, born Ireland.

WILSON, HUGH, 15, M, None listed, -, Scotland, 52, 52, KERS. In HH of Jas. Wilson, M, 29, born Scotland.

WILSON, JAMES, 48, M, Farmer, -, Scotland, 5, 5, COLL+.

WILSON, JANETTE, 69, F, None listed, -, Scotland, 547, 547, ABB. In HH of James Clatworthy, M, 45, born Ireland.

WILSON, JAS., 29, M, Merchant, -, Scotland, 52, 52, KERS.

WILSON, JOHN, 38, M, Machinist, -, Scotland, 470, 472, AND.

WILSON, JOHN, 37, M, Laborer, -, Scotland, 859, 836, CHAS%. In HH of H. Berry, M, 52, born Germany.

WILSON, LETITIA, 61, F, None listed, -, Scotland, 2309, 2309, ABB. In HH of William Wilson, M, 46, born SC.

WILSON, THOMAS, 25, M, Mariner, -, Scotland, 13, 16, CHAS. In HH of Anna Wilson, F, 25, born NY.

WITHERSPOON, C.M., 32, F, None listed, -, Scotland, 83, 83, KERS. In HH of Jas. K. Witherspoon, M, 33, born NC.

WOTHERSPOON, ROBERT, 55, M, Merchant, -, Scotland, 238, 213, CHAS*.

# Y

YOUNG, ALEXR., 67, M, Merchant, -, Scotland, 45, 45, KERS.

YOUNG, MARY, 59, F, None listed, -, Scotland, 532, 547, RICH.

YOUNG, WILLIAM, 52, M, Baker, -, Scotland, 509, 459, CHAS.

# Z

ZEWILL, WM., 65, M, None, -, Scotland, 1782, 1782, SUMT. In HH of G.W. Bradford, M, 27, born SC.

❖

# BORN IN GERMANY (1,943)

## A

ABRAHAMS, CATHERINE, 58, F, None listed, -, Germany, 78, 72, CHAS-. In HH of Elias Abrahams, M, 63, born England.

ADDIN, JOHN, 23, M, Shoemaker, -, Germany, 89, 90, ORNG+.

ADDIN, L., 31, M, Merchant, -, Germany, 74, 75, ORNG+.

ADICKS, DREDENCK, 10, M, None listed, -, Germany, 17, 15, CHAS-. In HH of John Adicks, M, 37, born Germany.

ADICKS, JOHN, 37, M, Shoemaker, -, Germany, 17, 15, CHAS-.

ADICKS, LOUISA, 28, F, None listed, -, Germany, 17, 15, CHAS-. In HH of John Adicks, M, 37, born Germany.

ADICKS, SOPHIA, 4, F, None listed, -, Germany, 17, 15, CHAS-. In HH of John Adicks, M, 37, born Germany.

AHRENS, JOHN, 35, M, Blacksmith, -, Germany, 541, 507, CHAS*.

AHRENS, MARY, 32, F, None listed, -, Germany, 541, 507, CHAS*. In HH of John Ahrens, M, 35, born Germany.

AHRENS, WILLIAM, 19, M, Clerk, -, Germany, 411, 409, CHAS%. In HH of H. Behr, M, 30, born Germany.

ALBERS, H., 19, M, Clerk, -, Germany, 370, 343, CHAS*. In HH of John Herkamp, M, 38, born Germany.

ALBRIGHT, DORKES, 30, F, None listed, -, Germany, 10, 10, CHAS*. In HH of Nicholas Albright, M, 40, born Germany.

ALBRIGHT, JOHN, 27, M, Clerk, -, Germany, 4, 4, CHAS*. In HH of Albert Finken, M, 23, born Germany.

ALBRIGHT, JOHN, 13, M, None listed, -, Germany, 10, 10, CHAS*. In HH of Nicholas Albright, M, 40, born Germany.

ALBRIGHT, NICHOLAS, 40, M, Grocer, -, Germany, 10, 10, CHAS*.

ALFS, C., 55, M, Castor Oil Mfg., -, Germany, 146, 146, CHAS%.

ALLAHALEY, FREDERICK, 27, M, Grocer, -, Germany, 50, 45, CHAS+.

ALLBRIGHT, CATHERINE, 60, F, None listed, -, Germany, 511, 469, CHAS+. In HH of John Rutzler, M, 45, born Germany.

ALLERS, CARSON, 50, M, Shopkeeper, -, Germany, 194, 194, CHAS%.

ALMER, JOHN, 29, M, Shopkeeper, -, Germany, 485, 443, CHAS+.

ALMER, LENAR, 25, F, None listed, -, Germany, 485, 443, CHAS+. In HH of John Almer, M, 29, born Germany.

ALMERS, FREDERICK J., 33, M, Grocer, -, Germany, 180, 165, CHAS*.

AMAN, GEORGE H., 52, M, Shopkeeper, -, Germany, 885, 862, CHAS%.

AMAN, METURF, 23, F, None listed, -, Germany, 885, 862, CHAS%. In HH of George H. Aman, M, 52, born Germany.

AMIE, CATHERINE, 23, F, None listed, -, Germany, 164, 154, CHAS-. In HH of D.A. Amie, M, 30, born Germany.

AMIE, D.A., 30, M, Grocer, -, Germany, 164, 154, CHAS-.

AMME, H., 28, M, Taylor, -, Germany, 365, 336, CHAS. In HH of C. Dorbaum, M, 30, born Germany.

AMYER, ANTONIO, 16, M, Clerk, -, Germany, 806, 786, CHAS-. In HH of Henry Bollman, M, 20, born Germany.

ANSEL, GERTRUDE, 29, F, None listed, -, Germany, 501, 467, CHAS*. In HH of William Ansel, M, 34, born Germany.

ANSEL, HANS, 23, M, Blacksmith, -, Germany, 501, 467, CHAS*. In HH of William Ansel, M, 34, born Germany.

ANSEL, WILLIAM, 34, M, Engineer, -, Germany, 501, 467, CHAS*.

ANSELL, FREDERICA, 38, F, None listed, -, Germany, 816, 796, CHAS-. In HH of John Ansell, M, 34, born Germany.

ANSELL, FREDERICK, 18, M, Cabinetmaker, -, Germany, 816, 796, CHAS-. In HH of John Ansell, M, 34, born Germany.

ANSELL, JOHN, 34, M, Cabinetmaker, -, Germany, 816, 796, CHAS-.

APELER, JOHN F., 32, M, Shopkeeper, -, Germany, 309, 309, CHAS%.

APELER, MARTHA, 30, F, None listed, -, Germany, 333, 333, CHAS%.

APLER, HERMAN, 25, M, Cabinetmaker, -, Germany, 667, 647, CHAS-. In Boarding House.

ARMOR, JOHN, 40, M, Grocer, -, Germany, 705, 697, CHAS%. In HH of Margt. Mintzingmeyer, F, 48, born Germany.

ARMS, JOHN H., 26, M, Clerk, -, Germany, 112, 104, CHAS+. In HH of Harman Werner, M, 30, born Germany.

ARNETZZ, ANN, 10, F, None listed, -, Germany, 335, 301, CHAS+. In HH of J.U. Boesch, M, 30, born Switzerland.

ASSMANN, WILLIAM, 42, M, Merchant, -, Germany, 1247, 1247, LEX.

AUGUSTE, GERARD, 27, M, Clerk, -, Germany, 172, 155, CHAS. In HH of Ann Marsh, F, 35, born SC.

B

BACHMAN, MARY Born UR, 23, F, None listed, -, Germany, 787, 770, CHAS%. In HH of Revd. John Bachman, M, 59, born NJ.

BADENHOF, HENRY, 17, M, None listed, -, Germany, 288, 288, CHAS%.

BAHULGE, F.W., 31, M, Shopkeeper, -, Germany, 466, 423, CHAS.

BALLSTER, JOHN, 35, M, Ordinance man, -, Germany, 1005, 982, CHAS%. Under command of Major P. Hagnes, Comg. Off. U.S. Arnsel.

BANCHAN, H., 20, M, Clerk, -, Germany, 48, 43, CHAS+. In HH of John

Grube, M, 18, born Germany.

BANKER, MARTINA, 14, F, None listed, -, Germany, 48, 58, CHAS.

BANSAMER, ____ 30, F, None listed, -, Germany, 504, 504, FAIR. In HH of J.F. Gamble, M, 42, Hotel keeper, born NC. no first name given. At the Winnsboro Hotel.

BARBER, LEWIS, 30, M, Baker, -, Germany, 285, 264, CHAS+. In HH of H. Wittschew, M, 23, born Germany.

BARKMAN, GEORGE, 37, M, Grocer, -, Germany, 133, 133, CHAS%.

BASE, HENRY, 24, M, Baker, -, Germany, 48, 57, CHAS.

BASE, HENRY, 22, M, Baker, -, Germany, 722, 680, CHAS+. In HH of Nicholas Kider, M, 34, born Germany.

BATIES, FRANZ, 38, M, Watch maker, -, Germany, 11, 11, CHAS+.

BATIES, MATILDA, 32, F, None listed, -, Germany, 11, 11, CHAS+. In HH of Franz Baties, M, 38, born Germany.

BAUCHAN, CHRIS, 28, M, Clerk, -, Germany, 100, 98, CHAS*. In HH of Peter Brewer, M, 42, born Germany.

BAUM, ELIZA, 32, M, None listed, -, Germany, 667, 647, CHAS-. In Boarding House.

BAUM, J.A., 46, M, Leather Merchant, -, Germany, 667, 647, CHAS-. In Boarding House.

BAUM, J.H., 18, M, Clerk, -, Germany, 667, 647, CHAS-. In Boarding House.

BAUMAN, ELIZABETH, 23, F, None listed, -, Germany, 744, 724, CHAS-. In HH of William Bauman, M, 26, born Germany.

BAUMAN, WILLIAM, 26, M, Shoemaker, -, Germany, 744, 724, CHAS-.

BAUNGER, BETTY, 20, F, Milliner, -, Germany, 852, 832, CHAS-. In HH of A.G. Parker, F, 38, born Germany.

BEAUFORD, SOPHIA, 24, F, None listed, -, Germany, 21, 17, CHAS+. In HH of Andrew Beauford, M, 36, born France.

BECKER, M.J.E., 20, M, Clerk, -, Germany, 179, 162, CHAS. In HH of Hans Jessen, M, 32, born Germany.

BEE, AMELIA, 26, F, None listed, -, Germany, 498, 491, CHAS%. In HH of Henry Williams, M, 50, born Denmark.

BEHLAN, ORTGIS, 18, M, Clerk, -, Germany, 53, 48, CHAS+. In HH of H. Oldenbuttle, M, 25, born Germany.

BEHLING, HENRY, 17, M, Clerk, -, Germany, 838, 818, CHAS-. In HH of T.M. Bristol, M, 30, born CT.

BEHMAN, CATHERINE, 29, F, None listed, -, Germany, 92, 90, CHAS*. In HH of Diederick Behman, M, 34, born Germany.

BEHMAN, CHRISTINA, 16, F, None listed, -, Germany, 92, 90, CHAS*. In HH of Diederick Behman, M, 34, born Germany.

BEHMAN, DIEDERICK, 34, M, Grocer, -, Germany, 92, 90, CHAS*.

**BEHMAN, HENRY**, 30, M, None listed, -, Germany, 92, 90, CHAS\*. In HH of Diederick Behman, M, 34, born Germany.

**BEHR, CATHARINE**, 6, F, None listed, -, Germany, 411, 409, CHAS%. In HH of H. Behr, M, 30, born Germany.

**BEHR, H.**, 30, M, Grocer, -, Germany, 411, 409, CHAS%.

**BEHR, LOUISA**, 27, F, None listed, -, Germany, 411, 409, CHAS%. In HH of H. Behr, M, 30, born Germany.

**BEHSONS, F.**, 33, M, Tailor, -, Germany, 400, 373, CHAS\*.

**BELITZER, CAROLINE**, 28, F, None listed, -, Germany, 725, 705, CHAS-. In HH of Isaac Belitzer, M, 36, born Germany.

**BELITZER, ISAAC**, 36, M, Merchant, -, Germany, 725, 705, CHAS-.

**BELITZER, JACOB**, 11, M, None listed, -, Germany, 725, 705, CHAS-. In HH of Isaac Belitzer, M, 36, born Germany.

**BELITZER, LAURA**, 4, F, None listed, -, Germany, 725, 705, CHAS-. In HH of Isaac Belitzer, M, 36, born Germany.

**BELITZER, THEODORE**, 7, M, None listed, -, Germany, 725, 705, CHAS-. In HH of Isaac Belitzer, M, 36, born Germany.

**BELLAIR, WILLIAM**, 35, M, Shopkeeper, -, Germany, 341, 315, CHAS.

**BELLIRE, GUSTAVIS**, 13, M, None listed, -, Germany, 1106, 1083, CHAS-. In Charleston Orphan House.

**BENGE, CHARLES**, 21, M, Clerk, -, Germany, 538, 504, CHAS\*. In HH of Henry Harinberg, M, 25, born Germany.

**BENNETT, FREDERICK**, 24, M, Baker, -, Germany, 269, 253, CHAS-. In HH of William Stratton, M, 44, born NY.

**BENSON, ELIZABETH**, 50, F, None listed, -, Germany, 123, 114, CHAS-.

**BENTEN, CHRISTON**, 28, M, Shopkeeper, -, Germany, 349, 349, CHAS%.

**BEQUEST, A.**, 40, F, None listed, -, Germany, 85, 95, CHAS. In HH of Harman Knee, M, 47, born Germany.

**BEQUEST, A.**, 16, F, None listed, -, Germany, 85, 95, CHAS. In HH of Harman Knee, M, 47, born Germany.

**BERENTS, LEWIS**, 21, M, Baker, -, Germany, 722, 680, CHAS+. In HH of Nicholas Kider, M, 34, born Germany.

**BERNEMAN, FREDERICK**, 24, M, Jeweler, -, Germany, 728, 708, CHAS-. In HH of Maria Spencer, F, 63, born England.

**BERNGER, C.R.**, 33, M, Clerk, -, Germany, 56, 50, CHAS+. In HH of Frederick Lampe, M, 30, born Germany.

**BERNGER, HENRY**, 18, M, Clerk, -, Germany, 56, 50, CHAS+. In HH of Frederick Lampe, M, 30, born Germany.

**BERRY, H.**, 52, M, Shopkeeper, -, Germany, 859, 836, CHAS%.

**BERYIE, CATHERINE**, 30, F, None listed, -, Germany, 343, 317, CHAS. In HH of Henry Beryie, M, 40, born Germany.

BERYIE, HENRY, 40, M, Shopkeeper, -, Germany, 343, 317, CHAS.
BESSMAN, JOHN, 30, M, Gardner, -, Germany, 1883, 1883, SUMT. In Hotel.
BETSCHUM, ANNE, 32, F, None listed, -, Germany, 763, 748, CHAS%. In
HH of John Betschum, M, 35, born Germany.
BETSCHUM, HENRY S., 11, M, None listed, -, Germany, 763, 748, CHAS%.
In HH of John Betschum, M, 35, born Germany.
BETSCHUM, JOHN, 35, M, Laborer, -, Germany, 763, 748, CHAS%.
BIANCIA, MARY S., 31, F, None listed, -, Germany, 32, 27, CHAS+. In HH
of Achille Biancia, M, 33, born Switzerland.
BIESARRER, HENRY, 35, M, Grocer, -, Germany, 345, 328, CHAS-.
BILLINGS, JULIA, 33, F, None listed, -, Germany, 867, 844, CHAS%.
BIRD, MARY ANN, 16, F, None listed, -, Germany, 546, 512, CHAS*. In HH
of Solomon Knepley, M, 58, born PA.
BISCHOFF, A., 35, M, Merchant, -, Germany, 97, 89, CHAS+.
BISCHOFF, HENRY, 22, M, Clerk, -, Germany, 287, 271, CHAS-. In HH of
Ann Myerhoff, F, 22, born Germany.
BISCHOFF, WILLIAM, 40, M, Farmer, -, Germany, 1017, 994, CHAS%.
BISCHOFFE, NICHOLAS, 19, M, Clerk, -, Germany, 199, 187, CHAS+. In
HH of Henry Wulburn, M, 21, born Germany.
BITZ, C., 37, M, Priv. U.S.A., -, Germany, 47, 43, CHAS$. In HH of John
Ewing, M, 50, born MA.
BLACK, SOPHIA, 26, F, None listed, -, Germany, 124, 116, CHAS*. In HH
of William Black, M, 28, born NY.
BLANKENSTEIN, CATHERINE, 43, F, None listed, -, Germany, 283, 289,
RICH. In HH of Jacob Blankenstein, M, 43, born Germany.
BLANKENSTEIN, ELIZABETH, 15, F, None listed, -, Germany, 283, 289,
RICH. In HH of Jacob Blankenstein, M, 43, born Germany.
BLANKENSTEIN, JACOB, 43, M, Gunsmith, -, Germany, 283, 289, RICH.
BLASIMIS, J., 29, M, Punter, -, Germany, 667, 647, CHAS-. In Boarding
House.
BLAUM, ANNA ELIZABETH, 26, F, None listed, -, Germany, 101, 99,
CHAS*. In HH of H. Blaum, M, 23, born Germany.
BLAUM, H., 23, M, Shopkeeper, -, Germany, 101, 99, CHAS*.
BLEPMAN, WILLIAM, 30, M, Upholsterer, -, Germany, 444, 441, CHAS%.
BLOCK, HENRY, 25, M, None listed, -, Germany, 836, 816, CHAS-. In
Boarding House.
BLOCK, WILLIAM, 21, M, Clerk, -, Germany, 596, 554, CHAS+.
BLOCKER, ALFRED, 39, M, Grocer, -, Germany, 710, 702, CHAS%.
BLOCKER, ANN, 36, F, None listed, -, Germany, 710, 702, CHAS%. In HH
of Ann Blocker, F, 36, born Germany.
BLOCKER, AUGUSTUS, 10, M, None listed, -, Germany, 710, 702, CHAS%.

In HH of Ann Blocker, F, 36, born Germany.

**BLOCKER, CAROLINE**, 8, F, None listed, -, Germany, 710, 702, CHAS%. In HH of Ann Blocker, F, 36, born Germany.

**BLUM, AUGUSTA**, 21, F, None listed, -, Germany, 188, 176, CHAS-. In HH of John Mintzing, M, 28, born Germany.

**BLUM, D. ELIZABETH**, 26, F, None listed, -, Germany, 1, 1, CHAS+. In HH of John P. Blum, M, 28, born Germany.

**BLUM, ELIZA**, 26, F, None listed, -, Germany, 196, 180, CHAS*. In HH of Lewis Muller, M, 31, born Germany.

**BLUM, ELIZA**, 20, F, None listed, -, Germany, 188, 176, CHAS-. In HH of John Mintzing, M, 28, born Germany.

**BLUM, JOHN P.**, 28, M, Grocer, -, Germany, 1, 1, CHAS+.

**BLUM, MARY S.**, 76, F, None listed, -, Germany, 820, 778, CHAS+. In HH of Saml. Lord, M, 54, born MA.

**BOCHMAN, CATHERINE**, 25, F, None listed, -, Germany, 662, 642, CHAS-.

**BOCKMAN, HENRY**, 22, M, Farmer, -, Germany, 1186, 1186, LEX.

**BOCKMAN, MARY**, 22, F, None listed, -, Germany, 1186, 1186, LEX. In HH of Henry Bockman, M, 22, born Germany.

**BOESCH, MARY**, 25, F, None listed, -, Germany, 335, 301, CHAS+. In HH of J.U. Boesch, M, 30, born Switzerland.

**BOHLES, LEO**, 47, M, Grocer, -, Germany, 16, 14, CHAS-.

**BOHLES, MEESA**, 40, F, None listed, -, Germany, 16, 14, CHAS-. In HH of Leo Bohles, M, 47, born Germany.

**BOHLIN, J.H.**, 20, M, Clerk, -, Germany, 160, 151, CHAS+. In HH of Henry Stams 20, born Germany.

**BOISE, A.**, 22, M, Clerk, -, Germany, 847, 827, CHAS-. In HH of Sophia Selle 34, born Germany.

**BOKLULY?, LUDER J.**, 35, M, Merchant, -, Germany, 770, 770, BARN.

**BOKLULY?, MARTHA**, 34, F, None listed, -, Germany, 770, 770, BARN. In HH of Luder F. Bokluly?, M, 35, born Germany.

**BOLACKEN, DIEDRICK**, 12, M, None listed, -, Germany, 696, 688, CHAS%. In HH of John Bolacken, M, 40, born Germany.

**BOLACKEN, JOHN**, 40, M, Grocer, -, Germany, 696, 688, CHAS%.

**BOLACKEN, MARY**, 37, F, None listed, -, Germany, 696, 688, CHAS%. In HH of John Bolacken, M, 40, born Germany.

**BOLLMAN, HENRY**, 20, M, Clerk, -, Germany, 806, 786, CHAS-.

**BORCHERS, J.**, 37, M, Grocer, -, Germany, 22, 22, CHAS%.

**BORNER, C.F.**, 29, M, Grocer, -, Germany, 352, 335, CHAS-.

**BORNER, CATHERINE**, 55, F, None listed, -, Germany, 352, 335, CHAS-. In HH of C.F. Borner, M, 29, born Germany.

**BORNER, CHRISTIAN**, 21, M, Clerk, -, Germany, 352, 335, CHAS-. In HH of C.F. Borner, M, 29, born Germany.

**BORNER, MARY**, 22, F, None listed, -, Germany, 352, 335, CHAS-. In HH of C.F. Borner, M, 29, born Germany.

**BORTELL, F.C.**, 30, M, Jeweller, -, Germany, 492, 496, And. In HH of Ann Morris, F, 36, born SC.

**BOSCH, J.H.**, 24, M, Grocer, -, Germany, 552, 511, CHAS+.

**BOSCH, JOHN D.**, 20, M, Shopkeeper, -, Germany, 185, 185, CHAS%.

**BOSE, HARMAN**, 26, M, Clerk, -, Germany, 677, 657, CHAS-. In HH of Elizabeth Fell, F, 40, born SC.

**BOSMAN, WM.**, 28, M, Tailor, -, Germany, 464, 421, CHAS.

**BOUGLE, GEORGE**, 42, M, Laborer, -, Germany, 535, 571, RICH.

**BOYD, DORA**, 30, F, None listed, -, Germany, 285, 269, CHAS-. In HH of James Harrale, M, 30, born GA.

**BRANDES, CATARIN**, 34, F, None listed, -, Germany, 1050, 1028, CHAS%. In HH of Claus Schleyer, M, 37, born Germany.

**BRANDES, HENRY**, 5, M, None listed, -, Germany, 1050, 1028, CHAS%. In HH of Claus Schleyer, M, 37, born Germany.

**BRANDES, PETER**, 39, M, Miller, -, Germany, 1050, 1028, CHAS%. In HH of Claus Schleyer, M, 37, born Germany.

**BRANDT, JOHN**, 25, M, Carpenter, -, Germany, 433, 392, CHAS+. In HH of H. Steinman, M, 28, born Germany.

**BRANDT, MARIA**, 20, F, None listed, -, Germany, 433, 392, CHAS+. In HH of H. Steinman, M, 28, born Germany.

**BRANDT, T.C.**, 55, M, Carriage Trimmer, -, Germany, 465, 423, CHAS+.

**BRANNACKER, CHARLES**, 26, M, Shoemaker, -, Germany, 412, 371, CHAS+.

**BRAUN, JOHN**, 26, M, Taylor, -, Germany, 379, 344, CHAS. In HH of N.R. Schineder, M, 32, born Germany.

**BREDENBERG, JOHN H.**, 26, M, Grocer, -, Germany, 380, 353, CHAS*.

**BREEDMAN, W.**, 27, M, Shopkeeper, -, Germany, 428, 387, CHAS+.

**BREGNAN, H.**, 24, M, Shopkeeper, -, Germany, 318, 293, CHAS.

**BREMAR, CAROLINE**, 21, F, None listed, -, Germany, 284, 263, CHAS+. In HH of F.H. Bremar, M, 33, born Germany.

**BREMAR, F.H.**, 33, M, Grocer, -, Germany, 284, 263, CHAS+.

**BREMAR, JOHN**, 34, M, Shoemaker, -, Germany, 183, 167, CHAS*.

**BRENSSEN, ANNE**, 34, F, None listed, -, Germany, 684, 676, CHAS%. In HH of C.H. Brenssen, M, 35, born Germany.

**BRENSSEN, C.H.**, 35, M, Shopkeeper, -, Germany, 684, 676, CHAS%.

**BRENSSEN, MATAR**, 4, F, None listed, -, Germany, 684, 676, CHAS%. In HH of C.H. Brenssen, M, 35, born Germany.

**BREWER, ANNA**, 25, F, None listed, -, Germany, 838, 818, CHAS-. In HH of

T.M. Bristol, M, 30, born CT.

**BREWER, DEDRICK**, 18, M, None listed, -, Germany, 666, 658, CHAS%. In HH of A. Lindstedt, M, 29, born Germany.

**BREWER, PETER**, 42, M, Grocer, -, Germany, 100, 98, CHAS*.

**BREY, CATHERINE**, 6, F, None listed, -, Germany, 517, 500, CHAS-. In HH of J.H. Keil, M, 32, born Germany.

**BREY, JOHN H.**, 4, M, None listed, -, Germany, 517, 500, CHAS-. In HH of J.H. Keil, M, 32, born Germany.

**BREY, REBECCA**, 22, F, None listed, -, Germany, 517, 500, CHAS-. In HH of J.H. Keil, M, 32, born Germany.

**BRIENER, WILLIAM**, 28, M, Clerk, -, Germany, 385, 383, CHAS%. In HH of Benjamin Wreden, M, 38, born Germany.

**BRIGAMAN, HENRY D.**, 32, M, Farmer, -, Germany, 732, 770, PICK.

**BRIGHAM, DOROTHY**, 36, F, None listed, -, Germany, 770, 753, CHAS%. In HH of William Brigham, M, 38, born Germany.

**BRIGHAM, FREDERICK**, 14, M, None listed, -, Germany, 770, 753, CHAS%. In HH of William Brigham, M, 38, born Germany.

**BRIGHAM, WILLIAM**, 38, M, Grocer, -, Germany, 770, 753, CHAS%.

**BROCKNEY, CHAS.**, 26, M, Wheel wright, -, Germany, 379, 344, CHAS. In HH of N.R. Schineder, M, 32, born Germany.

**BROCKNEY, W.**, 28, M, Wheel wright, -, Germany, 379, 344, CHAS. In HH of N.R. Schineder, M, 32, born Germany.

**BROODMAN, H.**, 32, M, Priv. U.S.A., -, Germany, 47, 43, CHAS$. In HH of John Ewing, M, 50, born MA.

**BROWN, JOSEPH**, 29, M, Hatter, -, Germany, 764, 744, CHAS-.

**BRUDENBERG, C.F.**, 25, M, Grocer, -, Germany, 4, 4, CHAS%.

**BRUHAS, H.**, 22, M, Clerk, -, Germany, 440, 437, CHAS%. In HH of John A. Cook, M, 52, born Germany.

**BRUNER, J.H.**, 25, M, Clerk, -, Germany, 407, 367, CHAS+. In HH of Stephen Bush, M, 26, born Germany.

**BRUNGER, WILLIAM**, 30, M, Grocer, -, Germany, 493, 476, CHAS-.

**BRUNS, H.**, 24, M, Grocer, -, Germany, 507, 465, CHAS+.

**BRYANT, MARY**, 25, F, None listed, -, Germany, 872, 849, CHAS%. In HH of William Bryant, M, 25, born Germany.

**BRYANT, MARY**, 6, F, None listed, -, Germany, 872, 849, CHAS%. In HH of William Bryant, M, 25, born Germany.

**BRYANT, WILLIAM**, 25, M, Laborer, -, Germany, 872, 849, CHAS%.

**BUCHEN, HENRY**, 21, M, Blacksmith, -, Germany, 143, 143, CHAS%. In HH of Jacob Hillan, M, 35, born Germany.

**BUCKELHOFF, WILHELMINA**, 30, F, Grocer, -, Germany, 486, 452, CHAS*.

**BUCKING, ADALINE**, 46, F, None listed, -, Germany, 870, 847, CHAS%. In

HH of John Bucking, M, 46, born Germany.
**BUCKING, ANN**, 12, F, None listed, -, Germany, 870, 847, CHAS%. In HH of John Bucking, M, 46, born Germany.
**BUCKING, FREDRICK**, 21, M, None listed, -, Germany, 870, 847, CHAS%. In HH of John Bucking, M, 46, born Germany.
**BUCKING, GEORGE**, 2, M, None listed, -, Germany, 870, 847, CHAS%. In HH of John Bucking, M, 46, born Germany.
**BUCKING, HENRY**, 10, M, None listed, -, Germany, 870, 847, CHAS%. In HH of John Bucking, M, 46, born Germany.
**BUCKING, JOHN**, 46, M, Painter, -, Germany, 870, 847, CHAS%.
**BUCKING, MARTHA**, 15, F, None listed, -, Germany, 870, 847, CHAS%. In HH of John Bucking, M, 46, born Germany.
**BUCKING, MARY**, 18, F, None listed, -, Germany, 870, 847, CHAS%. In HH of John Bucking, M, 46, born Germany.
**BUCKMAN, CAROLINE**, 18, F, None listed, -, Germany, 1174, 1174, LEX. In HH of John H. Buckman, M, 50, born Germany.
**BUCKMAN, JOHN H.**, 50, M, Bricklayer, -, Germany, 1174, 1174, LEX.
**BUCKMAN, MARY E.**, 58, F, None listed, -, Germany, 1174, 1174, LEX. In HH of John H. Buckman, M, 50, born Germany.
**BUKMAN, FREDERIC**, 50, M, Overseer, -, Germany, 378, 378, MARL.
**BULL, JOHN**, 38, M, Grocer, -, Germany, 95, 93, CHAS*.
**BULLWINKLE, DIEDRICK**, 22, M, Shopkeeper, -, Germany, 336, 336, CHAS%.
**BULLWINKLE, F.**, 22, M, Grocer, -, Germany, 479, 437, CHAS.
**BULLWINKLE, GEORGE**, 25, M, Baker, -, Germany, 69, 69, COLL.
**BULLWINKLE, HENRY**, 25, M, Store keeper, -, Germany, 177, 160, CHAS.
**BULLWINKLE, MARTIN**, 16, M, None listed, -, Germany, 596, 588, CHAS%. In HH of Henry Ehricks, M, 37, born Germany.
**BULWINCKLE, M.**, 22, M, Shopkeeper, -, Germany, 68, 78, CHAS.
**BULWINKLE, ANNE**, 28, F, None listed, -, Germany, 556, 548, CHAS%. In HH of George Bulwinkle, M, 29, born Germany.
**BULWINKLE, AULIDE**, 26, F, Servant, -, Germany, 160, 143, CHAS. In HH of John H. Ostendosff, M, 38, born Germany.
**BULWINKLE, DIEDERICK**, 30, M, Grocer, -, Germany, 470, 436, CHAS*.
**BULWINKLE, GEORGE**, 29, M, Shopkeeper, -, Germany, 556, 548, CHAS%.
**BULWINKLE, GEORGE**, 26, M, None listed, -, Germany, 1185, 1164, CHAS%. In HH of Mary Ann Sanders, F, 40 black, born SC.
**BULWINKLE, HENRY**, 45, M, Shopkeeper, -, Germany, 562, 554, CHAS%.
**BUNGER, CATHERINE**, 34, F, None listed, -, Germany, 636, 628, CHAS%. In HH of Nicholas Bunger, M, 36, born Germany.
**BUNGER, NICHOLAS**, 36, M, Shopkeeper, -, Germany, 636, 628, CHAS%.

BURDELL, E.T., 15, M, None listed, -, Germany, 279, 279, CHAS%.

BURGHMAN, B., 48, M, Grocer, -, Germany, 793, 776, CHAS%.

BURHEIT, FRANCES, 3, F, None listed, -, Germany, 894, 871, CHAS%. In HH of Philip Bucheit, M, 31, born Germany.

BURHEIT, LOUISA, 23, F, None listed, -, Germany, 894, 871, CHAS%. In HH of Philip Bucheit, M, 31, born Germany.

BURHEIT, PHILIP, 31, M, Engineer, -, Germany, 894, 871, CHAS%.

BURHEIT, PHILIP, 7, M, None listed, -, Germany, 894, 871, CHAS%. In HH of Philip Bucheit, M, 31, born Germany.

BURKMAN, ANDREW, 22, M, Baker, -, Germany, 1169, 1148, CHAS%.

BURMASTER, B., 20, M, Clerk, -, Germany, 847, 827, CHAS-. In HH of Sophia Selle 34, born Germany.

BURMASTER, CLAUS, 24, M, Tailor, -, Germany, 800, 758, CHAS+. In HH of Harman Sturke, M, 34, born Germany.

BURMASTER, FREDERICK, 20, M, Clerk, -, Germany, 374, 347, CHAS*. In HH of Harriot Gray, F, 45, born SC.

BURNHAM, CARSTEN, 24, M, Shopkeeper, -, Germany, 595, 553, CHAS+. In HH of William Burnham, M, 50, born England.

BURNHIEM, A., 22, M, Luth. Minister, -, Germany, 467, 450, CHAS-. In HH of Martha Mitchell, F, 30, born SC.

BURNS, HENRY, 33, M, Shoemaker, -, Germany, 245, 250, RICH. In HH of Gottlieb Eilhardt, M, 41, born Germany.

BURNS, WILLIAM, 22, M, Clerk, -, Germany, 180, 165, CHAS*. In HH of Frederick J. Almers, M, 33, born Germany.

BUSH, A., 45, M, Shopkeeper, -, Germany, 813, 793, CHAS-. In HH of Isaac Seckendorffe, M, 40, born Germany.

BUSH, ANNE, 25, F, None listed, -, Germany, 407, 367, CHAS+. In HH of Stephen Bush, M, 26, born Germany.

BUSH, STEPHEN, 26, M, Grocer, -, Germany, 407, 367, CHAS+.

BUSHKIN, F.W.H., 25, M, Clerk, -, Germany, 426, 385, CHAS+. In HH of C.F. Hankin, M, 26, born Germany.

BUSSAKER, CHARLES, 65, M, None listed, -, Germany, 237, 222, CHAS-. Poor House.

BYER, CATHERINE, 34, M, None listed, -, Germany, 162, 162, CHAS%. In HH of John Byer, M, 38, born Germany.

BYER, FRITZ, 11, M, None listed, -, Germany, 162, 162, CHAS%. In HH of John Byer, M, 38, born Germany.

BYER, JOHN, 38, M, Grocer, -, Germany, 162, 162, CHAS%.

# C

**CAGELAR, CHRISTINE**, 18, F, None listed, -, Germany, 2022, 2028, Edge. In HH of Charles Crouch, M, 34, born Germany.

**CAMPSEN, BERNARD**, 16, M, Clerk, -, Germany, 745, 725, CHAS-. In HH of Frederick Wittpen, M, 43, born Germany.

**CAMPSEND, J.**, 25, M, Store keeper, -, Germany, 342, 305, CHAS+. In HH of H.D. Ellerhorst, M, 35, born Germany.

**CAMPSON, FREDERICK**, 31, M, Laborer, -, Germany, 783, 766, CHAS%. In HH of Frederick Kracki, M, 41, born Germany.

**CANLIER, GEORGE**, 40, M, Physician, -, Germany, 111, 103, CHAS+.

**CARROLL, CLARA**, 39, F, None listed, -, Germany, 592, 609, RICH. In HH of Alexander Carroll, M, 32, born England.

**CARSTENS, A.**, 24, M, Miller, -, Germany, 110, 110, CHAS%. In HH of H. Oetjen, M, 35, born Germany.

**CARSTENS, H.**, 21, M, Clerk, -, Germany, 110, 110, CHAS%. In HH of H. Oetjen, M, 35, born Germany.

**CARSTIN, HENRY**, 21, M, Clerk, -, Germany, 630, 611, CHAS-. In HH of John A. Kerp, M, 26, born Germany.

**CASTELLA, ELIZABETH**, 28, F, None listed, -, Germany, 295, 272, CHAS+. In HH of Jose Castella, M, 32, born Spain.

**CAUSE, BETTY**, 25, F, None listed, -, Germany, 672, 652, CHAS-. In HH of Louisa Wilcox, F, 40, born England.

**CHIRAS, CHRISTOPHER**, 40, M, Drayman, -, Germany, 280, 254, CHAS*. In IIII of E. Messner, M, 28, born Germany.

**CHRISTOPHER, GEORGE**, 38, M, Miller, -, Germany, 190, 190, CHAS%.

**CINK, CAMROD**, 31, M, Cabinetmaker, -, Germany, 729, 767, PICK.

**CLANPEN, J.C.**, 38, M, Shopkeeper, -, Germany, 430, 428, CHAS%.

**CLANPEN, JACOB**, 13, M, None listed, -, Germany, 430, 428, CHAS%. In HH of J.C. Clanpen, M, 38, born Germany.

**CLANPEN, MARIA**, 34, F, None listed, -, Germany, 430, 428, CHAS%. In HH of J.C. Clanpen, M, 38, born Germany.

**CLAUSE, H.**, 35, M, Laborer, -, Germany, 467, 464, CHAS%. In HH of Peter Collison, M, 61, born Germany.

**CLAUSHERS, FREDERICK**, 22, M, Musician, -, Germany, 775, 733, CHAS+. In Boarding House

**CLAWSON, H.W.**, 51, M, None listed, -, Germany, 418, 377, CHAS+. In HH of William Cose, M, 41, born SC.

**CLAY, CLAUS**, 17, M, Shopkeeper, -, Germany, 683, 675, CHAS%. In HH of John H. Thu, M, 35, born Germany.

**CLINE, CHRISTINE**, 50, M, Clerk, -, Germany, 640, 621, CHAS-. In HH of

Benjamin Rash, M, 28, born Germany.

**CLINTSWITH, HAMMOND**, 29, M, Shopkeeper, -, Germany, 256, 256, CHAS%.

**CLINTSWITH, HENRY**, 26, M, Shopkeeper, -, Germany, 256, 256, CHAS%. In HH of Hammond Clintswith, M, 29, born Germany.

**COFFIN, ARABELLA**, 4, F, None listed, -, Germany, 631, 612, CHAS-. In HH of Thomas A. Coffin, M, 42, born Germany.

**COFFIN, CAROLINE**, 10, F, None listed, -, Germany, 631, 612, CHAS-. In HH of Thomas A. Coffin, M, 42, born Germany.

**COFFIN, CECELIA**, 38, F, None listed, -, Germany, 631, 612, CHAS-. In HH of Thomas A. Coffin, M, 42, born Germany.

**COFFIN, CHRISTINE**, 6, F, None listed, -, Germany, 631, 612, CHAS-. In HH of Thomas A. Coffin, M, 42, born Germany.

**COFFIN, HENRY**, 14, M, None listed, -, Germany, 631, 612, CHAS-. In HH of Thomas A. Coffin, M, 42, born Germany.

**COFFIN, JAMES**, 8, M, None listed, -, Germany, 631, 612, CHAS-. In HH of Thomas A. Coffin, M, 42, born Germany.

**COFFIN, JULET**, 12, F, None listed, -, Germany, 631, 612, CHAS-. In HH of Thomas A. Coffin, M, 42, born Germany.

**COFFIN, THOMAS A.**, 42, M, Planter, -, Germany, 631, 612, CHAS-.

**COHEN, ELIZAH**, 50, M, Pedler, -, Germany, 81, 73, CHAS+. In HH of Marcus Vetterhau, M, 39, born Germany.

**COHEN, HANNAH**, 34, F, None listed, -, Germany, 43, 38, CHAS+.

**COHEN, HARTWIG**, 66, M, Butcher, -, Germany, 899, 876, CHAS%.

**COHN, JACOB**, 38, M, Merchant, -, Germany, 24, 24, EDGE. Jacob Cohan, born Hamburg, Germany.

**COHRS, MARIA**, 23, F, None listed, -, Germany, 816, 796, CHAS-. In HH of John Ansell, M, 34, born Germany.

**COLLISON, PETER**, 61, M, Laborer, -, Germany, 467, 464, CHAS%.

**COMPSEN, CATHERINE**, 16, F, None listed, -, Germany, 878, 836, CHAS+. In HH of John H. Hartz, M, 39, born Germany.

**COMPSON, GEO.**, 18, M, Shoemaker, -, Germany, 412, 385, CHAS*. In HH of John Weber, M, 38, born Germany.

**CONOLLY, WILLIAM**, 80, M, Farmer, -, Germany, 684, 684, EDGE.

**CONRADE, ELLEN**, 28, F, None listed, -, Germany, 117, 109, CHAS-. In HH of John Conrade, M, 40, born Germany.

**CONRADE, JOHN**, 40, M, Shopkeeper, -, Germany, 117, 109, CHAS-.

**CONRADE, META**, 34, F, None listed, -, Germany, 117, 109, CHAS-. In HH of John Conrade, M, 40, born Germany.

**CONRADE, SEENA**, 16, F, None listed, -, Germany, 117, 109, CHAS-. In HH of John Conrade, M, 40, born Germany.

COOK, JOHN A., 52, M, Grocer, -, Germany, 440, 437, CHAS%.
COPES, HENRY, 23, M, None listed, -, Germany, 60, 62, PICK. In HH of James White, M, 29, born SC.
COPP, EDWARD, 40, M, Clerk, -, Germany, 819, 777, CHAS+. In HH of James Taylor, M, 30, born England.
CORDES, ALBRIGHT, 55, M, Baker, -, Germany, 963, 943, CHAS-.
CORDES, DIEDRICK, 31, M, Shopkeeper, -, Germany, 361, 361, CHAS%. In HH of Corat Dickhoff, M, 39, born Germany.
CORDES, G., 33, M, Grocer, -, Germany, 441, 400, CHAS+.
CORDES, GERTRUDE, 22, F, None listed, -, Germany, 441, 400, CHAS+. In HH of G. Cordes, M, 33, born Germany.
CORDES, HENRY, 40, M, Laborer, -, Germany, 1044, 1022, CHAS%. In HH of Peter Shira, M, 21, born Germany.
CORDES, JOHN, 26, M, Grocer, -, Germany, 152, 143, CHAS+.
CORDES, LAVINA, 36, F, None listed, -, Germany, 1044, 1022, CHAS%. In HH of Peter Shira, M, 21, born Germany.
CORDES, SOPHIA, 30, F, None listed, -, Germany, 963, 943, CHAS-. In HH of Albright Cordes, M, 55, born Germany.
CORDES, THEODORE, 35, M, Tavern keeper, -, Germany, 52, 47, CHAS+.
CORKER, CAROLINE, 15, F, None listed, -, Germany, 646, 626, CHAS-. In HH of Henry Corker, M, 39, born Germany.
CORKER, HENRY, 39, M, Grocer, -, Germany, 646, 626, CHAS-.
CORKER, MARGARET, 38, F, None listed, -, Germany, 646, 626, CHAS-. In IIII of Henry Corker, M, 39, born Germany.
CORONEILSEN, CLAUS, 14, M, Clerk, -, Germany, 644, 625, CHAS-. In HH of Jacob Hencken, M, 28, born Germany.
COSTWICK, CHRISTIANA, 25, F, None listed, -, Germany, 139, 123, CHAS. In HH of Barthohs Costwick, M, 50, born Austria.
COUGHMAN, BINHARD, 41, M, Planter, -, Germany, 1147, 1147, SUMT.
COVE, JNO., 65, M, Farmer, -, Germany, 92, 92, COLL+.
CRAMER, CATHARINE, 36, F, None listed, -, Germany, 1081, 1131, PICK. In HH of George Cramer, M, 44, born Germany.
CRAMER, FREDERICK, 4, M, None listed, -, Germany, 1081, 1131, PICK. In HH of George Cramer, M, 44, born Germany.
CRAMER, GEORGE, 44, M, Farmer, -, Germany, 1081, 1131, PICK.
CRAMER, LEWIS, 3, M, None listed, -, Germany, 1081, 1131, PICK. In HH of George Cramer, M, 44, born Germany.
CREWD, WILLIAM, 36, M, Sail maker, -, Germany, 10, 11, CHAS.
CREWS, LOUISA, 35, F, None listed, -, Germany, 1075, 1052, CHAS-. In HH of C.M. Arnold, M, 34, born GA.
CRONSTADT, MARY ANN, 73, F, None listed, -, Germany, 306, 283, CHAS.

73

In HH of Henry Lipscombe, M, 45, born Germany.

**CROSS, GEORGE**, 25, M, Clerk, -, Germany, 428, 387, CHAS+. In HH of W. Breedman, M, 27, born Germany.

**CROUCH, CHARLES**, 34, M, Shoemaker, -, Germany, 2022, 2028, EDGE.

**CROUCH, ELIZABETH**, 26, F, None listed, -, Germany, 2022, 2028, EDGE. In HH of Charles Crouch, M, 34, born Germany.

**CRUDUP, BARNET**, 25, M, None listed, -, Germany, 256, 256, LEX. In HH of Uriah Coogler, M, 74, born SC.

**CRUGER, CHRISTIAN**, 36, M, None, -, Germany, 538, 504, CHAS*. In HH of Henry Harinberg, M, 25, born Germany.

**CRUSER, JACOB**, 26, M, Clerk, -, Germany, 762, 742, CHAS-. In HH of Charles Agriel, M, 37, born Sweden.

**CURLES, JOHN**, 25, M, Boiler maker, -, Germany, 678, 636, CHAS+.

# D

**DAILEY, JOHN**, 30, M, Farmer, -, Germany, 1227, 1228, AND*.

**DAMISH, CHRIS**, 19, M, Baker, -, Germany, 28, 28, BARN. In HH of John Damish, M, 53, born Germany.

**DAMISH, FRED**, 16, M, Baker, -, Germany, 28, 28, BARN. In HH of John Damish, M, 53, born Germany.

**DAMISH, JOHN**, 53, M, Baker, -, Germany, 28, 28, BARN.

**DASCHER, C.**, 27, M, Clerk, -, Germany, 802, 785, CHAS%. In HH of W. Steffers, M, 25, born Germany.

**DASCHER, HANNAH**, 22, M, None listed, -, Germany, 129, 120, CHAS+.

**DAVIDSON, G.**, 27, M, Clerk, -, Germany, 7, 7, Chas-. In HH of J.F. Ficken, M, 40, born Germany.

**DAVIS, HENRY**, 28, M, Grocer, -, Germany, 298, 275, CHAS+.

**DEDIMANN, CATHARINE**, 31, F, None listed, -, Germany, 403, 401, CHAS%. In HH of T.S. Dedimann, M, 36, born Germany.

**DEDIMANN, T.S.**, 36, M, Grocer, -, Germany, 403, 401, CHAS%.

**DEH, BENJAMIN**, 30, M, None listed, -, Germany, 898, 875, CHAS%. In HH of Dedrick Meinarders, M, 36, born Germany.

**DELAND, JOHN**, 19, M, Clerk, -, Germany, 100, 92, CHAS+. In HH of G.H. Rumple, M, 43, born Germany.

**DENEMAN, CARLOS**, 27, M, Carpenter, -, Germany, 143, 143, CHAS%. In HH of Jacob Hillan, M, 35, born Germany.

**DENGGER, FREDERICK**, 20, M, Shopkeeper, -, Germany, 349, 349, CHAS%. In HH of Christon Benten, M, 28, born Germany.

**DETZ, LEWIS**, 16, M, Clerk, -, Germany, 416, 388, CHAS*. In HH of John H. Renneker, M, 30, born Germany.

DEVERMANN, HENRY, 22, M, Chemist, -, Germany, 989, 968, CHAS-. In HH of Benjn. Garden, M, 45, born Prussia.

DIAL, WILLIAM H., 48, M, Baker, -, Germany, 602, 619, RICH.

DICKHOFF, CORAT, 39, M, Shopkeeper, -, Germany, 361, 361, CHAS%.

DICKHOFF, MARGARET, 24, F, None listed, -, Germany, 361, 361, CHAS%. In HH of Corat Dickhoff, M, 39, born Germany.

DIEFENBACK, C., 39, M, Poutcher, -, Germany, 34, 30, CHAS$.

DIEFENBACK, M., 35, F, None listed, -, Germany, 34, 30, CHAS$. In HH of C. Diefenback, M, 39, born Germany.

DIEGETS, GEO., 40, M, Overseer, -, Germany, 1295, 1295, SUMT.

DIERSON, ELIZABETH, 24, F, None listed, -, Germany, 119, 119, CHAS%. In HH of William Dierson, M, 39, born Germany.

DIERSON, FRITZ L., 4, M, None listed, -, Germany, 119, 119, CHAS%. In HH of William Dierson, M, 39, born Germany.

DIERSON, MARIA, 6, F, None listed, -, Germany, 119, 119, CHAS%. In HH of William Dierson, M, 39, born Germany.

DIERSON, WILLIAM, 39, M, Grocer, -, Germany, 119, 119, CHAS%.

DINBLAN, CONSTANTINE, 31, M, Taylor, -, Germany, 69, 69, BEAU+.

DOHLENAN, HENRY, 21, M, Shopkeeper, -, Germany, 171, 137, CHAS*. In HH of Diederick Tietyew, M, 23, born Germany.

DOLAY, ELIZA, 26, F, None listed, -, Germany, 213, 200, CHAS+. In HH of Joseph Dolay, M, 27, born Germany.

DOLAY, JOSEPH, 27, M, Blacksmith, -, Germany, 213, 200, CHAS+.

DOLE, JACOB, 26, M, Corpl. U.S.A., -, Germany, 47, 43, CHAS$. In HH of John Ewing, M, 50, born MA.

DORBAUM, C., 30, M, Taylor, -, Germany, 365, 336, CHAS.

DORRELL, LOUISA, 50, F, None listed, -, Germany, 798, 781, CHAS%. In HH of William Dorrell, M, 25, born Germany.

DORRELL, LOUISA B., 22, F, None listed, -, Germany, 798, 781, CHAS%. In HH of William Dorrell, M, 25, born Germany.

DORRELL, WILLIAM, 25, M, Baker, -, Germany, 798, 781, CHAS%.

DORSHEA, CATHERINE, 22, F, None listed, -, Germany, 662, 642, CHAS-. In HH of Catherine Bochman, F, 25, born Germany.

DRAGMAN, CATHERINE, 73, F, None listed, -, Germany, 36, 36, CHAS*. In HH of George O. Rosenbaum, M, 37, born Germany.

DRAGMAN, JOSEPH, 38, M, Pedler, -, Germany, 501, 453, CHAS. In HH of James Doyle, M, 32, born Ireland.

DRAGMAN, PAULINE, 34, F, None listed, -, Germany, 501, 453, CHAS. In HH of James Doyle, M, 32, born Ireland.

DREDER, DIEDERICK, 28, M, Clerk, -, Germany, 802, 760, CHAS+. In HH of William Masher, M, 28, born Germany.

DROGER, HENRY, 21, M, Merchant, -, Germany, 18, 18, BEAU+.
DRUCKER, MOSES, 45, M, Merchant, -, Germany, 24, 24, KERS.
DRYER, CORBET, 24, M, Shopkeeper, -, Germany, 650, 642, CHAS%.
DRYER, EURNARK, 29, M, Clerk, -, Germany, 471, 468, CHAS%. In HH of
Herman Meyer, M, 33, born Germany.
DUBTENHOFFER, CATHAREN, 38, F, None listed, -, Germany, 96, 96,
BEAU. In HH of Jacob Dubtenhoffer, M, 37, born Germany.
DUBTENHOFFER, JACOB, 37, M, Shoemaker, -, Germany, 96, 96, BEAU.
DUBTENHOFFER, JOSEPH, 11, M, None listed, -, Germany, 96, 96, BEAU.
In HH of Jacob Dubtenhoffer, M, 37, born Germany.
DUHANS, HENRY, 19, M, Clerk, -, Germany, 337, 320, CHAS-. In HH of
Martin Von Glahn, M, 26, born Germany.
DUKIN, HENRY J., 20, M, None listed, -, Germany, 925, 902, CHAS%. In HH
of Emeline Taylor, F, 45, born SC.
DULLS, JACOB, 19, M, Clerk, -, Germany, 121, 112, CHAS+. In HH of J.B.
Rankin, M, 29, born Germany.
DUPING, ANNA, 37, F, None listed, -, Germany, 112, 112, BEAU. In HH of
E.F.J. Duping, M, 38, born Germany.
DUPING, E.F.J., 38, M, Shopkeeper, -, Germany, 112, 112, BEAU.
DUPING, JOSEPH, 12, M, None listed, -, Germany, 112, 112, BEAU. In HH
of E.F.J. Duping, M, 38, born Gemany.
DURNSTUCKS, ELIZABETTE, 23, F, None listed, -, Germany, 294, 271,
CHAS+. In HH of W. Durnstucks, M, 28, born Germany.
DURNSTUCKS, W., 28, M, Shoemaker, -, Germany, 294, 271, CHAS+.
DURVING, MEIRTENS, 20, F, None listed, -, Germany, 48, 58, CHAS.

E

EASON, C.D., 60, F, Boarding House, -, Germany, 937, 917, CHAS-.
EBERHART, CHARLES, 24, M, Tailor, -, Germany, 414, 425, RICH. In HH of
James H. Wells, M, 56, born GA.
EBERLE, C., 30, M, Upholsterer, -, Germany, 720, 700, CHAS-. In HH of L.
Schackmand, M, 45, born Germany.
EGG, EDWARD, 30, M, Watchmaker, -, Germany, 347, 353, RICH. In HH of
Jane E. Reeder, F, 37, born MA.
EHRICKS, HENRY, 37, M, Shopkeeper, -, Germany, 596, 588, CHAS%.
EHRICKS, MARIA, 25, F, None listed, -, Germany, 596, 588, CHAS%. In HH
of Henry Ehricks, M, 37, born Germany.
EHRLICH, MICHAEL, 42, M, Shoemaker, -, Germany, 349, 355, RICH.
EILHARDT, CHARLES, 28, M, Shoemaker, -, Germany, 245, 250, RICH. In
HH of Gottlieb Eilhardt, M, 41, born Germany.

**EILHARDT, GOTTLIEB**, 41, M, Bootmaker, -, Germany, 245, 250, RICH.
**EILHARDT, JOHANNA**, 28, F, None listed, -, Germany, 245, 250, RICH. In HH of Gottlieb Eilhardt, M, 41, born Germany.
**EILHARDT, LOUISA**, 5, F, None listed, -, Germany, 245, 250, RICH. In HH of Gottlieb Eilhardt, M, 41, born Germany.
**EISEMANN, JACOB F.**, 28, M, Tailor, -, Germany, 192, 196, RICH.
**ELBERS, C.**, 23, M, Clerk, -, Germany, 342, 305, CHAS+. In HH of H.D. Ellerhorst, M, 35, born Germany.
**ELFERS, C.F.M.**, 20, M, None listed, -, Germany, 5, 5, BEAU+. In HH of William F. Jackson, M, 28, jailor, born SC. C.F.M. Elfers injaid (vagrant).
**ELIAS, DAVID**, 35, M, Merchant, -, Germany, 249, 254, RICH.
**ELLERHORST, H. D.**, 35, M, Store keeper, -, Germany, 342, 305, CHAS+.
**ELLERHORST, H. D.**, 29, M, Clerk, -, Germany, 1001, 979, CHAS-.
**ELLERHORST, WILLIAM**, 25, M, Store keeper, -, Germany, 342, 305, CHAS+. In HH of H.D. Ellerhorst, M, 35, born Germany.
**ELLIS, ANNA**, 22, F, None listed, -, Germany, 265, 239, CHAS*. In HH of Nicholas Ellis, M, 26, born Germany.
**ELLIS, NICHOLAS**, 26, M, Grocer, -, Germany, 265, 239, CHAS*.
**ENGLAND, CHARLES**, 6, M, None listed, -, Germany, 366, 337, CHAS. In HH of Wm. England, M, 45, born Germany.
**ENGLAND, MARGARET**, 35, F, None listed, -, Germany, 366, 337, CHAS. In HH of Wm. England, M, 45, born Germany.
**ENGLAND, WILLIAM**, 9, M, None listed, -, Germany, 366, 337, CHAS. In HH of Wm. England, M, 45, born Germany.
**ENGLAND, WM.**, 45, M, Shoemaker, -, Germany, 366, 337, CHAS.
**ENGLEBERG, HENRIETTA**, 23, F, None listed, -, Germany, 45, 40, CHAS+. In HH of M. Engleberg, M, 33, born Germany.
**ENGLEBERG, M.**, 33, M, Tailor, -, Germany, 45, 40, CHAS+.
**ENGLESBERG, LEWIS**, 28, M, Dyer, -, Germany, 220, 197, CHAS*. In HH of Nicholas Boesch, M, 28, born Switzerland.
**EPLER, CATHERINE**, 23, F, None listed, -, Germany, 446, 443, CHAS%. In HH of D. Epler, M, 27, born Germany.
**EPLER, D.**, 27, M, Grocer, -, Germany, 446, 443, CHAS%.
**EPPING, ANNA**, 22, F, None listed, -, Germany, 730, 710, CHAS-. In HH of J. P. M. Epping, M, 33, born Germany.
**EPPING, CARL**, 28, M, Merchant, -, Germany, 301, 278, CHAS.
**EPPING, J.P.M.**, 33, M, Druggest, -, Germany, 730, 710, CHAS-.
**EPPING, WILLIAM**, 23, M, Clerk, -, Germany, 997, 976, CHAS-. In HH of Jasper Christiansen, M, 46, born Denmark.
**ESPEN, W.D.**, 18, M, Clerk, -, Germany, 120, 120, CHAS%. In HH of H. Von Holland, M, 24, born Germany.

EWEN, GEORGE, 15, M, Clerk, -, Germany, 8, 8, CHAS+. In HH of Thomas Ewen, M, 34, born Germany.

EWEN, THOMAS, 34, M, Painter, -, Germany, 8, 8, CHAS+.

EWEN, WILLIELMINA, 36, F, None listed, -, Germany, 8, 8, CHAS+. In HH of Thomas Ewen, M, 34, born Germany.

**F**

FAIRCHELL, ANNA, 46, F, None listed, -, Germany, 472, 469, CHAS%. In HH of Henry Ruffer, M, 50, born France.

FAIRCHELL, FRITZ, 18, M, Laborer, -, Germany, 472, 469, CHAS%. In HH of Henry Ruffer, M, 50, born France.

FAIRCHELL, JOHN, 5, M, None listed, -, Germany, 472, 469, CHAS%. In HH of Henry Ruffer, M, 50, born France.

FANFENBANKS, MARY, 38, F, None listed, -, Germany, 1047, 1025, CHAS%. In HH of Lekmont Fanfenbanks, M, 40, born Germany.

FANFENBANKS, SEKMONT, 40, M, Laborer, -, Germany, 1047, 1025, CHAS%.

FASTBENDER, MARTHA, 66, F, None listed, -, Germany, 17, 15, CHAS+.

FECHTMANN, RICHARD, 27, M, Tobacconist, -, Germany, 754, 734, CHAS-. In HH of Bernard Volger, M, 30, born Germany.

FEDGEN, ANGUSTA, 26, F, None listed, -, Germany, 421, 444, PICK. In HH of Herman Fedgen, M, 30, born Germany.

FEDGEN, HERMAN, 30, M, Taylor, -, Germany, 421, 444, PICK.

FENNER, FREDERICK, 20, M, Blacksmith, -, Germany, 338, 312, CHAS. In HH of Henry Pluger, M, 25, born Germany.

FETYAN, JAMES, 35, M, Laborer, -, Germany, 1132, 1111, CHAS%.

FICKEN, J.F., 40, M, Grocer, -, Germany, 7, 7, Chas-.

FICKEN, REBECCA, 33, F, None listed, -, Germany, 7, 7, CHAS-. In HH of J.F. Ficken, M, 40, born Germany.

FICKLER, ANNA, 25, F, None listed, -, Germany, 49, 44, CHAS+. In HH of August Fickler, M, 35, born Germany.

FICKLER, AUGUST, 35, M, Fruiterer, -, Germany, 49, 44, CHAS+.

FIDGEN, AUGUSTA, 26, F, None listed, -, Germany, 421, 444, PICK. In HH of Herman Fidgen, M, 30, born Germany.

FIDGEN, HERMAN, 30, M, Taylor, -, Germany, 421, 444, PICK.

FIEGAL, JACOB, 23, M, Store keeper, -, Germany, 813, 793, CHAS-. In HH of Isaac Seckendorffe, M, 40, born Germany.

FIESCHER, J.H., 27, M, Tailor, -, Germany, 378, 361, CHAS-.

FINCKEN, ALBERT, 18, M, Clerk, -, Germany, 562, 554, CHAS%. In HH of Henry Bulwinkle, M, 45, born Germany.

FINK, B.H., 26, M, Apothecary, -, Germany, 1096, 1073, CHAS-.
FINK, HAMMOND, 22, M, Baker, -, Germany, 285, 264, CHAS+. In HH of H.
Wittschew, M, 23, born Germany.
FINK, HARMAN, 40, M, Laborer, -, Germany, 697, 689, CHAS%.
FINK, JOHN, 60, M, None, -, Germany, 109, 102, CHAS-.
FINK, P.J., 21, M, Chemist, -, Germany, 271, 255, CHAS-. In HH of C.H.
Pancknin, M, 46, born Prussia.
FINK, SOPHIA, 36, F, None listed, -, Germany, 697, 689, CHAS%. In HH of
Harman Fink, M, 40, born Germany.
FINKEN, ALBERT, 23, M, Grocer, -, Germany, 4, 4, CHAS*.
FIREGHTESH, R., 22, M, Clerk, -, Germany, 379, 344, CHAS. In HH of N.R.
Schineder, M, 32, born Germany.
FLACH, GEORGE W., 65, M, Watch maker, -, Germany, 432, 391, CHAS+.
FLAGG, GEORGE, 40, M, Clerk, -, Germany, 202, 190, CHAS+. In Boarding
House.
FLEGER, FREDRICK, 40, M, Laborer, -, Germany, 913, 890, CHAS%.
FLEMMAN, CAROLINE, 30, F, None listed, -, Germany, 364, 335, CHAS. In
HH of Peter Weber, M, 50, born Germany.
FLEMMAN, GEORGE, 35, M, Shoemaker, -, Germany, 364, 335, CHAS. In
HH of Peter Weber, M, 50, born Germany.
FLONACKER, J., 26, M, Blacksmith, -, Germany, 47, 42, CHAS+.
FLONACKER, JOSEPH, 23, M, Blacksmith, -, Germany, 47, 42, CHAS+. In
HH of J. Flonacker, M, 26, born Germany.
FLONACKER, SARAH, 29, F, None listed, -, Germany, 47, 42, CHAS+. In
HH of J. Flonacker, M, 26, born Germany.
FLOTE, WILLIAM, 22, M, Watch maker, -, Germany, 374, 347, CHAS*. In
HH of Harriot Gray, F, 45, born SC.
FOLK, ELIZA F., 28, F, None listed, -, Germany, 296, 273, CHAS+. In HH of
John D. Folk, M, 30, born Germany.
FOLK, JOHN D., 30, M, Grocer, -, Germany, 296, 273, CHAS+.
FRANCIS, MARY, 25, F, None listed, -, Germany, 141, 125, CHAS.
FRANK, CATHERINE, 30, F, None listed, -, Germany, 638, 647, RICH+. In
HH of John Frank, M, 47, born Germany.
FRANK, CATHERINE, 25, M, None listed, -, Germany, 254, 259, RICH. In
HH of Harmon C. Frank, M, 28, born Germany.
FRANK, CATHERINE, 23, F, None listed, -, Germany, 553, 519, CHAS*. In
Catholic Seminary.
FRANK, CHRISTIAN, 34, M, Shoemaker, -, Germany, 153, 153, LEX. In HH
of Barbara Corly, F, 80, born SC. Census states Christian Frank, born
Witenburg, Germany.
FRANK, DOROTHY, 13, F, None listed, -, Germany, 638, 647, RICH+. In HH

of John Frank, M, 47, born Germany.

**FRANK, ELIZABETH**, 19, F, None listed, -, Germany, 848, 828, CHAS-. In HH of B. Figeroux, M, 42, born West Indies.

**FRANK, HARMON C.**, 28, M, Merchant, -, Germany, 254, 259, RICH.

**FRANK, HENRY**, 15, M, None listed, -, Germany, 638, 647, RICH+. In HH of John Frank, M, 47, born Germany.

**FRANK, JOHN**, 47, M, Tailor, -, Germany, 638, 647, RICH+.

**FRANK, JOHN**, 11, M, None listed, -, Germany, 638, 647, RICH+. In HH of John Frank, M, 47, born Germany.

**FRANKS, C.**, 28, M, Merchant, -, Germany, 1066, 1066, DARL.

**FRANKY, CHS.**, 26, M, Merchant, -, Germany, 388, 388, DARL.

**FREDERIC, CATHERINE**, 23, F, None listed, -, Germany, 67, 67, LEX. In HH of Frederic Frederic, M, 33, born Bavaria, Germany. The census states that Catherine Frederic, born Bavaria, Germany.

**FREDERIC, FREDERIC**, 33, M, Shoemaker, -, Germany, 67, 67, LEX. The census states that Frederic Frederic, born Bavaria, Germany.

**FREE, FREDERICK**, 30, M, Planter, -, Germany, 1173, 1152, CHAS%.

**FREELANDER, ISAAC**, 26, M, Merchant, -, Germany, 537, 520, CHAS-. In HH of Samuel Valentine, M, 50, born Prussia.

**FREINDER, E.**, 22, M, Clerk, -, Germany, 140, 124, CHAS. In HH of J.H. Nienmeths, M, 60, born Germany.

**FRENEY, ADOLPH**, 15, M, None listed, -, Germany, 205, 193, CHAS+. In HH of Frederick Franey, M, 47, born Germany.

**FRENEY, FREDERICK**, 47, M, Locksmith, -, Germany, 205, 193, CHAS+.

**FRENEY, LOUISA**, 31, F, None listed, -, Germany, 205, 193, CHAS+. In HH of Frederick Franey, M, 47, born Germany.

**FRIEZE, JOHN**, 35, M, Farmer, -, Germany, 123, 103, CHAS$.

**FRIEZE, LEWIS**, 28, M, Farmer, -, Germany, 160, 139, CHAS$.

**FRIEZO, FREDRICK**, 38, M, Farmer, -, Germany, 1020, 997, CHAS%.

**FRIEZO, LEWIS**, 27, M, Farmer, -, Germany, 1020, 997, CHAS%. In HH of Fredrick Friezo, M, 38, born Germany.

**FRITZMAN, SEBASTIAN**, 52, M, Tailor, -, Germany, 1391, 1391, NEWB.

**FRONE, F.**, 18, M, Tailor, -, Germany, 661, 641, CHAS-. In HH of W. Hieze, M, 34, born Germany.

**FROST, ANNA**, 2, F, None listed, M, Germany, 531, 546, RICH. In HH of Henry Frost, M, 26 Mulatto, born Germany.

**FROST, HENRY**, 26, M, Shoemaker, M, Germany, 531, 546, RICH.

**FROST, HENRY**, 3, M, None listed, M, Germany, 531, 546, RICH. In HH of Henry Frost, M, 26 mulatto, born Germany.

**FROST, LYDIA**, 25, F, None listed, M, Germany, 531, 546, RICH. In HH of Henry Frost, M, 26 mulatto, born Germany.

FRY, JOSEPH, 40, M, Musician, -, Germany, 139, 130, CHAS+.
FRY, MARGARET, 28, F, None listed, -, Germany, 139, 130, CHAS+. In HH of Joseph Fry, M, 40, born Germany.
FULLINGWEIDER, JACOB, 40, M, Planter, -, Germany, 233, 237, PICK+.
FUNKENSTEADT, BECKE, 28, F, None listed, -, Germany, 94, 92, CHAS*. In HH of George Funkensteadt, M, 38, born Germany.
FUNKENSTEADT, GEORGE, 38, M, Grocer, -, Germany, 94, 92, CHAS*.
FURLMAN, MARTIN, 60, M, None listed, -, Germany, 1827, 1827, SPART. In HH of Jane Willigar, F, 75, born SC.
FURTH, DANIEL, 40, M, Carpenter, -, Germany, 329, 304, CHAS.
FURTH, HENRICK, 33, M, Clerk, -, Germany, 24, 22, CHAS-.

# G

GALFORD, HARMOND, 20, M, Baker, -, Germany, 285, 264, CHAS+. In HH of H. Wittschew, M, 23, born Germany.
GARBER, FREDERICK, 29, M, Druggest, -, Germany, 473, 439, CHAS*. In HH of S. Wierfelder, M, 30, born Germany.
GARBER, JOHN, 49, M, Shopkeeper, -, Germany, 231, 231, CHAS%.
GARICK, FRANCIS, 35, M, Saddler, -, Germany, 533, 533, FAIR.
GEADTS, E., 31, M, Grocer, -, Germany, 1110, 1088, CHAS%.
GEADTS, FRITZ, 10, M, Clerk, -, Germany, 1110, 1088, CHAS%. In HH of E. Geadts, M, 31, born Germany.
GEADTS, MARGARET, 28, F, None listed, -, Germany, 1110, 1088, CHAS%. In HH of E. Geadts, M, 31, born Germany.
GEKINGS, FERNAFORDE, 36, M, Shopkeeper, -, Germany, 334, 334, COLL*.
GEKINGS, FRANCES, 33, F, None listed, -, Germany, 334, 334, COLL*. In HH of Fernaforde Gekings, M, 36, born Germany.
GERBETH, FREDERICK, 19, M, Carpenter, -, Germany, 59, 61, PICK. In HH of John Bundt, M, 20, born SC.
GERDTS, ALEMINA, 25, F, None listed, -, Germany, 151, 142, CHAS+. In HH of H. Gerdts, M, 38, born Germany.
GERDTS, H., 38, M, Grocer, -, Germany, 151, 142, CHAS+.
GERDTZ, CHARLES H., 33, M, Clerk, -, Germany, 3, 3, CHAS-. In HH of John E. Lee, M, 29, born Germany.
GERMAN, JAMES, 40, M, Planter, -, Germany, 52, 52, FAIR.
GERRICK, FRANCIS, 47, M, Cabinetmaker, -, Germany, 1167, 1146, CHAS%.
GERRICK, LOUISA, 30, F, None listed, -, Germany, 1167, 1146, CHAS%. In HH of Francis Gerrick, M, 47, born Germany.

**GERTYN, JOHN**, 19, M, None listed, -, Germany, 562, 554, CHAS%. In HH of Henry Bulwinkle, M, 45, born Germany.

**GESLER, BARNET**, 1, M, None listed, -, Germany, 187, 176, CHAS+. In HH of Eleanor Pelska, F, 26, born Germany.

**GESLER, ROSA**, 35, F, None listed, -, Germany, 187, 176, CHAS+. In HH of Eleanor Pelska, F, 26, born Germany.

**GESSEL, H.**, 32, M, Grocer, -, Germany, 553, 512, CHAS+.

**GETSEN, HENRY**, 24, M, Clerk, -, Germany, 68, 68, CHAS%. In HH of Jacob Meyer, M, 38, born Germany.

**GIDEL, JOANA**, 30, F, Milliner, -, Germany, 852, 832, CHAS-. In HH of A.G. Parker, F, 38, born Germany.

**GILFERS, AUGUST**, 19, M, Clerk, -, Germany, 328, 303, CHAS. In HH of Henry Gilfers, M, 56, born Germany.

**GILFERS, CHARLES**, 15, M, None, -, Germany, 328, 303, CHAS. In HH of Henry Gilfers, M, 56, born Germany.

**GILFERS, HENRY**, 56, M, Fruiterer, -, Germany, 328, 303, CHAS.

**GILFERS, HENRY**, 8, M, None listed, -, Germany, 328, 303, CHAS. In HH of Henry Gilfers, M, 56, born Germany.

**GILFERS, HERMAN**, 18, M, None, -, Germany, 328, 303, CHAS. In HH of Henry Gilfers, M, 56, born Germany.

**GILFERS, MARGARET**, 32, F, None listed, -, Germany, 328, 303, CHAS. In HH of Henry Gilfers, M, 56, born Germany.

**GILFERS, MINA**, 14, F, None listed, -, Germany, 328, 303, CHAS. In HH of Henry Gilfers, M, 56, born Germany.

**GIVENRATH, ELIZABETH**, 43, F, None listed, -, Germany, 339, 345, RICH.

**GIVENRATH, JOSEPH**, 17, M, Laborer, -, Germany, 339, 345, RICH. In HH of Elizabeth Givenrath, F, 43, born Germany.

**GIVIN, CONRAD**, 33, M, Shoemaker, -, Germany, 790, 770, CHAS-.

**GIVIN, FREDERICA**, 30, F, None listed, -, Germany, 790, 770, CHAS-. In HH of Conrad Givin, M, 33, born Germany.

**GLADZ, DORILLA**, 27, M, None listed, -, Germany, 351, 313, CHAS+. In HH of Herman Gladz, M, 40, born Germany.

**GLADZ, FREDERICK**, 25, M, Carpenter, -, Germany, 351, 313, CHAS+. In HH of Herman Gladz, M, 40, born Germany.

**GLADZ, HANS**, 9, M, None listed, -, Germany, 351, 313, CHAS+. In HH of Herman Gladz, M, 40, born Germany.

**GLADZ, HENRIETTA**, 36, F, None listed, -, Germany, 351, 313, CHAS+. In HH of Herman Gladz, M, 40, born Germany.

**GLADZ, HENRIETTA**, 7, F, None listed, -, Germany, 351, 313, CHAS+. In HH of Herman Gladz, M, 40, born Germany.

**GLADZ, HERMAN**, 40, M, Builder, -, Germany, 351, 313, CHAS+.

GOHIS, JOHN H., 20, M, Clerk, -, Germany, 97, 89, CHAS+. In HH of A. Bischoff, M, 35, born Germany.

GOLDBERG, JACOB, 38, M, Store keeper, -, Germany, 638, 597, CHAS+.

GOLDBERG, MARIAM, 34, F, None listed, -, Germany, 638, 597, CHAS+. In HH of Jacob Goldberg, M, 38, born Germany.

GOLDBERG, MOSES, 24, M, Tailor, -, Germany, 638, 597, CHAS+. In HH of Jacob Goldberg, M, 38, born Germany.

GOODMAN, BENJAMIN, 17, M, Clerk, -, Germany, 264, 269, RICH. In HH of Samuel Keeling, M, 30, born Germany.

GOODMAN, CHARLES, 25, M, Jeweller, -, Germany, 221, 207, CHAS-.

GOODSTRUCT, H., 40, M, Blacksmith, -, Germany, 163, 153, CHAS-. In HH of F. Rissler, M, 30, born Germany.

GOTSCHON, H., 40, M, Farmer, -, Germany, 151, 130, CHAS$.

GOTSHAM, J.F., 34, M, Brick layer, -, Germany, 818, 818, NEWB.

GOULDING, MARY, 73, F, None listed, -, Germany, 1227, 1206, CHAS%. In HH of Thomas D. Condy, M, 52, born SC.

GOVENEUR, ELIZABETH, 44, F, None listed, -, Germany, 383, 347, CHAS. In HH of Peter Goveneur, M, 44, born France.

GRANT, FRANCES, 29, F, None listed, -, Germany, 758, 743, CHAS%.

GRAY, CHRIS, 40, M, None listed, -, Germany, 849, 807, CHAS+.

GRAY, MARY, 36, F, None listed, -, Germany, 849, 807, CHAS+. In HH of Chris Gray, M, 40, born Germany.

GRAY, YANCEY, 73, F, None listed, -, Germany, 821, 779, CHAS+. In HH of John B. Gray, M, 50, born SC.

GREEN, C.F., 56, M, Shopkeeper, -, Germany, 149, 133, CHAS.

GREEN, G.G., 19, M, Clerk, -, Germany, 149, 133, CHAS. In HH of C.F. Green, M, 56, born Germany.

GREEN, JOHN, 40, M, Grocer, -, Germany, 2021, 2027, EDGE.

GREEN, PAULINE, 13, F, None listed, -, Germany, 149, 133, CHAS. In HH of C.F. Green, M, 56, born Germany.

GREENWAULD, BARNEY, 35, M, Merchant, -, Germany, 704, 704, WILL.

GREENWAULD, ESTHER, 22, F, None listed, -, Germany, 704, 704, WILL. In HH of Barney Greenwauld, M, 35, born Germany.

GREENWAULD, FERDINAND, 30, M, Merchant, -, Germany, 704, 704, WILL. In HH of Barney Greenwauld, M, 35, born Germany.

GREN, MARTHA, 19, F, None listed, -, Germany, 918, 895, CHAS%. In HH of Dedrick Ohen, M, 35, born Germany.

GRINDELL, A., 29, M, Whitesmith, -, Germany, 178, 167, CHAS+. In HH of C. Leo Meyer, M, 30, born Germany.

GRINDELL, C. SHLAGER, 25, M, Iron dealer, -, Germany, 179, 168, CHAS+.

GRINDELL, MINA, 23, F, None listed, -, Germany, 179, 168, CHAS+. In HH of C. Shlager Grindell, M, 25, born Germany.

**GRINDELL, ROSA**, 3, F, None listed, -, Germany, 179, 168, CHAS+. In HH of C. Shlager Grindell, M, 25, born Germany.

**GRINDELL, WILHELMINA**, 22, F, None listed, -, Germany, 178, 167, CHAS+. In HH of C. Leo Meyer, M, 30, born Germany.

**GRINER, ELIZABETH**, 33, F, None listed, -, Germany, 24, 24, SPART. In HH of F. Griner, M, 33, born Germany.

**GRINER, F.**, 33, M, Boot maker, -, Germany, 24, 24, SPART.

**GRINER, GEORGE O.**, 21, M, None listed, -, Germany, 24, 24, SPART. In HH of F. Griner, M, 33, born Germany.

**GROWSLING, J.F.**, 45, M, Musician, -, Germany, 429, 388, CHAS+. In HH of W. Breedman, M, 27, born Germany.

**GRUBE, HENRY**, 29, M, Grocer, -, Germany, 48, 43, CHAS+. In HH of John Grube, M, 18, born Germany.

**GRUBE, JOHN**, 18, M, Grocer, -, Germany, 48, 43, CHAS+.

**GRUNLAN, FREDK.**, 46, M, Clerk, -, Germany, 527, 510, CHAS-. In HH of C.F. Kohncke, M, 45, born Germany.

**GUESWEIN, ANNIE**, 18, F, None listed, -, Germany, 11, 10, CHAS$. In HH of Edward Semecke, M, 35, born Germany.

**GURCHIN, MELER**, 22, F, Servant, -, Germany, 188, 171, CHAS. In HH of J.D. Habenech, M, 37, born Germany.

**H**

**HABENECH, J.D.**, 37, M, Grocer, -, Germany, 188, 171, CHAS.

**HABENECH, LOUISA**, 24, F, None listed, -, Germany, 188, 171, CHAS. In HH of J.D. Habenech, M, 37, born Germany.

**HABERHAUSEN, JOHN**, 47, M, Physician, -, Germany, 273, 253, CHAS+.

**HABERNICH, ANNA**, 23, F, None listed, -, Germany, 51, 46, CHAS+. In HH of J.H. Wilkenning, M, 32, born Germany.

**HABERSON, LAWRENCE**, 38, M, Mariner, -, Germany, 167, 153, CHAS*.

**HAHN, H.H.**, 25, M, Grocer, -, Germany, 343, 305, CHAS+.

**HAHN, JOHN**, 17, M, Clerk, -, Germany, 343, 305, CHAS+. In HH of H.H. Hahn, M, 25, born Germany.

**HAHNEWINKLE, H.**, 25, F, Clerk, -, Germany, 847, 827, CHAS-. In HH of Sophia Selle 34, born Germany.

**HAHNS, DIEDRICK**, 18, M, Clerk, -, Germany, 718, 709, CHAS%. In HH of John Schroder, M, 30, born Germany.

**HALLOWAY, HENRY**, 27, M, Laborer, -, Germany, 868, 845, CHAS%.

**HAMMARSKOLD, EMIMLY**, 30, F, None listed, -, Germany, 416, 374, CHAS. In HH of P.U. Hammarskold, M, 35, born Germany.

HAMMARSKOLD, P.U., 35, M, Architect, -, Germany, 416, 374, CHAS.
HAMMELL, W., 36, M, Druggist, -, Germany, 145, 145, CHAS%.
HANCK, CHRIST., 20, M, None listed, -, Germany, 10, 10, CHAS*. In HH of
Nicholas Albright, M, 40, born Germany.
HANDLWALKER, CHAS., 23, M, Clerk, -, Germany, 167, 149, CHAS. In
Boarding house.
HANKIN, C.F., 26, M, Grocer, -, Germany, 426, 385, CHAS+.
HANKRAM, UTTO, 25, M, None listed, -, Germany, 1200, 1200, LEX. In HH
of John Lain, M, 55, born SC.
HANS, CAROLINE, 25, F, None listed, -, Germany, 705, 697, CHAS%. In
HH of Margt. Mintzingmeyer, F, 48, born Germany.
HANSCHILD, PETER, 59, M, Grocer, -, Germany, 113, 105, CHAS+.
HAPPOLD, CHS. D., 45, M, Coach trimmer, -, Germany, 713, 673, CHAS+.
HAPPOLDT, JOHN M., 47, M, Gunsmith, -, Germany, 173, 163, CHAS+.
HAPPOLETT, ALBERT, 45, M, Butcher, -, Germany, 1138, 1117, CHAS%.
HAPPOLETT, EDWARD, 35, M, None, -, Germany, 1138, 1117, CHAS%. In
HH of Albert Happolett, M, 45, born Germany.
HARBERS, ANNE, 48, F, None listed, -, Germany, 321, 321, CHAS%. In HH
of C.H. Harbers, M, 50, born Germany.
HARBERS, C.H., 50, M, Shopkeeper, -, Germany, 321, 321, CHAS%.
HARBERS, H., 21, M, None listed, -, Germany, 415, 387, CHAS*. In HH of
J.H. Konig, M, 35, born Germany.
HARBERS, JOHN, 19, M, Clerk, -, Germany, 321, 321, CHAS%. In HH of
C.H. Harbers, M, 50, born Germany.
HARBERS, MARGARET, 33, F, None listed, -, Germany, 486, 469, CHAS-.
In HH of R.H. Harbers, M, 27, born Germany.
HARBERS, R.H., 27, M, Grocer, -, Germany, 486, 469, CHAS-.
HARBERT, FREDERIC, 39, M, Lace weaver, -, Germany, 546, 547, AND*.
HARISBERG, HENRY, 25, M, Grocer, -, Germany, 538, 504, CHAS*.
HARMAN, HENRY, 30, M, Shopkeeper, -, Germany, 757, 742, CHAS%.
HARMAN, MARY P., 28, F, None listed, -, Germany, 757, 742, CHAS%. In
HH of Henry Harman, M, 30, born Germany.
HARMS, G., 26, F, None listed, -, Germany, 370, 343, CHAS*. In HH of John
Herkamp, M, 38, born Germany.
HARMS, HENRY, 33, M, Miller, -, Germany, 458, 472, RICH.
HARMS, HENRY, 24, M, Clerk, -, Germany, 386, 384, CHAS%. In HH of
John Kreet, M, 36, born Germany.
HARTMAN, HANNAH, 27, F, None listed, -, Germany, 1191, 1170, CHAS%.
HARTMAN, JOHN T., 29, M, Shopkeeper, -, Germany, 187, 187, CHAS%.
HARTMAN, MARGT., 16, F, None listed, -, Germany, 495, 488, CHAS%. In
HH of Francis Metcherf, M, 24, born Germany.

HARTMAN, REBECCA, 28, F, None listed, -, Germany, 187, 187, CHAS%. In HH of John T. Hartman, M, 29, born Germany.

HARTZ, AMOYLEA, 35, F, None listed, -, Germany, 878, 836, CHAS+. In HH of John H. Hartz, M, 39, born Germany.

HARTZ, CAROLINE, 32, F, None listed, -, Germany, 26, 24, CHAS-. In HH of F.P. Hartz, M, 40, born Germany.

HARTZ, F.P., 40, M, Carter, -, Germany, 26, 24, CHAS-.

HARTZ, FREDERICK, 21, M, Boot maker, -, Germany, 128, 119, CHAS+. In HH of Martin Lanse, M, 34, born Germany.

HARTZ, JOHN H., 39, M, Grocer, -, Germany, 878, 836, CHAS+.

HARVERS, DIEDERICK, 30, M, Grocer, -, Germany, 432, 415, CHAS-.

HARVERS, SOPHIA, 31, F, None listed, -, Germany, 432, 415, CHAS-. In HH of Diederick Harvers, M, 30, born Germany.

HARVERS, SUDICA, 62, M, Clerk, -, Germany, 432, 415, CHAS-. In HH of Diederick Harvers, M, 30, born Germany.

HASDALE, HERMAN, 31, M, Grocer, -, Germany, 452, 449, CHAS%.

HASDALE, MEETA, 30, F, None listed, -, Germany, 452, 449, CHAS%. In HH of Herman Hasdale, M, 31, born Germany.

HASELL, JEREMIAH, 45, M, Teacher, -, Germany, 687, 706, RICH.

HASELL, MARIE, 44, F, None listed, -, Germany, 687, 706, RICH. In HH of Jeremiah Hasell, M, 45, born Germany.

HASEMAN, MARIA, 20, F, None listed, -, Germany, 75, 67, CHAS+. In HH of Gerhard Reicks, M, 44, born Germany.

HAY, ANN, 20, F, None listed, -, Germany, 647, 639, CHAS%. In HH of Avery Hay, M, 27, born Germany.

HAY, ARBY, 10, F, None listed, -, Germany, 647, 639, CHAS%. In HH of Avery Hay, M, 27, born Germany.

HAY, AVERY, 27, M, Shopkeeper, -, Germany, 647, 639, CHAS%.

HAY, CATHERINE, 27, F, None listed, -, Germany, 647, 639, CHAS%. In HH of Avery Hay, M, 27, born Germany.

HAY, HENRY, 13, M, None listed, -, Germany, 647, 639, CHAS%. In HH of Avery Hay, M, 27, born Germany.

HEATH, MARGART, 18, F, None listed, -, Germany, 238, 238, PICK+. In HH of Isaak Heath, M, 24, born NC.

HEEDT, FRANCES, 10, F, None listed, -, Germany, 763, 743, CHAS-. In HH of Valentine Heedt, M, 40, born Germany.

HEEDT, HENRY, 8, M, None listed, -, Germany, 763, 743, CHAS-. In HH of Valentine Heedt, M, 40, born Germany.

HEEDT, MARY, 25, F, None listed, -, Germany, 763, 743, CHAS-. In HH of Valentine Heedt, M, 40, born Germany.

HEEDT, MARY, 11, F, None listed, -, Germany, 763, 743, CHAS-. In HH of

Valentine Heedt, M, 40, born Germany.
HEEDT, VALENTINE, 40, M, Shopkeeper, -, Germany, 763, 743, CHAS-.
HEFENS, HENRY, 35, M, Grocer, -, Germany, 8, 8, CHAS-.
HEFENS, JULIA, 23, F, None listed, -, Germany, 8, 8, CHAS-. In HH of
Henry Hefens, M, 35, born Germany.
HEIM, J.F., 33, M, Farmer, -, Germany, 2345, 2345, GREE.
HEIMSETH, H., 26, M, Grocer, -, Germany, 484, 442, CHAS+.
HEINE, MEETA, 15, F, None listed, -, Germany, 661, 641, CHAS-. In HH of
W. Hieze, M, 34, born Germany.
HEINE, W., 34, M, Tailor, -, Germany, 661, 641, CHAS-.
HEISENBUTTLE, GERARD, 25, M, Baker, -, Germany, 448, 445, CHAS%. In
HH of Martin Van Zoostein, M, 22, born Germany.
HEITZFELDS, JOHN, 12, M, None listed, -, Germany, 1106, 1083, CHAS-. In
Charleston Orphan House.
HELDMAN, GEORGE, 31, M, Sadler, -, Germany, 2293, 2293, GREE.
HELDMAN, MATHEIU, 19, M, Sadler, -, Germany, 2293, 2293, GREE. In HH
of George Heldman, M, 31, born Germany
HENCKE, DIEDERICK, 30, M, Grocer, -, Germany, 498, 456, CHAS+.
HENCKE, HANS, 7, M, None listed, -, Germany, 498, 456, CHAS+. In HH of
Diederick Hencke, M, 30, born Germany.
HENCKE, META, 24, F, None listed, -, Germany, 498, 456, CHAS+. In HH of
Diederick Hencke, M, 30, born Germany.
HENCKEN, JACOB, 28, M, Grocer, -, Germany, 644, 625, CHAS-.
HENIS, D., 22, M, Grocer, -, Germany, 1013, 990, CHAS-.
HENKEN, BELLOMA, 1, F, None listed, -, Germany, 758, 796, PICK. In HH
of John M. Henken, M, 29, born Germany.
HENKEN, DOROTHEA, 26, F, None listed, -, Germany, 758, 796, PICK. In
HH of John M. Henken, M, 29, born Germany.
HENKEN, H., 25, M, Grocer, -, Germany, 505, 498, CHAS%.
HENKEN, JOHN, 4, M, None listed, -, Germany, 758, 796, PICK. In HH of
John M. Henken, M, 29, born Germany.
HENKEN, JOHN M., 29, M, Farmer, -, Germany, 758, 796, PICK.
HENNIES, CHRISTIANNA, 35, F, None listed, -, Germany, 338, 344, RICH.
In HH of William Hennies, M, 44, born Germany
HENNIES, WILLIAM, 44, M, Cooper, -, Germany, 338, 344, RICH.
HENRICHSON, HENRY, 33, M, Merchant, -, Germany, 367, 376, RICH.
HENRICKSON, FREDERICK, 40, M, Grocer, -, Germany, 815, 798, CHAS%.
HENSHAW, JACOB S., 68, M, Mariner, -, Germany, 42, 42, CHAS!.
HEOSTELLOH, JOHN, 29, M, Farmer, -, Germany, 30, 30, EDGE*.
HERKEN, BELLOMA, 1, F, None listed, -, Germany, 758, 596, PICK. In HH
of John M. Herken, M, 29, born Germany.

HERKEN, DOROTHEA, 26, F, None listed, -, Germany, 758, 596, PICK. In HH of John M. Herken, M, 29, born Germany.
HERKEN, JOHN, 4, M, None listed, -, Germany, 758, 596, PICK. In HH of John M. Herken, M, 29, born Germany.
HERKEN, JOHN M., 29, M, Farmer, -, Germany, 758, 596, PICK.
HERLING, CHARLES, 30, M, Shoemaker, -, Germany, 359, 331, CHAS.
HERLING, FRANCES, 28, M, Shoemaker, -, Germany, 359, 331, CHAS. In HH of Charles Herling, M, 30, born Germany.
HERLING, LOUISA, 25, F, None listed, -, Germany, 359, 331, CHAS. In HH of Charles Herling, M, 30, born Germany.
HERMER, HENRY, 22, M, Clerk, -, Germany, 284, 263, CHAS+. In HH of F.H. Bremar, M, 33, born Germany.
HERMKE, CORDE, 24, M, Clerk, -, Germany, 27, 32, CHAS. In HH of L. Subkin, M, 24, born Germany.
HERSCH, SAMUEL, 24, M, None listed, -, Germany, 523, 473, CHAS. In HH of John P. Neibuhr, M, 31, born Germany.
HERSCHEL, ANNA, 37, F, None listed, -, Germany, 116, 108, CHAS-. In HH of L. Herschel, M, 40, born Germany.
HERSCHEL, FREDERICK, 13, M, None listed, -, Germany, 116, 108, CHAS-. In HH of L. Herschel, M, 40, born Germany.
HERSCHEL, HENRIETTA, 15, F, None listed, -, Germany, 116, 108, CHAS-. In HH of L. Herschel, M, 40, born Germany.
HERSCHEL, L., 40, M, Grocer, -, Germany, 116, 108, CHAS-.
HERTWICH, CHRISTIANA, 24, F, None listed, -, Germany, 1059, 1036, CHAS-. In HH of Florance Hertwich, M, 26, born Germany.
HERTWICH, FLORANCE, 26, M, Shoemaker, -, Germany, 1059, 1036, CHAS-.
HERWIG, W., 37, M, Music Store, -, Germany, 721, 701, CHAS-. In Boarding House.
HESS, ADELINE, 28, F, None listed, -, Germany, 686, 695, RICH. In HH of Henry Hess, M, 45, born Germany.
HESS, HENRY, 45, M, Merchant, -, Germany, 686, 695, RICH.
HESS, JACOB, 40, M, Servant, -, Germany, 882, 840, CHAS+. In Charleston Hotel.
HESS, JOHN, 28, M, None listed, -, Germany, 541, 507, CHAS*. In HH of John Ahrens, M, 35, born Germany.
HESSELMIER, LENA, 21, F, None listed, -, Germany, 436, 395, CHAS+. In HH of H. Werkermann, M, 34, born Germany.
HETT, ANDREW, 32, M, Musician, -, Germany, 34, 29, CHAS+.
HETT, CATHERINE, 8, F, None listed, -, Germany, 34, 29, CHAS+. In HH of Andrew Hett, M, 32, born Germany.

HETT, EDWARD, 5, M, None listed, -, Germany, 34, 29, CHAS+. In HH of
Andrew Hett, M, 32, born Germany.
HETT, GERTRUDE, 28, F, None listed, -, Germany, 34, 29, CHAS+. In HH of
Andrew Hett, M, 32, born Germany.
HETT, MARY, 3, F, None listed, -, Germany, 34, 29, CHAS+. In HH of
Andrew Hett, M, 32, born Germany.
HEY, ERBE H., 32, M, Clerk, -, Germany, 380, 353, CHAS*. In HH of John H.
Bredenberg, M, 26, born Germany.
HEYER, CHARLES, 26, M, Musician, -, Germany, 86, 78, CHAS+. In
Boarding House.
HEYES, JOHN H., 30, M, Shopkeeper, -, Germany, 1178, 1157, CHAS%.
HEYES, MARGARET, 30, F, None listed, -, Germany, 1178, 1157, CHAS%.
In HH of John H. Heyes, M, 30, born Germany.
HEYES, MARTHA, 2, F, None listed, -, Germany, 1178, 1157, CHAS%. In
HH of John H. Heyes, M, 30, born Germany.
HEZMAN, GEO., 33, M, Merchant, -, Germany, 21, 21, Lanc. In HH of H.R.
Price, M, 40, born SC.
HEZMAN, J., 22, M, Merchant, -, Germany, 21, 21, Lanc. In HH of H.R.
Price, M, 40, born SC.
HIGHTOWER, ERNEST, 28, M, Merchant., -, Germany, 855, 855, BARN.
HIGHTOWER, FREDERKA, 27, F, None listed, -, Germany, 855, 855, BARN.
In HH of Ernest Hightower, M, 28, born Germany.
HILDEBRAND, HENRY, 30, M, Clerk, -, Germany, 40, 37, CHAS-. Listed as
prisoner.
HILLAN, JACOB, 35, M, Boot maker, -, Germany, 143, 143, CHAS%.
HILLAN, SOPHIA, 34, F, None listed, -, Germany, 143, 143, CHAS%. In HH
of Jacob Hillan, M, 35, born Germany.
HILLER, CHARLES, 50, M, Planter, -, Germany, 635, 644, RICH+.
HILLIGAN, ALTAR, 25, M, Shopkeeper, -, Germany, 969, 946, CHAS%.
HILLIGAN, ANNA, 25, F, None listed, -, Germany, 969, 946, CHAS%. In HH
of Altar Hilligan, M, 25, born Germany.
HILSON, JOHN, 40, M, Planter, -, Germany, 630, 622, CHAS%.
HINES, HENRY, 17, M, Grocer, -, Germany, 281, 265, CHAS-.
HINES, MADELINE, 17, F, None listed, -, Germany, 211, 197, CHAS-. In HH
of Jacob Small, M, 30, born Germany.
HINNES, H.F., 30, M, Clerk, -, Germany, 176, 166, CHAS+. In HH of B.H.
Myer, M, 46, born Germany.
HITCHFELDEN, HARMON, 37, M, R.R. Laborer, -, Germany, 968, 945,
CHAS%. In HH of Christopher Volmer, M, 35, born Germany.
HITCHFELDEN, HENRIETTA, 30, F, None listed, -, Germany, 968, 945,

CHAS%. In HH of Christopher Volmer, M, 35, born Germany.

**HITCHFIELD, WILLIAM**, 19, M, Clerk, -, Germany, 69, 61, CHAS+.

**HOFFMAN, HENRY**, 24, M, Shopkeeper, -, Germany, 772, 755, CHAS%. In HH of Frederick State, M, 58, born Germany.

**HOFFMANN, J.**, 27, M, Merchant, -, Germany, 2264, 2264, GREE. In HH of T.R. Roberts, M, 29, born SC.

**HOGEFF, MICHAEL**, 30, M, Baker, -, Germany, 253, 231, CHAS. In HH of John T. Marshal, M, 48, born Scotland.

**HOGUE, JAMES**, 30, M, Tailor, -, Germany, 339, 345, RICH. In HH of Elizabeth Givenrath, F, 43, born Germany.

**HOLLENBACK, FETZ**, 28, M, Tavern keeper, -, Germany, 58, 52, CHAS+.

**HOLM, DIEDERICK**, 9, M, None listed, -, Germany, 644, 625, CHAS-. In HH of Jacob Hencken, M, 28, born Germany.

**HOLMBERG, AMORA**, 56, F, None listed, -, Germany, 416, 374, CHAS. In HH of P.U. Hammarskold, M, 35, born Germany. '

**HOLTON, ANN**, 40, F, None listed, -, Germany, 295, 279, CHAS-.

**HOLTON, CAROLINE**, 5, F, None listed, -, Germany, 295, 279, CHAS-. In HH of Ann Holton, F, 40, born Germany.

**HOLTON, CHARLOTTE**, 11, F, None listed, -, Germany, 295, 279, CHAS-. In HH of Ann Holton, F, 40, born Germany.

**HOLTON, FREDERICK**, 12, M, None listed, -, Germany, 295, 279, CHAS-. In HH of Ann Holton, F, 40, born Germany.

**HOLTON, JOANA A.**, 8, F, None listed, -, Germany, 295, 279, CHAS-. In HH of Ann Holton, F, 40, born Germany.

**HOLTON, WILLIAM**, 42, M, Gas fitter, -, Germany, 295, 279, CHAS-. In HH of Ann Holton, F, 40, born Germany.

**HOPE, L.D.**, 30, M, Stage driver, -, Germany, 1842, 1842, SUMT. In Hotel.

**HOPMAN, JOHN**, 40, M, Boot maker, -, Germany, 987, 966, CHAS-.

**HOPMAN, JOSEPH**, 22, M, Boot maker, -, Germany, 987, 966, CHAS-. In HH of John Hopman, M, 40, born Germany.

**HOPMAN, MARY**, 35, F, None listed, -, Germany, 987, 966, CHAS-. In HH of John Hopman, M, 40, born Germany.

**HORNHOLM, SOPHIA**, 29, F, None listed, -, Germany, 747, 727, CHAS-. In HH of E. Hornholm, M, 29, born Sweden.

**HUDE, A.**, 36, M, Clerk, -, Germany, 74, 74, CHAS%. In HH of F. Niliams, M, 40, born Germany.

**HUFFER, FRANCIS**, 21, M, Sadler, -, Germany, 233, 211, CHAS. In HH of Charles Love, M, 40, born Scotland.

**HUFFMAN, JOSEPH**, 30, M, Merchant, -, Germany, 318, 318, LEX. In HH of Hariet Veal, F, 45, born SC.

**HUFFNER, A.**, 37, M, Shoemaker, -, Germany, 457, 455, CHAS%.

**HUFFNER, JOANA CATHERINE**, 34, F, None listed, -, Germany, 457, 455, CHAS%. In HH of A. Huffner, M, 37, born Germany.

**HULSBERG, HENRY**, 25, M, Shopkeeper, -, Germany, 166, 153, CHAS*.

**HUMAN, GEORGE**, 18, M, None listed, -, Germany, 754, 734, CHAS-. In HH of Bernard Volger, M, 30, born Germany.

**HUNTAMANN, J.G.**, 23, M, Druggist, -, Germany, 730, 710, CHAS-. In HH of J.P.M.Epping, M, 33, born Germany.

**HURKAMP, JANNA M.**, 35, F, None listed, -, Germany, 370, 343, CHAS*. In HH of John Herkamp, M, 38, born Germany.

**HURKAMP, JOHN**, 38, M, Grocer, -, Germany, 370, 343, CHAS*.

**HURSTMAN, DEDRICK**, 80, M, Mechanic, -, Germany, 632, 641, RICH+. In HH of John Winthron, M, 48, born Germany.

**HURSTMAN, DEDRICK**, 35, M, Overseer, -, Germany, 698, 648, RICH+.

**HUSENBUTTLE, MATHEW**, 18, M, Clerk, -, Germany, 677, 635, CHAS+. In HH of Henry Piedemann, M, 26, born Germany.

**HUSMAN, HENRY**, 38, M, Merchant, -, Germany, 83, 83, BEAU.

**HUSMAN, JOHN**, 22, M, Clerk, -, Germany, 385, 349, CHAS. In HH of Geo. F. Meldan, M, 27, born Germany.

**HUSMAN, MATER**, 22, M, None listed, -, Germany, 83, 83, BEAU. In HH of Henry Husman, M, 38, born Germany.

**HUTLLENDER, HENRY**, 17, M, Clerk, -, Germany, 384, 357, CHAS*. In HH of F. Wehman, M, 24, born Germany.

# I

**INGINER, JNO.**, 36, M, Farmer, -, Germany, 29, 29, LEX. Census date stated Jno. Inginer, born Baden, Germany.

**ISEMAN, ISAAC**, 30, M, None listed, -, Germany, 367, 367, DARL. In HH of Mark Iseman, M, 20, born Germany.

**ISEMAN, MANUEL**, 45, M, Merchant, -, Germany, 10, 11, MAR.

**ISEMAN, MARK**, 20, M, Merchant, -, Germany, 367, 367, DARL.

**ISEMAN, ROSENA**, 25, F, None listed, -, Germany, 367, 367, DARL. In HH of Mark Iseman, M, 20, born Germany.

**ISENBUTTLE, JOHN**, 15, M, Clerk, -, Germany, 453, 420, CHAS*. In HH of Martin Spinkin, M, 34, born Germany.

**ISENHOOT, JNO.**, 24, M, Shoemaker, -, Germany, 153, 153, LEX. In HH of Barbara Corly, F, 80, born SC. Census states Jno. Isenhoot born Witenburg, Germany.

# J

**JACOBS, JOHN**, 35, M, Merchant, -, Germany, 315, 290, CHAS.

**JACOBS, SARAH**, 50, F, None listed, -, Germany, 41, 36, CHAS+. In HH of Jacob Simon Jacobs, M, 56, born Denmark.

**JACOBSON, J.**, 24, M, Merchant, -, Germany, 813, 793, CHAS-. In HH of Isaac Seckendorffe, M, 40, born Germany.

**JAGER, ADOLPH**, 4, M, None listed, -, Germany, 254, 239, CHAS+. In HH of J.A. Jager, M, 30, born Germany.

**JAGER, ALBERT**, 26, F, None listed, -, Germany, 254, 239, CHAS+. In HH of J.A. Jager, M, 30, born Germany.

**JAGER, AMELIA**, 5, F, None listed, -, Germany, 589, 571, CHAS-. In HH of Hans Jager, M, 51, born Germany.

**JAGER, ANTONIO**, 9, M, None listed, -, Germany, 589, 571, CHAS-. In HH of Hans Jager, M, 51, born Germany.

**JAGER, CARL**, 2, M, None listed, -, Germany, 254, 239, CHAS+. In HH of J.A. Jager, M, 30, born Germany.

**JAGER, FREDERICK**, 13, M, None listed, -, Germany, 589, 571, CHAS-. In HH of Hans Jager, M, 51, born Germany.

**JAGER, HANS**, 51, M, Shopkeeper, -, Germany, 589, 571, CHAS-.

**JAGER, J.A.**, 30, M, Glazier, -, Germany, 254, 239, CHAS+.

**JAGER, JOANA**, 49, F, None listed, -, Germany, 589, 571, CHAS-. In HH of Hans Jager, M, 51, born Germany.

**JANSEN, COLINA**, 16, F, None listed, -, Germany, 117, 109, CHAS-. In HH of John Conrade, M, 40, born Germany.

**JANSEN, FREDERICK**, 18, M, Clerk, -, Germany, 117, 109, CHAS-. In HH of John Conrade, M, 40, born Germany.

**JESSEN, CHARLOTTE**, 26, F, None listed, -, Germany, 179, 162, CHAS. In HH of Hans Jessen, M, 32, born Germany.

**JESSEN, HANS**, 32, M, Store keeper, -, Germany, 179, 162, CHAS.

**JESSON, F.**, 21, M, Clerk, -, Germany, 196, 179, CHAS. In HH of C. Ollen, M, 28, born Germany.

**JOHN, HENRY**, 45, M, Locksmith, -, Germany, 86, 78, CHAS+. In Boarding House.

**JOHNS, DIEDERICK**, 21, M, Blacksmith, -, Germany, 163, 153, CHAS-. In HH of F. Rissler, M, 30, born Germany.

**JOHNSON, GEORGE**, 26, M, Mariner, -, Germany, 341, 315, CHAS. In HH of William Bellair, M, 35, born Germany.

**JOHNSON, JAMES**, 36, M, Shoemaker, -, Germany, 259, 237, CHAS.

**JOHNSON, LUDER**, 35, M, Grocer, -, Germany, 99, 92, CHAS-.

**JOHNSTON, JOHN**, 47, M, Rigger, -, Germany, 90, 101, CHAS.

**JUGLER, CHRISTIANA**, 50, F, None listed, -, Germany, 372, 372, CHAS%.

**JUNGBLUTH, JOHN**, 26, M, Tavern Keeper, -, Germany, 86, 78, CHAS+. In Boarding House.

**JUNGHIEM, WM.**, 16, M, Clerk, -, Germany, 779, 759, CHAS-. In HH of John Ogeman, M, 26, born Germany.

**JUST, GEORGE**, 65, M, Wharf Builder, -, Germany, 460, 443, CHAS-.

# K

**KAARMAN, JOHN B.**, 37, M, Laborer, -, Germany, 345, 328, CHAS-. In HH of Henry Biesarrer, M, 35, born Germany.

**KAHAHALL, MICHAEL C.**, 38, M, RR officer, -, Germany, 885, 895, RICH+.

**KAHR, GERTRUDE**, 49, F, None listed, -, Germany, 122, 138, CHAS. In HH of John J. Kahr, M, 37, born Germany.

**KAHR, JASPER**, 36, M, Clerk, -, Germany, 122, 138, CHAS. In HH of John J. Kahr, M, 37, born Germany.

**KAHR, JOHN J.**, 37, M, Grocer, -, Germany, 122, 138, CHAS.

**KAISER, CHRISTIAN**, 44, M, Silversmith, -, Germany, 557, 557, UNION. In Hotel.

**KAISER, JULIUS**, 18, M, Painter, -, Germany, 556, 556, UNION. In Hotel. Occp: listed as Painter (fancy).

**KALB, EMMELINE**, 6, F, None listed, -, Germany, 139, 139, CHAS%. In HH of J.H. Kalb, M, 45, born Germany.

**KALB, J.C.**, 32, F, None listed, -, Germany, 139, 139, CHAS%. In HH of J.H. Kalb, M, 45, born Germany.

**KALB, J.H.**, 45, M, Baker, -, Germany, 139, 139, CHAS%.

**KALB, JOHN**, 10, M, None listed, -, Germany, 139, 139, CHAS%. In HH of J.H. Kalb, M, 45, born Germany.

**KALB, JULIA ANNA**, 8, F, None listed, -, Germany, 139, 139, CHAS%. In HH of J.H. Kalb, M, 45, born Germany.

**KALB, LOUISA**, 12, F, None listed, -, Germany, 139, 139, CHAS%. In HH of J.H. Kalb, M, 45, born Germany.

**KAPPLEMAN, M.H.**, 47, M, Bookseller, -, Germany, 272, 256, CHAS-.

**KAUFMAN, FRANCES**, 24, M, None listed, -, Germany, 292, 298, RICH. In HH of Henry Kaufman, M, 35, born Germany.

**KAUFMAN, HENRY**, 35, M, Merchant, -, Germany, 292, 298, RICH.

**KAUFMAN, ISAAC**, 80, M, None, -, Germany, 292, 298, RICH. In HH of Henry Kaufman, M, 35, born Germany.

**KEELING, EMILY**, 22, F, None listed, -, Germany, 264, 269, RICH. In HH of Samuel Keeling, M, 30, born Germany.

**KEELING, GABRIEL**, 27, M, Merchant, -, Germany, 264, 269, RICH. In HH of Samuel Keeling, M, 30, born Germany.

**KEELING, JEANNETTE**, 25, F, None listed, -, Germany, 264, 269, RICH. In HH of Samuel Keeling, M, 30, born Germany.

KEELING, MARY A., 18, F, None listed, -, Germany, 264, 269, RICH. In HH of Samuel Keeling, M, 30, born Germany.

KEELING, SAMUEL, 30, M, Merchant, -, Germany, 264, 269, RICH.

KEIL, J.H., 32, M, Store keeper, -, Germany, 517, 500, CHAS-.

KEIL, MARGARET, 28, F, None listed, -, Germany, 517, 500, CHAS-. In HH of J.H. Keil, M, 32, born Germany.

KEITZBER, CAROLINE, 29, F, None listed, -, Germany, 1079, 1101, CHAS%. In HH of Hans Keitzber, M, 34, born Germany.

KEITZBER, CLAUS, 10, M, None listed, -, Germany, 1079, 1101, CHAS%. In HH of Hans Keitzber, M, 34, born Germany.

KEITZBER, FRITZ, 7, M, None listed, -, Germany, 1079, 1101, CHAS%. In HH of Hans Keitzber, M, 34, born Germany.

KEITZBER, HANS, 34, M, Grocer, -, Germany, 1079, 1101, CHAS%.

KEITZBER, MARY, 4, F, None listed, -, Germany, 1079, 1101, CHAS%. In HH of Hans Keitzber, M, 34, born Germany.

KELLARS, C., 35, M, Merchant, -, Germany, 284, 263, CHAS+. In HH of F.H. Bremar, M, 33, born Germany.

KELLERMAN, GEO., 28, M, Baker, -, Germany, 667, 647, CHAS-. In Boarding House.

KENNEY, DEAS H., 31, M, Tailor, -, Germany, 311, 287, CHAS+.

KERCHER, F.E., 21, M, Shoemaker, -, Germany, 414, 373, CHAS+. In HH of W. Woolfe, M, 23, born Germany.

KERNE, CHARLES, 21, M, Shoemaker, -, Germany, 414, 373, CHAS+. In HH of W. Woolfe, M, 23, born Germany.

KERP, JOHN A., 26, M, Grocer, -, Germany, 630, 611, CHAS-.

KIDER, NICHOLAS, 23, M, Baker, -, Germany, 722, 680, CHAS+.

KIEFFER, HANSIN, 35, F, None listed, -, Germany, 68, 60, CHAS+. In HH of John Kieffer, M, 38, born Germany.

KIEFFER, JOHN, 38, M, Shopkeeper, -, Germany, 68, 60, CHAS+.

KIEP, CATHERINE, 67, F, None listed, -, Germany, 444, 403, CHAS+. In HH of Jergen Henry Kiep, M, 31, born Germany.

KIEP, FREDERICA D., 23, F, None listed, -, Germany, 444, 403, CHAS+. In HH of Jergen Henry Kiep, M, 31, born Germany.

KIEP, JERGEN HENRY, 31, M, Grocer, -, Germany, 444, 403, CHAS+.

KIEP, MARY CATHERINE, 22, F, None listed, -, Germany, 444, 403, CHAS+. In HH of Jergen Henry Kiep, M, 31, born Germany.

KINDELL, FREDERICK, 18, M, Baker, -, Germany, 139, 139, CHAS%. In HH of J.H. Kalb, M, 45, born Germany.

KING, FREDERICK, 24, M, Clerk, -, Germany, 116, 108, CHAS-. In HH of L. Herschel, M, 40, born Germany.

KINSLER, MICHAEL, 45, M, Farmer, -, Germany, 277, 279, And. In HH of

Mary McCrary, F, 56, born SC.

**KIPELSTEIN, FREDERICK**, 27, M, Merchant, -, Germany, 393, 403, RICH. In Hotel.

**KIRKLER, HARTWIG**, 31, M, Finisher, -, Germany, 1043, 1021, CHAS%.

**KIRKLER, WINNA**, 32, F, None listed, -, Germany, 1043, 1021, CHAS%. In HH of Hartwig Kirkler, M, 31, born Germany.

**KISELSTEIN, JULIUS**, 58, M, Pianist, -, Germany, 131, 134, RICH.

**KISKER, AUGUSTUS**, 33, M, Musician, -, Germany, 86, 78, CHAS+. In Boarding House.

**KLEESIG, AUGUST**, 30, M, Clerk, -, Germany, 306, 290, CHAS-.

**KLEESIG, AUGUST**, 1, M, None listed, -, Germany, 306, 290, CHAS-. In HH of August Kleesig, M, 30, born Germany.

**KLEESIG, CHARLOTTE**, 5, F, None listed, -, Germany, 306, 290, CHAS-. In HH of August Kleesig, M, 30, born Germany.

**KLEESIG, LOUISA**, 30, F, None listed, -, Germany, 306, 290, CHAS-. In HH of August Kleesig, M, 30, born Germany.

**KLEESIG, MEETA**, 4, F, None listed, -, Germany, 306, 290, CHAS-. In HH of August Kleesig, M, 30, born Germany.

**KLENKA, ANDREW**, 25, M, Shopkeeper, -, Germany, 556, 548, CHAS%. In HH of George Bulwinkle, M, 29, born Germany.

**KLIBER, AMBROSE**, 22, M, None listed, -, Germany, 902, 879, CHAS%. In HH of Fredrick Kliber, M, 50, born Germany.

**KLIBER, FREDRICK**, 50, M, None listed, -, Germany, 902, 879, CHAS%.

**KLIBER, MARTHA**, 50, F, None listed, -, Germany, 902, 879, CHAS% In HH of Fredrick Kliber, M, 50, born Germany.

**KLINCK, BINAH**, 34, F, None listed, -, Germany, 764, 749, CHAS%. In HH of Harman Klinck, M, 38, born Germany.

**KLINCK, C.**, 22, M, Chymist, -, Germany, 523, 473, CHAS. In HH of John P. Neibuhr, M, 31, born Germany.

**KLINCK, GEORGE**, 30, M, Carpenter, -, Germany, 558, 524, CHAS*. In HH of Gerd. St.Records, M, 50, born Germany.

**KLINCK, HARMAN**, 36, M, Clerk, -, Germany, 558, 524, CHAS*. In HH of Gerd. St.Records, M, 50, born Germany.

**KLINCK, HARMAN.**, 38, M, Grocer, -, Germany, 764, 749, CHAS%.

**KLINCK, HENRY**, 19, M, Clerk, -, Germany, 95, 93, CHAS*. In HH of John Bull, M, 38, born Germany.

**KLINCK, JOANA**, 12, F, None listed, -, Germany, 764, 749, CHAS%. In HH of Harman Klinck, M, 38, born Germany.

**KLINCK, JOHN**, 53, M, Merchant, -, Germany, 434, 417, CHAS-.

**KLINE, AUGUSTA**, 25, F, None listed, -, Germany, 798, 781, CHAS%. In HH of William Dorrell, M, 25, born Germany.

KLINE, CAROLINE, 28, F, None listed, -, Germany, 357, 329, CHAS. In HH of E. Groves, F, 50, runs boarding house, born SC.
KLINE, CHRISTIAN, 38, M, Laborer, -, Germany, 529, 544, RICH.
KLINE, DIEDERICK, 18, M, Laborer, -, Germany, 4, 4, CHAS%. In HH of C.F. Breedenberg, M, 25, born Germany.
KLINE, FREDERICK, 34, M, Baker, -, Germany, 48, 57, CHAS. In HH of Henry Base, M, 24, born Germany.
KLINE, W., 30, M, Merchant, -, Germany, 357, 329, CHAS. In HH of E. Groves, F, 50, runns boarding house, born SC.
KNABLE, ANNA, 25, F, None listed, -, Germany, 1013, 990, CHAS-. In HH of D. Henis, M, 22, born Germany.
KNEE, CHRISTIANA, 34, F, None listed, -, Germany, 85, 95, CHAS. In HH of Harman Knee, M, 47, born Germany.
KNEE, HARMAN, 47, M, Shopkeeper, -, Germany, 85, 95, CHAS.
KNEUFFER, F., 50, M, Physician, -, Germany, 477, 443, CHAS*. In HH of Charles P. Frazer, M, 45, born SC.
KNOBLER, SUSAN, 32, F, None listed, -, Germany, 803, 761, CHAS+. In HH of William Knobler, M, 33, born Germany.
KNOBLER, WILLIAM, 33, M, Baker, -, Germany, 803, 761, CHAS+.
KNOCKE, ANON, 26, M, Ordinance man, -, Germany, 1005, 982, CHAS%. Under command of Major P. Hagnes, Comg. Off. U.S. Arnsel.
KNOLPHEN, C., 33, M, Gardner, -, Germany, 164, 154, CHAS-. In HH of D.A. Amie, M, 30, born Germany.
KOCH, WILLIAM, 21, M, Cigar maker, -, Germany, 556, 556, UNION. In Hotel.
KOHNARHEM, ANNE, 22, F, None listed, -, Germany, 520, 513, CHAS%. In HH of John H. Kohnarhem, M, 40, born Germany.
KOHNARHEM, JOHN H., 40, M, Shopkeeper, -, Germany, 520, 513, CHAS%.
KOHNCKE, C.F., 45, M, Grocer, -, Germany, 527, 510, CHAS-.
KOHNE, J.C., 22, M, Clerk, -, Germany, 4, 4, CHAS%. In HH of C.F. Breedenberg, M, 25, born Germany.
KOLLMAN, ALBERT, 22, M, Clerk, -, Germany, 216, 194, CHAS. In HH of D. Kollman, M, 35, born Germany.
KOLLMAN, D., 35, M, Shopkeeper, -, Germany, 216, 194, CHAS.
KOLMECKE, A., 50, M, Shopkeeper, -, Germany, 287, 287, CHAS%.
KOLMECKE, FRANCIS, 40, F, None listed, -, Germany, 287, 287, CHAS%. In HH of A. Kolmecke, M, 50, born Germany.
KONER, FREDERICK, 15, M, None listed, -, Germany, 35, 35, CHAS%. In HH of Henry Zerbet, M, 31, born Germany.
KONIG, HANNAH, 26, F, None listed, -, Germany, 415, 387, CHAS*. In HH

of J.H. Konig, M, 35, born Germany.

**KONIG, J.H.**, 35, M, Grocer, -, Germany, 415, 387, CHAS*.

**KONOCHKEY, ALBERT**, 19, M, Clerk, -, Germany, 404, 368, CHAS. In HH of Jacob Von Been, M, 24, born Germany

**KOOPMAN, B.**, 26, M, Merchant, -, Germany, 19, 19, KERS.

**KOPMAN, JACOB**, 34, M, Baker, -, Germany, 478, 475, CHAS%.

**KORHANS, JOHN**, 12, M, None listed, -, Germany, 466, 463, CHAS%. In HH of Christian Slippergrel, M, 30, born France.

**KOSTER, JOHN**, 25, M, None listed, -, Germany, 470, 467, CHAS%. In HH of C. Vandelkin, M, 24, born Germany.

**KOSTER, JOHN**, 25, M, Carpenter, -, Germany, 892, 869, CHAS%. In HH of Nicholas Newman, M, 38, born Germany.

**KRAATZ, LEWIS**, 30, M, Locksmith, -, Germany, 86, 78, CHAS+. In Boarding House.

**KRACKE, FREDERICK**, 41, M, Grocer, -, Germany, 783, 766, CHAS%.

**KRACKE, SOPHIA**, 39, F, None listed, -, Germany, 783, 766, CHAS%. In HH of Frederick Kracki, M, 41, born Germany.

**KRAFT, J.M.**, 40, M, Boot maker, -, Germany, 9, 9, NEWB.

**KRAFT, SEBASTIAN**, 32, M, Whitesmith, -, Germany, 9, 9, NEWB. In HH of J.M. Kraft 40, M, born Germany.

**KRAKE, DAVID**, 38, M, Watchmaker, -, Germany, 513, 513, FAIR. In HH of J.M. Cranford, M, 27, born Ireland. At the Fairfield Hotel.

**KRAMER, AUGUSTA**, 14, M, None listed, -, Germany, 500, 493, CHAS%. In HH of William Kramer, M, 55, born Germany.

**KRAMER, BERTRAM**, 9, M, None listed, -, Germany, 500, 493, CHAS%. In HH of William Kramer, M, 55, born Germany.

**KRAMER, ELIZA**, 23, F, None listed, -, Germany, 895, 872, CHAS%. In HH of Jacob Kramer, M, 26, born Germany.

**KRAMER, JACOB**, 26, M, None listed, -, Germany, 895, 872, CHAS%.

**KRAMER, LOUISA**, 37, F, None listed, -, Germany, 500, 493, CHAS%. In HH of William Kramer, M, 55, born Germany.

**KRAMER, WILLIAM**, 55, M, Cabinetmaker, -, Germany, 500, 493, CHAS%.

**KREAYE, HENRY**, 21, M, Clerk, -, Germany, 527, 510, CHAS-. In HH of C.F. Kohncke, M, 45, born Germany.

**KREET, CHRISTIANA**, 30, F, None listed, -, Germany, 386, 384, CHAS%. In HH of John Kreet, M, 36, born Germany.

**KREET, JASPER NICHOLAS**, 12, M, None listed, -, Germany, 386, 384, CHAS%. In HH of John Kreet, M, 36, born Germany.

**KREET, JOHN**, 36, M, Grocer, -, Germany, 386, 384, CHAS%.

**KREKI, FREDRICK**, 35, M, None listed, -, Germany, 676, 668, CHAS%.

**KREKI, MARY**, 32, F, None listed, -, Germany, 676, 668, CHAS%. In HH of

Fredrick Kreki, M, 35, born Germany.

**KRIETE, FREDERICK**, 55, M, None listed, -, Germany, 237, 222, CHAS-. Poor House.

**KROPP, JOHN F.**, 33, M, Apt. Burser, -, Germany, 11, 11, RICH. Occupation: Apt. Burser SC Colo.

**KROSS, HENRY**, 24, M, Clerk, -, Germany, 795, 778, CHAS%. In HH of William Zeleo, M, 38, born Germany.

**KRUSE, CATHERINE**, 35, F, None listed, -, Germany, 795, 805, RICH+. In HH of Herman Kruse, M, 45, born Germany.

**KRUSE, HERMAN**, 45, M, Laborer, -, Germany, 795, 805, RICH+.

**KUHNEE, H. K.**, 15, M, Clerk, -, Germany, 68, 78, CHAS. In HH of M. Bulwinckle, M, 22, born Germany.

**KUHTMANN, H.W.**, 35, M, Merchant, -, Germany, 531, 490, CHAS+.

**KUNHARDT, WILLIAM**, 64, M, Port Warden, -, Germany, 567, 525, CHAS+.

**KUSEL, J.H.**, 29, M, Grocer, -, Germany, 120, 112, CHAS-.


# L

**LAEB, CATHARINE**, 60, F, None listed, -, Germany, 806, 807, ORNG+. In HH of D. Laeb or Laele), M, 37, born Germany.

**LAEB, D.**, 37, M, Merchant, -, Germany, 806, 807, ORNG+.

**LAEB, HENRIETTA**, 30, F, None listed, -, Germany, 806, 807, ORNG+. In HH of D. Laeb or Laele), M, 37, born Germany.

**LAMPE, FREDERICK**, 30, M, Grocer, -, Germany, 56, 50, CHAS+. In HH of Frederick Lampe, M, 30, born Germany.

**LANCK, NICHOLAS**, 22, M, Baker, -, Germany, 285, 264, CHAS+. In HH of H. Wittschew, M, 23, born Germany.

**LANG, HENRY M.**, 49, M, Waggon maker, -, Germany, 274, 274, GREE. In HH of Stephen Philips, M, 40, born SC.

**LANGER, WILLIAM**, 36, M, Farmer, -, Germany, 788, 789, And*.

**LANSE, MARTIN**, 34, M, Boot maker, -, Germany, 128, 119, CHAS+.

**LANSE, SUSANAH**, 23, F, Boot maker, -, Germany, 128, 119, CHAS+. In HH of Martin Lanse, M, 34, born Germany.

**LAPALE, WILLIAM**, 33, M, Shoemaker, -, Germany, 413, 424, RICH. In HH of Theodore Vogel, M, 30, born Germany.

**LARK, CHARLES**, 34, M, Farmer, -, Germany, 937, 937, PICK+.

**LARK, ELIMINA**, 41, F, None listed, -, Germany, 937, 937, PICK+. In HH of Charles Lark, M, 34, born Germany

**LARK, HENRY**, 50, M, Farmer, -, Germany, 943, 943, PICK+.

**LAWRENCE, JOHAN**, 21, M, Clerk, -, Germany, 287, 271, CHAS-. In HH of Ann Myerhoff, F, 22, born Germany.

LAWRENCE, JOSEPH, 52, M, Cabinetmaker, -, Germany, 287, 271, CHAS-. In HH of Ann Myerhoff, F, 22, born Germany.

LEAR, LEWIS, 25, M, Clerk, -, Germany, 433, 392, CHAS+. In HH of H. Steinman, M, 28, born Germany.

LECLAIR, CONRAD, 32, M, Clerk, -, Germany, 789, 769, CHAS-. In HH of George Reicke, M, 56, born Germany.

LEDUS, WILLIAM, 30, M, Shopkeeper, -, Germany, 231, 231, CHAS%. In HH of John Garber, M, 49, born Germany.

LEE, JOHN E., 29, M, Grocer, -, Germany, 3, 3, CHAS-.

LEHAY, ANN D., 34, F, None listed, -, Germany, 412, 410, CHAS%. In HH of John Lehay, M, 37, born Germany.

LEHAY, JOHN, 37, M, Grocer, -, Germany, 412, 410, CHAS%.

LEHAY, MARGARET E., 13, F, None listed, -, Germany, 412, 410, CHAS%. In HH of John Lehay, M, 37, born Germany.

LEHAY, MARY, 10, F, None listed, -, Germany, 412, 410, CHAS%. In HH of John Lehay, M, 37, born Germany.

LEIRNTRETT, ELIZABETH, 26, F, None listed, -, Germany, 538, 538, FAIR. In HH of G.M. Leirntrett, M, 30, born Germany.

LEIRNTRETT, G.M., 39, M, Merchant, -, Germany, 538, 538, FAIR.

LELLLENTAL, IRAN, 23, M, Oil Manufacture, -, Germany, 146, 146, CHAS%. In HH of C. Alfs, M, 55, born Germany.

LEMAN, CHRIS, 25, M, Tavern keeper, -, Germany, 58, 52, CHAS+. In HH of Fetz Hallenback, M, 28, born Germany.

LEMAN, HANNAH, 22, F, None listed, -, Germany, 43, 38, CHAS+. In HH of Hannah Cohen, F, 34, born Germany.

LENS, H., 21, M, Grocer, -, Germany, 660, 618, CHAS+.

LENTHE, HENRY, 19, M, Clerk, -, Germany, 58, 52, CHAS+. In HH of Fetz Hallenback, M, 28, born Germany.

LEOPOLD, FREDRICK, 35, M, Shopkeeper, -, Germany, 652, 644, CHAS%.

LEOPOLD, J., MR., 42, M, Farmer, -, Germany, 10, 10, CHAS#.

LEOPOLD, REBECCA, 25, F, None listed, -, Germany, 652, 644, CHAS%. In HH of Fredrick Leopold, M, 35, born Germany.

LEOPOLD, W., MR., 26, M, Farmer, -, Germany, 29, 29, CHAS#.

LEPACK, DORIS, 9, F, None listed, -, Germany, 803, 783, CHAS-. In HH of J.J. Lepack, M, 40, born Poland.

LESEMAN, F.W., 27, M, Clerk, -, Germany, 440, 437, CHAS%. In HH of John A. Cook, M, 52, born Germany.

LESESNE, D., 22, M, None listed, -, Germany, 151, 142, CHAS+. In HH of H. Gerdts, M, 38, born Germany.

LESESNE, PRISCELLA, 20, F, None listed, -, Germany, 151, 142, CHAS+. In HH of H. Gerdts, M, 38, born Germany.

**LEVER, DOROTHY**, 26, F, None listed, -, Germany, 9, 9, RICH. In HH of George Lever, M, 29, born SC.

**LEVEREN, W.**, 23, M, Sadler, -, Germany, 391, 355, CHAS. In HH of F.W. Theus, M, 28, born Germany.

**LEVY, ELIAS**, 50, M, Merchant, -, Germany, 221, 226, RICH. Page out of order, follow HH 177/181.

**LEVY, T.Z.**, 29, M, Merchant, -, Germany, 27, 27, NEWB.

**LEWIS, JOHN**, 16, M, Clerk, -, Germany, 484, 442, CHAS+. In HH of H. Heimseth, M, 26, born Germany.

**LIEBER, MATILDA**, 40, F, None listed, -, Germany, 688, 697, RICH. In HH of Francis Lieber, M, 50, born Prussia.

**LIGHTNER, SOPHIA**, 19, F, None listed, -, Germany, 886, 866, CHAS-. In HH of William Searle, M, 36, born England.

**LILANDORFF, HENRY**, 24, M, Shoemaker, -, Germany, 183, 167, CHAS*. In HH of John Bremar, M, 34, born Germany.

**LILENTHAL, SILAS**, 32, M, Merchant, -, Germany, 1178, 1178, EDGE. In HH of Richard Parks, M, 59, born GA

**LILIENTHAL, LIN**, 27, M, Merchant, -, Germany, 287, 293, RICH.

**LILIENTHAL, MOSES**, 24, M, Merchant, -, Germany, 686, 695, RICH. In HH of Henry Hess, M, 45, born Germany.

**LINDENTHALL, CARSTEN**, 22, M, Clerk, -, Germany, 166, 153, CHAS*. In HH of Henry Hulsberg, M, 25, born Germany.

**LINDSTEDT, A.**, 29, M, Shopkeeper, -, Germany, 666, 658, CHAS%.

**LINDSTEDT, MARY**, 29, F, None listed, -, Germany, 666, 658, CHAS%. In HH of A. Lindstedt, M, 29, born Germany.

**LINGE, HENRY**, 27, M, None listed, -, Germany, 562, 554, CHAS%. In HH of Henry Bulwinkle, M, 45, born Germany.

**LINSTEDT, C.**, 28, M, None listed, -, Germany, 353, 326, CHAS*. In HH of G. Linstedt, M, 28, born Germany.

**LINSTEDT, G.**, 21, M, Grocer, -, Germany, 353, 326, CHAS*.

**LIPMAN, MARY**, 28, F, None listed, -, Germany, 275, 259, CHAS-. In HH of William Lipman, M, 30, born Germany.

**LIPMAN, WILLIAM**, 30, M, Confectioner, -, Germany, 275, 259, CHAS-.

**LIPP, FREDERICK**, 21, M, Clerk, -, Germany, 160, 160, CHAS%. In HH of Frederick Mehrtens, M, 38, born Germany.

**LIPPS, FREDERICK**, 23, M, Clerk, -, Germany, 188, 171, CHAS. In HH of J.D. Habenech, M, 37, born Germany.

**LIPSCOMBE, FREDERICA**, 42, F, None listed, -, Germany, 306, 283, CHAS. In HH of Henry Lipscombe, M, 45, born Germany.

**LIPSCOMBE, FREDERICK**, 18, M, None listed, -, Germany, 306, 283, CHAS. In HH of Henry Lipscombe, M, 45, born Germany.

**LIPSCOMBE, HENRY**, 45, M, Grocer, -, Germany, 306, 283, CHAS.

**LIPSCOMBE, JOANA C.**, 20, F, None listed, -, Germany, 306, 283, CHAS. In HH of Henry Lipscombe, M, 45, born Germany.

**LIVERPOOL, JOHN**, 17, M, Clerk, -, Germany, 640, 621, CHAS-. In HH of Benjamin Rash, M, 28, born Germany.

**LLYER, HENRY**, 34, M, Carpenter, -, Germany, 380, 342, CHAS+.

**LOELE, CATHERINE**, 60, F, None listed, -, Germany, 806, 806, ORNG+. In HH of D. Loele, M, 37, born Germany.

**LOELE, D.**, 37, M, Merchant, -, Germany, 806, 806, ORNG+.

**LOELE, HENRIETTA**, 30, F, None listed, -, Germany, 806, 806, ORNG+. In HH of D. Loele, M, 37, born Germany.

**LUBKIN, HARMAN**, 28, M, Clerk, -, Germany, 27, 32, CHAS. In HH of L. Subkin, M, 24, born Germany.

**LUBKIN, HENRIETTA**, 25, F, None listed, -, Germany, 27, 32, CHAS. In HH of L. Subkin, M, 24, born Germany.

**LUCINS, FREDERICK**, 83, M, Farmer, -, Germany, 1167, 1167, EDGE. In HH of Thomas Chamberlin, M, 50, born VA.

**LUDES, DEIDERICK**, 21, M, Clerk, -, Germany, 610, 591, CHAS-. In HH of H. Stemmermann, M, 34, born Germany.

**LUDOVIC, AMELIA**, 32, F, None listed, -, Germany, 28, 34, CHAS. In HH of Frances Roberts, M, 41, born Germany.

**LUDZ, B.**, 38, M, Shoemaker, -, Germany, 40, 40, BARN.

**LUDZ, MARGARET**, 24, F, None listed, -, Germany, 40, 40, BARN. In HH of B. Ludz, M, 38, born Germany.

**LUFIS, HENRY**, 25, M, Shopkeeper, -, Germany, 635, 627, CHAS%. In HH of Carson Renner, M, 25, born Germany.

**LUNDT, AUGUSTUS**, 24, M, Mariner, -, Germany, 341, 305, CHAS+. In HH of Jane Hamilton, F, 49, born England.

**LYNCH, F.**, 35, M, None listed, -, Germany, 400, 373, CHAS*. In HH of F. Behrens, M, 33, born Germany.


# M

**MABUS, ELIZABETH**, 60, F, None listed, -, Germany, 50, 50, LEX. In HH of Manly Yartman, M, 21, born SC. Census date stated ElizabaethMabus, born Gats, Germany. Her age torn 6_.

**MAIRS, A.**, 46, M, Merchant, -, Germany, 438, 438, LAU.

**MAIRS, S.**, 50, M, Merchant, -, Germany, 802, 782, CHAS-. In HH of George Prince, M, 33, born Poland.

**MANCKO, P.**, 30, M, Shopkeeper, -, Germany, 342, 316, CHAS.

**MANGLIS, HENRY**, 20, M, Clerk, -, Germany, 646, 626, CHAS-. In HH of

Henry Corker, M, 39, born Germany.
MANN, GEORGE A., 40, M, Confectioner, -, Germany, 24, 24, BEAU.
MANN, HANS, 32, M, None listed, -, Germany, 24, 24, BEAU. In HH of
George A Mann, M, 40, born Germany.
MANN, PETER, 26, M, Mariner, -, Germany, 60, 70, CHAS.
MANN, PETER JR., 20, M, Mariner, -, Germany, 60, 70, CHAS. In HH of
Peter Mann, M, 26, born Germany.
MAPUS, CATHARINE, 41, F, None listed, -, Germany, 1215, 1215, LEX. In
HH of William Mapus, M, 47, born Germany.
MAPUS, GEORGE, 40, M, Farmer, -, Germany, 911, 911, LEX.
MAPUS, WILLIAM., 47, M, Overseer, -, Germany, 1215, 1215, LEX.
MARERER, ADAM, 24, M, Oil Manufacture, -, Germany, 146, 146, CHAS%.
In HH of C. Alfs, M, 55, born Germany.
MARGENHOFF, E.H., 39, M, Grocer, -, Germany, 98, 90, CHAS+.
MARGENHOFF, J., 26, M, Merchant, -, Germany, 1360, 1360, BARN.
MARGENHOFF, WILLEMINA, 30, F, None listed, -, Germany, 98, 90,
CHAS+. In HH of E.H. Margenhoff, M, 39, born Germany.
MARGRAF, HENRY, 32, M, Shoemaker, -, Germany, 231, 236, RICH.
MARINHOFF, HENRY, 33, M, Tavern keeper, -, Germany, 158, 141, CHAS.
MARINHOFF, MARIA, 25, F, None listed, -, Germany, 158, 141, CHAS. In
HH of Henry Marinhoff, M, 33, born Germany.
MARK, LOUISA, 28, M, None listed, -, Germany, 194, 194, CHAS%. In HH
of Carson Allers, M, 50, born Germany.
MARSHALL, M. W., 53, M, Dentist, -, Germany, 44, 44, BARN.
MARSHALL, MARTIN, 21, M, Clerk, -, Germany, 152, 143, CHAS+. In HH
of John Cordes, M, 26, born Germany.
MARTEN, JOHN, 30, M, Mariner, -, Germany, 337, 311, CHAS. In HH of
William H. Fowler, M, 38 running Boarding house, born England.
MARTEN, THEODORE, 18, M, Bar Keeper, -, Germany, 337, 311, CHAS. In
HH of William H. Fowler, M, 38 running Boarding house, born England.
MARTINS, FREDERICK W., 45, M, Tailor, -, Germany, 484, 441, CHAS.
MARTINS, MEETA, 40, F, None listed, -, Germany, 484, 441, CHAS. In HH
of Frederick W. Martins, M, 45, born Germany.
MASHER, WILLIAM, 28, M, Store keeper, -, Germany, 802, 760, CHAS+.
MASKY, CATHERINE, 18, F, None listed, -, Germany, 333, 333, CHAS%. In
HH of Martha Apeler, F, 30, born Germany.
MATHUSSEN, C.F., 72, M, Merchant, -, Germany, 421, 379, CHAS.
MAYBLUM, N., 25, M, Merchant, -, Germany, 357, 357, KERS.
MAYER, JULIA, 27, F, None listed, -, Germany, 28, 26, CHAS-. In HH of
Louis Mayer, M, 25, born Germany.
MAYER, LOUIS, 25, M, Grocer, -, Germany, 28, 26, CHAS-.

MAYER, OTTO, 35, M, Grocer, -, Germany, 739, 727, CHAS%.
MAYER, OTTO, 27, M, Musician, -, Germany, 379, 344, CHAS. In HH of
N.R. Schineder, M, 32, born Germany.
MAYER, OTTO, 10, M, None listed, -, Germany, 739, 727, CHAS%. In HH of
Otto Mayer, M, 35, born Germany.
MAYER, TERESA, 30, F, None listed, -, Germany, 739, 727, CHAS%. In HH
of Otto Mayer, M, 35, born Germany.
MCKENBERGER, CHARLOTTE, 35, F, None listed, -, Germany, 1188, 1167,
CHAS%. In HH of Fredrick T. McKenberger, M, 39, born Germany.
MCKENBERGER, FREDRICK T., 39, M, R.R. Laborer, -, Germany, 1188,
1167, CHAS%.
MEHRTENS, DIEDRICK, 8, M, None listed, -, Germany, 160, 160, CHAS%.
In HH of Frederick Mehrtens, M, 38, born Germany.
MEHRTENS, FREDERICK, 38, M, Grocer, -, Germany, 160, 160, CHAS%.
MEHRTENS, HENRY, 25, M, Shopkeeper, -, Germany, 278, 278, CHAS%.
MEHRTENS, HENRY, 23, M, Shopkeeper, -, Germany, 226, 226, CHAS%.
MEHRTENS, JOANA, 35, F, None listed, -, Germany, 160, 160, CHAS%. In
HH of Frederick Mehrtens, M, 38, born Germany.
MEHRTENS, LEWIS, 19, M, None listed, -, Germany, 278, 278, CHAS%. In
HH of Henry Mehrtens, M, 25, born Germany.
MEHRTENS, RUDOLPH, 18, M, Shopkeeper, -, Germany, 226, 226, CHAS%.
In HH of Henry Mehrtens, M, 23, born Germany.
MEHRTENS, WILLIAM, 28, M, Painter, -, Germany, 160, 160, CHAS%. In
HH of Frederick Mehrtens, M, 38, born Germany.
MEHRTEUS, J.C., 32, M, Grocer, -, Germany, 219, 205, CHAS-.
MEHRTNS, GEORGE, 16, M, Shopkeeper, -, Germany, 561, 553, CHAS%. In
HH of J. Mehrtns, M, 27, born Germany.
MEHRTNS, J., 27, M, Shopkeeper, -, Germany, 561, 553, CHAS%.
MEHRTNS, JOHN, 66, M, Shopkeeper, -, Germany, 561, 553, CHAS%. In
HH of J. Mehrtns, M, 27, born Germany.
MEHRTNS, REBECCA, 63, F, None listed, -, Germany, 561, 553, CHAS%. In
HH of J. Mehrtns, M, 27, born Germany.
MEHRTNS, WILLIAM, 20, M, Shopkeeper, -, Germany, 561, 553, CHAS%.
In HH of J. Mehrtns, M, 27, born Germany.
MEINARDERS, CORNELIA, 9, F, None listed, -, Germany, 898, 875,
CHAS%. In HH of Dedrick Meinarders, M, 36, born Germany.
MEINARDERS, DEDRICK, 36, M, Shopkeeper, -, Germany, 898, 875,
CHAS%.
MEINARDERS, EDWARD, 4, M, None listed, -, Germany, 898, 875, CHAS%.
In HH of Dedrick Meinarders, M, 36, born Germany.
MEINARDERS, HENRY, 12, M, None listed, -, Germany, 898, 875, CHAS%.

In HH of Dedrick Meinarders, M, 36, born Germany.

**MEINARDERS, MARTHA**, 31, F, None listed, -, Germany, 898, 875, CHAS%.
In HH of Dedrick Meinarders, M, 36, born Germany.

**MELCARD, JOHN**, 30, M, Drayman, -, Germany, 1031, 1009, CHAS%.

**MELCARD, MARGARET**, 45, F, None listed, -, Germany, 1031, 1009,
CHAS%. In HH of John Melcard, M, 30, born Germany.

**MELDAN, GEO. F.**, 27, M, Shopkeeper, -, Germany, 385, 349, CHAS.

**MELNLUS, REBECCA**, 14, F, None listed, -, Germany, 938, 915, CHAS%. In
HH of James M. Eason 31, born SC.

**MEMMINGER, C.G.**, 47, M, Atty at Law, -, Germany, 1103, 1080, CHAS-.

**MENDY, CAROLINE**, 50, F, None listed, -, Germany, 176, 176, CHAS%. In
HH of Jacob Mendy, M, 60, born Germany.

**MENDY, HELENA**, 5, F, None listed, -, Germany, 176, 176, CHAS%. In HH
of Jacob Mendy, M, 60, born Germany.

**MENDY, JACOB**, 60, M, Shopkeeper, -, Germany, 176, 176, CHAS%.

**MENTZING, HENRY**, 19, M, Tailor, -, Germany, 661, 641, CHAS-. In HH of
W. Hieze, M, 34, born Germany.

**MERKHERDT, ANCHIN**, 26, F, None listed, -, Germany, 1022, 999, CHAS%.
In HH of M. Merkherdt, M, 23, born Germany.

**MERKHERDT, FREDRICK**, 7, M, None listed, -, Germany, 1022, 999,
CHAS%. In HH of M. Merkherdt, M, 23, born Germany.

**MERKHERDT, M.**, 23, M, R.R. Laborer, -, Germany, 1022, 999, CHAS%.

**MERRING, MARY**, 15, F, None listed, -, Germany, 819, 802, CHAS%. In HH
of John Schacte, M, 38, born Germany.

**MESSNER, E.**, 28, M, Grocer, -, Germany, 280, 254, CHAS*.

**METZLER, CHARLES**, 20, M, Shoemaker, -, Germany, 25, 20, CHAS+. In
HH of John Metzler, M, 34, born Germany.

**METZLER, JACOB**, 27, M, Shoemaker, -, Germany, 163, 154, CHAS+.

**METZLER, JOHN**, 23, M, Shoemaker, -, Germany, 25, 20, CHAS+.

**METZLER, PAULINA**, 26, F, None listed, -, Germany, 163, 154, CHAS+. In
HH of Jacob Metzler, M, 27, born Germany.

**MEYER, C.**, 36, M, Clerk, -, Germany, 801, 784, CHAS%. In HH of G.
Oldenbuttle, M, 28, born Germany.

**MEYER, CATHERINE**, 31, F, None listed, -, Germany, 177, 167, CHAS+. In
HH of G. Meyer, M, 46, born Germany.

**MEYER, CLAUSE**, 25, M, Shopkeeper, -, Germany, 204, 204, CHAS%.

**MEYER, F.**, 18, M, Clerk, -, Germany, 505, 498, CHAS%. In HH of H. Henken,
M, 25, born Germany.

**MEYER, FREDERICK**, 20, M, Cabinetmaker, -, Germany, 667, 647, CHAS-.
In Boarding House.

**MEYER, FREDERICK C.**, 54, M, Merchant, -, Germany, 419, 378, CHAS+.

MEYER, G., 46, M, Shoemaker, -, Germany, 177, 167, CHAS+.
MEYER, HENRY, 19, M, Miller, -, Germany, 110, 110, CHAS%. In HH of H.
Oetjen, M, 35, born Germany.
MEYER, HERMAN, 33, M, Tavern keeper, -, Germany, 471, 468, CHAS%.
MEYER, JACOB, 38, M, Grocer, -, Germany, 68, 68, CHAS%.
MEYER, JACOB, 28, M, Boot maker, -, Germany, 128, 119, CHAS+. In HH
of Martin Lanse, M, 34, born Germany.
MEYER, JOHN, 24, M, Clerk, -, Germany, 175, 158, CHAS. In HH of M.
Meyer, M, 26, born Germany.
MEYER, JOHN D., 36, M, Grocer, -, Germany, 738, 718, CHAS-.
MEYER, LEO C., 30, M, Founder, -, Germany, 178, 167, CHAS+.
MEYER, LORRETTE, 30, F, None listed, -, Germany, 68, 68, CHAS%. In HH
of Jacob Meyer, M, 38, born Germany.
MEYER, M., 26, M, Shopkeeper, -, Germany, 175, 158, CHAS.
MEYER, MARGARET, 27, F, None listed, -, Germany, 738, 718, CHAS-. In
HH of John D. Meyer, M, 36, born Germany.
MEYER, MORRIS, 37, M, Merchant, -, Germany, 1079, 1056, CHAS-.
MEYER, SOPHIA, 12, F, None listed, -, Germany, 68, 68, CHAS%. In HH of
Jacob Meyer, M, 38, born Germany.
MEYERS, LUCY, 17, F, None listed, -, Germany, 321, 321, CHAS%. In HH of
C.H. Harbers, M, 50, born Germany.
MILLER, C., 28, M, Shoemaker, -, Germany, 491, 446, CHAS. In HH of
Henry Rancken, M, 26, born Germany.
MILLER, CONRAD, 35, M, Shoemaker, -, Germany, 330, 305, CHAS.
MILLER, F., 35, M, Mercht., -, Germany, 24, 24, BARN.
MILLER, FREDERICA, 23, F, None listed, -, Germany, 999, 978, CHAS-. In
HH of Otto Switzer, M, 38, born Switzerland.
MILLER, HANNAH, 77, F, None listed, -, Germany, 486, 452, CHAS*. In HH
of Wilhelmina Buckelhoff, F, 30, born Germany.
MILLER, HENRY, 75, M, Merchant, -, Germany, 1187, 1187, LEX.
MILLER, HENRY, 27, M, Clerk, -, Germany, 662, 642, CHAS-. In HH of
Catherine Bochman, F, 25, born Germany.
MILLER, J.P.R., 32, M, Merchant, -, Germany, 13, 13, ORNG*.
MILLER, JOHN, 59, M, Custom House, -, Germany, 109, 122, CHAS.
MILLER, JOHN, 38, M, Music teacher, -, Germany, 562, 562, UNION. In HH
of Wallace Thomson, M, 60, born SC.
MILLER, JOHN, 38, M, Music teacher, -, Germany, 563, 563, UNION. In HH
of Wallace Thomson, M, 60, born SC.
MILLER, JOHN L., 46, M, Farmer, -, Germany, 1184, 1184, LEX.
MILLER, LEWIS, 27, M, Grocer, -, Germany, 89, 87, CHAS*.
MILLER, MARGARET, 35, F, None listed, -, Germany, 24, 24, BARN. In HH

of F. Miller, M, 35, born Germany.

MILLER, MARIA, 30, F, None listed, -, Germany, 330, 305, CHAS. In HH of Conrad Miller, M, 35, born Germany.

MILLER, MARIA, 25, F, None listed, -, Germany, 491, 446, CHAS. In HH of Henry Rancken, M, 26, born Germany.

MILLER, PHILIP, 47, M, Tavern Keeper, -, Germany, 70, 70, MARL.

MILLER, RACHEL, 49, F, None listed, -, Germany, 1184, 1184, LEX. In HH of John L. Miller, M, 46, born Germany.

MILLER, STEPHEN, 21, M, Grocer, -, Germany, 1, 1, CHAS*.

MILLER, W., 60, M, Pedler, -, Germany, 180, 169, CHAS+. In HH of Joseph Gabriel, M, 29, born Mexico.

MILLET, JOHN, 18, M, None listed, -, Germany, 562, 562, HORR. In HH of John Willson, M, 35, born SC.

MINAH, META, 22, F, None listed, -, Germany, 164, 154, CHAS-. In HH of D.A. Amie, M, 30, born Germany.

MINTZING, CONRAD, 22, M, Grocer, -, Germany, 405, 388, CHAS-. In HH of H. Mintzzing, M, 22, born Germany. Twin of H. Mintzing.

MINTZING, H., 22, M, Grocer, -, Germany, 405, 388, CHAS-. A twin.

MINTZING, JOHN, 28, M, Grocer, -, Germany, 188, 176, CHAS-.

MINTZING, JOHN H., 22, M, Clerk, -, Germany, 188, 176, CHAS-. In HH of John Mintzing, M, 28, born Germany.

MINTZINGMEYER MARGT., 48, F, None listed, -, Germany, 705, 697, CHAS%.

MINTZINGMEYER, CHARLES, 18, M, Sausage maker, -, Germany, 705, 697, CHAS%. In HH of Margt. Mintzingmeyer, F, 48, born Germany.

MINTZINGMEYER, LOUISA, 16, F, None listed, -, Germany, 705, 697, CHAS%. In HH of Margt. Mintzingmeyer, F, 48, born Germany.

MITCHERF, FRANCIS, 24, M, Grocer, -, Germany, 495, 488, CHAS%.

MITCHERF, MARIA, 24, F, None listed, -, Germany, 495, 488, CHAS%. In HH of Francis Metcherf, M, 24, born Germany.

MITCHERF, THEODORE, 17, M, Clerk, -, Germany, 495, 488, CHAS%. In HH of Francis Metcherf, M, 24, born Germany.

MOHART, FEDRICK J., 24, M, None, -, Germany, 1210, 1210, LEX.

MOLLER, MARTIN, 33, M, Shopkeeper, -, Germany, 601, 593, CHAS%. In HH of John Van Harden, M, 19, born Germany.

MONCKEN, DIEDRICK, 17, M, Shopkeeper, -, Germany, 185, 185, CHAS%. In HH of John D. Bosch, M, 20, born Germany.

MOORE, HENRY, 40, M, None listed, -, Germany, 704, 704, WILL. In HH of Barney Greenwauld, M, 35, born Germany.

MOSES, ISAIAH, 77, M, Merchant, -, Germany, 231, 217, CHAS-.

MOSES, LEVI, 43, M, Merchant, -, Germany, 231, 217, CHAS-. In HH of

Isaiah Moses, M, 77, born Germany.
MOSES, LEVY SR., 76, M, None listed, -, Germany, 678, 670, CHAS%.
MOSTINDART, CATHERINE, 4, F, None listed, -, Germany, 717, 708, CHAS%. In HH of John Mostindart, M, 28, born Germany.
MOSTINDART, ELIZA, 22, F, None listed, -, Germany, 717, 708, CHAS%. In HH of John Mostindart, M, 28, born Germany.
MOSTINDART, JOHN, 28, M, Grocer, -, Germany, 717, 708, CHAS%.
MOSTINDART, JOHN F., 18, M, Clerk, -, Germany, 717, 708, CHAS%. In HH of John Mostindart, M, 28, born Germany.
MULER, HENRY, 26, M, Clerk, -, Germany, 341, 315, CHAS. In HH of William Bellair, M, 35, born Germany.
MULLER, CAROLINE, 26, F, None listed, -, Germany, 196, 180, CHAS*. In HH of Lewis Muller, M, 31, born Germany.
MULLER, FREDERECK, 18, M, Clerk, -, Germany, 1247, 1247, LEX. In HH of William Assmann, M, 42, born Germany.
MULLER, LEWIS, 31, M, Minister, -, Germany, 196, 180, CHAS*. Occupation: D.D. Luthern.
MUN, AGNESS, 24, F, None listed, -, Germany, 123, 123, BEAU. In HH of Daniel Mun, M, 26, born Gemany.
MUN, CHARLES, 4, M, None listed, -, Germany, 123, 123, BEAU. In HH of Daniel Mun, M, 26, born Gemany.
MUN, DANIEL, 26, M, None listed, -, Germany, 123, 123, BEAU.
MUN, MARTHA, 3, F, None listed, -, Germany, 123, 123, BEAU. In HH of Daniel Mun, M, 26, born Gemany.
MUNCH, DIEDERICK, 48, M, Shopkeeper, -, Germany, 7, 7, CHAS%.
MUNCH, FRITZ J., 14, M, None listed, -, Germany, 7, 7, CHAS%. In HH of Diederick Munch, M, 48, born Germany.
MUNCH, MEETA, 43, F, None listed, -, Germany, 7, 7, CHAS%. In HH of Diederick Munch, M, 48, born Germany.
MUNCH, SOPHIA, 17, F, None listed, -, Germany, 7, 7, CHAS%. In HH of Diederick Munch, M, 48, born Germany.
MYER, B.H., 46, M, Tavern Keeper, -, Germany, 176, 166, CHAS+.
MYER, DOROTHEA, 20, F, None listed, -, Germany, 518, 468, CHAS. In HH of John Stetting, M, 38, born Germany.
MYER, H., 60, M, Clerk, -, Germany, 806, 786, CHAS-. In HH of Henry Bollman, M, 20, born Germany.
MYER, HELENA, 18, F, None listed, -, Germany, 518, 468, CHAS. In HH of John Stetting, M, 38, born Germany.
MYER, HERMAN, 41, M, Merchant, -, Germany, 315, 290, CHAS. In HH of John Jacobs, M, 35, born Germany.
MYER, LENA, 15, F, None listed, -, Germany, 108, 100, CHAS+. In HH of E.

Vonderlieth, M, 33, born Germany.
**MYER, WM.**, 30, M, None listed, -, Germany, 280, 254, CHAS*. In HH of E. Messner, M, 28, born Germany.
**MYERHOFF, ANN**, 22, F, Shopkeeper, -, Germany, 287, 271, CHAS-.
**MYERHOFF, ANNA**, 25, F, Servant, -, Germany, 85, 95, CHAS. In HH of Harman Knee, M, 47, born Germany.
**MYERHOFF, ANNET**, 24, F, None listed, -, Germany, 287, 271, CHAS-. In HH of Ann Myerhoff, F, 22, born Germany.
**MYERHOFF, B.**, 21, M, Grocer, -, Germany, 491, 449, CHAS+.
**MYERS, DOORIS**, 34, F, None listed, -, Germany, 945, 922, CHAS%. In HH of F.C. Myers, M, 36, born Germany.
**MYERS, F.**, 33, M, Shoemaker, -, Germany, 1880, 1880, SUMT.
**MYERS, F.C.**, 36, M, Shopkeeper, -, Germany, 945, 922, CHAS%.
**MYERS, H.**, 22, M, Grocer, -, Germany, 1016, 993, CHAS%.
**MYERS, HARMON**, 15, M, Clerk, -, Germany, 1016, 993, CHAS%. In HH of H. Myers, M, 22, born Germany.
**MYERS, HERMON**, 41, M, Farmer, -, Germany, 3, 3, GREE.
**MYERS, M.**, 39, M, Merchant, -, Germany, 498, 464, CHAS*.
**MYERS, MARY**, 20, F, None listed, -, Germany, 484, 441, CHAS. In HH of Frederick W. Martins, M, 45, born Germany.

**N**
**NABOR, FREDRICK**, 30, M, None listed, -, Germany, 676, 668, CHAS%. In HH of Fredrick Kreki, M, 35, born Germany.
**NABOR, MARY**, 28, F, None listed, -, Germany, 676, 668, CHAS%. In HH of Fredrick Kreki, M, 35, born Germany.
**NATHANS, ANN**, 37, F, None listed, -, Germany, 250, 255, RICH. In HH of Meyer Nathans, M, 40, born England.
**NAUGHTMAN, ABRAHAM**, 50, M, Shopkeeper, -, Germany, 807, 765, CHAS+.
**NAUGHTMAN, AUGUSTUS**, 21, M, Shopkeeper, -, Germany, 506, 499, CHAS%.
**NAUGHTMAN, FANNY**, 20, F, None listed, -, Germany, 506, 499, CHAS%. In HH of Augustus Naughtman, M, 21, born Germany.
**NAUGHTMAN, FRANCES**, 50, F, None listed, -, Germany, 807, 765, CHAS+. In HH of Abraham Naughtman, M, 50, born Germany.
**NEALE, CATHARINE**, 67, F, None listed, -, Germany, 200, 200, BEAU+. In HH of John Neale, M, 44, born SC.
**NEAMANN, MARY**, 23, F, None listed, -, Germany, 989, 968, CHAS-. In HH of Benjn. Garden, M, 45, born Prussia.

NEIBUHR, JOHN P., 31, M, Druggist, -, Germany, 523, 473, CHAS.
NEIBUHR, REBECCA, 21, F, None listed, -, Germany, 523, 473, CHAS. In
HH of John P. Neibuhr, M, 31, born Germany.
NEIMYER, H., 28, M, Priv. U.S.A., -, Germany, 47, 43, CHAS$. In HH of
John Ewing, M, 50, born MA.
NELSON, WILLIAM, 48, M, Tavern Keeper, -, Germany, 203, 190, CHAS-.
NESLEY, JOHN, 26, M, Confectioner, -, Germany, 20, 20, NEWB.
NETTS, BARTHOLAMEW, 52, M, Farmer, -, Germany, 1275, 1275, ABB.
NETTS, MARY, 56, F, None listed, -, Germany, 1275, 1275, ABB. In HH of
Bartholamew Netts, M, 52, born Germany.
NETTS, PHILLIP, 22, M, Hireling, -, Germany, 1268, 1268, ABB. In HH of
John Y Clinkseale, M, 33, born SC.
NEUFFER, AUGUSTUS, 26, M, Carpenter, -, Germany, 451, 464, RICH. In
HH of Charles Neuffer, M, 44, born Germany.
NEUFFER, CHARLES, 44, M, Depty.Sheriff, -, Germany, 451, 464, RICH.
NEUMEYER, L., 22, M, Clerk, -, Germany, 720, 700, CHAS-. In HH of L.
Schackmand, M, 45, born Germany.
NEWBERGER, A., 31, M, Shoemaker, -, Germany, 1345, 1345, BARN.
NEWBERGER, CHRISTINA, 38, F, None listed, -, Germany, 1345, 1345,
BARN. In HH of A. Newberger, M, 31, born Germany.
NEWMAN, DORRIS, 10, M, None listed, -, Germany, 892, 869, CHAS%. In
HH of Nicholas Newman, M, 38, born Germany.
NEWMAN, MARGARET, 39, F, None listed, -, Germany, 892, 869, CHAS%.
In HH of Nicholas Newman, M, 38, born Germany.
NEWMAN, NICHOLAS, 38, M, Laborer, -, Germany, 892, 869, CHAS%.
NEWMAN, NICHOLAS, 3, M, None listed, -, Germany, 892, 869, CHAS%.
In HH of Nicholas Newman, M, 38, born Germany.
NIENMETHS, J.H, 60, M, Tavern Keeper, -, Germany, 140, 124, CHAS.
NIENMETHS, MARY, 50, F, None listed, -, Germany, 140, 124, CHAS. In HH
of J.H Nienmeths, M, 60, born Germany.
NIGHTIN, PETER, 55, M, Blacksmith, -, Germany, 542, 557, RICH. Date 1834
by name. In Lunatic Asylum.
NILIANS, F., 74, M, Grocer, -, Germany, 74, 74, CHAS%.
NINEMETZ, ADOLPH, 26, M, Store keeper, -, Germany, 177, 160, CHAS. In
HH of Henry Bullwinkle, M, 25, born Germany.
NIPPER, HARMAN, 20, M, Clerk, -, Germany, 296, 273, CHAS+. In HH of
John D. Folk, M, 30, born Germany.
NODD, FREDERICK, 25, M, Farmer, -, Germany, 732, 770, PICK. In HH of
Henry D. Brigaman, M, 32, born Germany.
NORMAN, CHARLES, 26, M, Cooper, -, Germany, 838, 848, RICH+.
NORMAN, FREDERIKA, 20, F, None listed, -, Germany, 838, 848, RICH+. In

HH of Charles Norman, M, 26, born Germany.
NORTON, ANN, 16, F, None listed, -, Germany, 666, 658, CHAS%. In HH of
A. Lindstedt, M, 29, born Germany.
NUMAN, JOHN, 28, M, Laborer, -, Germany, 712, 704, CHAS%. In HH of
John Steckeley, M, 40, born Germany.

## O

OAKS, AMBROSE, 62, M, Farmer, -, Germany, 1132, 1132, DARL.
OAKS, F.J., 30, M, None listed, -, Germany, 34, 34, KERS.
OAKS, MARY, 58, F, None listed, -, Germany, 1132, 1132, DARL. In HH of
Ambrose Oaks, M, 62, born Germany.
OAKS, PETER, 24, M, Saddler, -, Germany, 34, 34, KERS. In HH of F. J.
Oaks, M, 30, born Germany.
OAKS, PRISCILLA, 18, F, None listed, -, Germany, 34, 34, KERS. In HH of
F.. J. Oaks, M, 30, born Germany.
OBACH, WILHELMINA, 18, F, None listed, -, Germany, 386, 350, CHAS. In
HH of Francis Stien, M, 45, born Germany.
OELAICH, CHARLES, 29, M, Piano maker, -, Germany, 674, 654, CHAS-.
OELAICH, FREDERICA W., 58, F, None listed, -, Germany, 674, 654,
CHAS-. In HH of Charles Oelaich, M, 29, born Germany.
OELAICH, HENRETTA W., 24, F, None listed, -, Germany, 674, 654, CHAS-.
In HH of Charles Oelaich, M, 29, born Germany.
OELRICK, CHARLES, 30, M, Piano builder, -, Germany, 421, 393, CHAS*.
In HH of M. Deavaux 67, born SC.
OETJEN, H., 35, M, Miller, -, Germany, 110, 110, CHAS%.
OETJEN, JANE, 30, F, None listed, -, Germany, 110, 110, CHAS%. In HH of
H. Oetjen, M, 35, born Germany.
OETMANS, H., 46, M, Clerk, -, Germany, 446, 443, CHAS%. In HH of D.
Epler, M, 27, born Germany.
OFFENESSETRFFE, D., 56, M, Painter, -, Germany, 450, 433, CHAS-.
OGEMAN, JOHN, 26, M, Grocer, -, Germany, 779, 759, CHAS-.
OHACHIO?, CHAS., 24, M, Merchant, -, Germany, 753, 753, BARN.
OHEN, DEDRICK, 35, M, Laborer, -, Germany, 918, 895, CHAS%.
OHEN, GUSTINA, 36, F, None listed, -, Germany, 918, 895, CHAS%. In HH
of Dedrick Ohen, M, 35, born Germany.
OLAND, CATHERINE, 37, F, None listed, -, Germany, 27, 25, CHAS-. In HH
of Diederick Oland, M, 44, born Germany.
OLAND, DIEDERICK, 44, M, Grocer, -, Germany, 27, 25, CHAS-.
OLAND, HENRY, 29, M, Clerk, -, Germany, 239, 244, RICH.
OLDENBERG, HENRY, 32, M, Farmer, -, Germany, 305, 282, CHAS.

OLDENBERG, MARY JANE, 27, F, None listed, -, Germany, 305, 282, CHAS. In HH of Henry Oldenberg, M, 32, born Germany.

OLDENBUTTLE, H., 25, M, Shopkeeper, -, Germany, 53, 48, CHAS+.

OLDENDORFF, C., 36, F, None listed, -, Germany, 68, 69, ORNG+. In HH of F. Oldendorff, M, 35, born Germany.

OLDENDORFF, F., 35, M, Merchant, -, Germany, 68, 69, ORNG+.

OLDENDORFF, M., 14, F, None listed, -, Germany, 68, 69, ORNG+. In HH of F. Oldendorff, M, 35, born Germany.

OLDLENBUTTLE, G., 28, M, Grocer, -, Germany, 801, 784, CHAS%.

OLENDORFF, HENRICO, 16, F, None listed, -, Germany, 306, 290, CHAS-. In HH of August Kleesig, M, 30, born Germany.

OLLEN, C., 28, M, None listed, -, Germany, 196, 179, CHAS.

OLLEN, CATHERINE, 20, F, None listed, -, Germany, 196, 179, CHAS. In HH of C. Ollen, M, 28, born Germany.

OLTEN, HENRY, 26, M, Grocer, -, Germany, 435, 394, CHAS+.

OLUNDT, WILLIAM H., 23, M, Clerk, -, Germany, 553, 512, CHAS+. In HH of H. Gessel, M, 32, born Germany.

OLUNELS, WILLIAM, 22, M, Clerk, -, Germany, 510, 468, CHAS+. In HH of Claus Spriggs, M, 25, born Germany.

OSTENDOSFF, CATHERN, 28, F, None listed, -, Germany, 160, 143, CHAS. In HH of John H. Ostendosff, M, 38, born Germany.

OSTENDOSFF, JOHN H., 38, M, Store Keeper, -, Germany, 160, 143, CHAS.

OSTENHOLTZ, FREDRICK, 17, M, Shopkeeper, -, Germany, 652, 644, CHAS%. In HH of Fredrick Leopold, M, 35, born Germany.

OSTEREICHER, ANDREW, 21, M, Labourer, -, Germany, 412, 412, BEAU-. In HH of Godfrey F.H. Ostereicher, M, 59, born Germany.

OSTEREICHER, CATHARINE, 56, F, None listed, -, Germany, 412, 412, BEAU-. In HH of Godfrey F.H. Ostereicher, M, 59, born Germany.

OSTEREICHER, CATHARINE, 14, F, None listed, -, Germany, 412, 412, BEAU-. In HH of Godfrey F.H. Ostereicher, M, 59, born Germany.

OSTEREICHER, DAVID, 16, M, Labourer, -, Germany, 412, 412, BEAU-. In HH of Godfrey F.H. Ostereicher, M, 59, born Germany.

OSTEREICHER, GODFREY F.H., 59, M, Labourer, -, Germany, 412, 412, BEAU-.

OSTEREICHER, JACOB, 27, M, Labourer, -, Germany, 412, 412, BEAU-. In HH of Godfrey F.H. Ostereicher, M, 59, born Germany.

OSTEREICHER, JOSEPH, 11, M, None listed, -, Germany, 412, 412, BEAU-. In HH of Godfrey F.H. Ostereicher, M, 59, born Germany.

OSTEREICHER, WILLIAM, 18, M, Labourer, -, Germany, 412, 412, BEAU-. In HH of Godfrey F.H. Ostereicher, M, 59, born Germany.

OSTERHOLTZ, ELIZA, 22, F, None listed, -, Germany, 495, 488, CHAS%.

111

In HH of Francis Metcherf, M, 24, born Germany.

**OSTIEN, FREDERICK**, 17, M, Clerk, -, Germany, 201, 189, CHAS+. In HH of Henry Powell, M, 30, born Germany.

**OSTSERHOLTS, ANNA**, 20, F, None listed, -, Germany, 79, 79, CHAS%. In HH of J.D. Osterholts, M, 27, born Germany.

**OSTSERHOLTS, J.D.**, 27, M, Grocer, -, Germany, 79, 79, CHAS%.

**OTTEN, JOHN B.**, 29, M, Store keeper, -, Germany, 165, 165, CHAS%.

**OTTGEN, J.C.**, 35, M, Store keeper, -, Germany, 165, 148, CHAS.

**OUGTS?, MARY**, 62, F, None listed, -, Germany, 259, 259, EDGE.

**OVERSURE, CHRISTOPHER**, 20, M, Baker, -, Germany, 48, 57, CHAS. In HH of Henry Base, M, 24, born Germany.

**OVERSURE, FREDERICK**, 30, M, Baker, -, Germany, 48, 57, CHAS. In HH of Henry Base, M, 24, born Germany.

**OWENS, FRITZ**, 18, M, None listed, -, Germany, 448, 445, CHAS%. In HH of Martin Van Zoostein, M, 22, born Germany.

**OWENS, HENRY**, 40, M, Clerk, -, Germany, 281, 265, CHAS-. In HH of Henry Hines, M, 17, born Germany.

**OZIMANN, M.**, 60, F, None listed, -, Germany, 730, 710, CHAS-. In HH of J.P.M.Epping, M, 33, born Germany.


**P**

**PAPE, FREDERICK**, 15, M, None listed, -, Germany, 66, 67, RICH. In HH of Philip Pape, M, 48, born Germany.

**PAPE, JOHN**, 25, M, Clerk, -, Germany, 180, 165, CHAS*. In HH of Frederick J. Almers, M, 33, born Germany.

**PAPE, KUYUNDA**, 46, F, None listed, -, Germany, 66, 67, RICH. In HH of Philip Pape, M, 48, born Germany.

**PAPE, PHILIP**, 48, M, Tailor, -, Germany, 66, 67, RICH.

**PARKER, A.G.**, 38, F, Milliner, -, Germany, 852, 832, CHAS-.

**PATTERSON, CATHERINA**, 16, F, None listed, -, Germany, 5, 5, CHAS%. In HH of John H. Peterson, M, 40, born Germany.

**PATTERSON, CLARA**, 19, F, None listed, -, Germany, 5, 5, CHAS%. In HH of John H. Peterson, M, 40, born Germany.

**PATTERSON, JOHN H.**, 40, M, Mariner, -, Germany, 5, 5, CHAS%.

**PATTERSON, SOPHIA**, 37, F, None listed, -, Germany, 5, 5, CHAS%. In HH of John H. Peterson, M, 40, born Germany.

**PEHART, HENRY**, 52, M, Farmer, -, Germany, 549, 549, LEX.

**PELSKA, ELEANOR**, 26, F, Shopkeeper, -, Germany, 187, 176, CHAS+.

**PELTING, C.**, 26, M, Boot maker, -, Germany, 128, 119, CHAS+. In HH of Martin Lanse, M, 34, born Germany.

112

PEPPER, ANNA C., 30, F, None listed, -, Germany, 387, 385, CHAS%. In HH of L.M. Pepper, M, 35, born Germany.

PEPPER, L.M., 35, M, Grocer, -, Germany, 387, 385, CHAS%.

PEPPER, LEONORA, 10, F, None listed, -, Germany, 387, 385, CHAS%. In HH of L.M. Pepper, M, 35, born Germany.

PETERMAN, FRANCIS, 1, M, None listed, -, Germany, 25, 25, BEAU. In HH of Peter Peterman, M, 28, born Germany.

PETERMAN, MARTHA, 25, F, None listed, -, Germany, 25, 25, BEAU. In HH of Peter Peterman, M, 28, born Germany.

PETERMAN, PETER, 28, M, Cooper, -, Germany, 25, 25, BEAU.

PETERS, JNO., 35, M, Fireman, -, Germany, 1650, 1650, BARN.

PICKENPACK, DORATHA, 86, F, None listed, -, Germany, 34, 34, SPART. In HH of John Pickenpack, M, 80, born Germany.

PICKENPACK, JOHN, 80, M, Farmer, -, Germany, 34, 34, SPART.

PICKETS, GEORGE, 28, M, Cropper, -, Germany, 1344, 1344, ABB.

PIEDEMANN, HENRY, 26, M, Grocer, -, Germany, 677, 635, CHAS+.

PIEDEMANN, MARY, 20, F, None listed, -, Germany, 677, 635, CHAS+. In HH of Henry Piedemann, M, 26, born Germany.

PLATTS, L., 35, M, Boot/Shoemaker, -, Germany, 37, 37, NEWB.

PLATTS, THERISSA, 30, F, None listed, -, Germany, 37, 37, NEWB. In HH of L. Platts 35, M, born Germany.

PLEIN, CATHERINE, 52, F, None listed, -, Germany, 350, 333, CHAS-. In HH of H. Plein, M, 39, born Germany.

PLEIN, II., 39, M, Grocer, -, Germany, 350, 333, CHAS-.

PLENCE, C., 23, M, Tailor, -, Germany, 18, 16, CHAS+.

PLOGER, F.H., 35, M, Boot maker, -, Germany, 143, 143, CHAS%. In HH of Jacob Hillan, M, 35, born Germany.

PLUGER, HENRY, 25, M, Blacksmith, -, Germany, 338, 312, CHAS.

POMPKE, F., 90, F, None listed, -, Germany, 478, 475, CHAS%. In HH of Jacob Kopoman, M, 34, born Germany.

POWELL, HENRY, 30, M, Shopkeeper, -, Germany, 201, 189, CHAS+.

POWERS, F., 36, M, Grocer, -, Germany, 87, 85, CHAS*.

POWERS, HANNAH, 31, F, None listed, -, Germany, 87, 85, CHAS*. In HH of F. Powers, M, 36, born Germany.

PRICE, CATHARIN, 66, F, None listed, -, Germany, 730, 730, LEX. In HH of Jacob Price, M, 66 Farmer, born SC.

PRIGGE, CLAUS, 40, M, Shopkeeper, -, Germany, 226, 226, CHAS%. In HH of Henry Mehrtens, M, 23, born Germany.

PRIGGE, JULIA, 30, F, None listed, -, Germany, 226, 226, CHAS%. In HH of Henry Mehrtens, M, 23, born Germany.

PRINGLE, JOHN H., 32, M, Shopkeeper, -, Germany, 173, 173, CHAS%.

113

PROWMAN, AUGUSTIN, 50, M, Gardiner, -, Germany, 382, 382, BEAU-.
PROWMAN, AUGUSTUS, 9, M, None listed, -, Germany, 383, 383, BEAU-.
In HH of William Prowman, M, 30, born Germany.
PROWMAN, LEWIS, 25, M, Labourer, -, Germany, 111, 111, BEAU+.
PROWMAN, LEWIS, 1, M, None listed, -, Germany, 383, 383, BEAU-. In
HH of William Prowman, M, 30, born Germany.
PROWMAN, MARGARET, 21, F, None listed, -, Germany, 383, 383, BEAU-.
In HH of William Prowman, M, 30, born Germany.
PROWMAN, WILLIAM, 30, M, Labourer, -, Germany, 383, 383, BEAU-.
PUCKERHABER, JOHN, 33, M, Grocer, -, Germany, 1077, 1055, CHAS%.
PUCKERHABER, LEOPOLD, 10, M, None listed, -, Germany, 1077, 1055,
CHAS%. In HH of John Puckerhaber, M, 33, born Germany.
PUCKERHABER, LOUISA, 22, F, None listed, -, Germany, 1077, 1055,
CHAS%. In HH of John Puckerhaber, M, 33, born Germany.
PUNDS, JOHN, 52, M, Grocer, -, Germany, 553, 512, CHAS+. In HH of H.
Gessel, M, 32, born Germany.
PUNDT, AUGUST, 22, M, Baker, -, Germany, 285, 264, CHAS+. In HH of H.
Wittschew, M, 23, born Germany.

R
RANCKEN, HENRY, 26, M, Grocer, -, Germany, 491, 446, CHAS.
RANKIN, CATHERINE, 30, F, None listed, -, Germany, 249, 249, CHAS%. In
HH of John Rankin, M, 30, born Germany.
RANKIN, CATHERINE, 25, F, None listed, -, Germany, 121, 112, CHAS+. In
HH of J.B. Rankin, M, 29, born Germany.
RANKIN, GEO., 22, M, Tailor, -, Germany, 661, 641, CHAS-. In HH of W.
Hieze, M, 34, born Germany.
RANKIN, J.B., 29, M, Tavern keeper, -, Germany, 121, 112, CHAS+.
RANKIN, JOHN, 30, M, Painter, -, Germany, 249, 249, CHAS%.
RANKIN, JOHN, 22, M, Grocer, -, Germany, 10, 10, CHAS.
RASH, BENJAMIN, 28, M, Grocer, -, Germany, 640, 621, CHAS-.
READ, GEORGE, 19, M, Clerk, -, Germany, 470, 436, CHAS*. In HH of
Diederick Bulwinkle, M, 30, born Germany.
READER, RANDOLPH, 31, M, Hireling, -, Germany, 400, 403, ABB. In HH
of Daniel Reidge, M, 40, born SC.
RECKLING, HENRY, 38, M, Gunsmith, -, Germany, 265, 270, RICH.
REDCLOUF, H., 32, M, Taylor, -, Germany, 382, 346, CHAS.
REDCLOUF, REBECCA, 30, F, None listed, -, Germany, 382, 346, CHAS. In
HH of H. Reeclouf, M, 32, born Germany.
REED, SARAH, 22, F, None listed, -, Germany, 204, 204, PICK+. In HH of

Jacob Reed, M, 23, born TN.

**REICHTER, EDWIN**, 29, M, Clerk, -, Germany, 86, 78, CHAS+. In Boarding House.

**REICKE, ELIZABETH**, 41, F, None listed, -, Germany, 789, 769, CHAS-. In HH of George Reicke, M, 56, born Germany.

**REICKE, GEORGE**, 56, M, Grocer, -, Germany, 789, 769, CHAS-.

**REICKER, F.G.**, 23, M, Cabinetmaker, -, Germany, 816, 796, CHAS-. In HH of John Ansell, M, 34, born Germany.

**REICKS, ANNA**, 41, F, None listed, -, Germany, 75, 67, CHAS+. In HH of Gerhard Reicks, M, 44, born Germany.

**REICKS, GERHARD**, 44, M, Shopkeeper, -, Germany, 75, 67, CHAS+.

**REICKS, GERTRUDE**, 7, F, None listed, -, Germany, 75, 67, CHAS+. In HH of Gerhard Reicks, M, 44, born Germany.

**REICKS, JULIA ANN**, 10, F, None listed, -, Germany, 75, 67, CHAS+. In HH of Gerhard Reicks, M, 44, born Germany.

**REINHART, GEORGE**, 29, M, Baker, -, Germany, 981, 960, CHAS-.

**REINHART, TERESA**, 29, F, None listed, -, Germany, 981, 960, CHAS-. In HH of George Reinhart, M, 29, born Germany.

**RENNEKER, JOHN H.**, 30, M, Grocer, -, Germany, 416, 388, CHAS*.

**RENNER, CARSON**, 25, M, Shopkeeper, -, Germany, 635, 627, CHAS%.

**RENNUD, BERNARD**, 22, M, Clerk, -, Germany, 8, 8, CHAS-. In HH of Henry Hefens, M, 35, born Germany.

**REUSS, H.**, 26, M, Watch maker, -, Germany, 667, 647, CHAS-. In Boarding House.

**RICE, HANNAH**, 40, F, None listed, -, Germany, 67, 59, CHAS+.

**RICHTER, CHISTOPHER**, 58, M, Farmer, -, Germany, 1166, 1166, LEX.

**RICHTER, CHRISTIAN J.**, 17, M, None listed, -, Germany, 1166, 1166, LEX. In HH of Cristopher Richter, M, 58, born Germany.

**RICHTER, EVE M.**, 51, F, None listed, -, Germany, 1166, 1166, LEX. In HH of Cristopher Richter, M, 58, born Germany.

**RICHTER, JOHN**, 23, M, None, -, Germany, 161, 164, Rick+.

**RICKETTS, JOHN**, 30, M, Farmer, -, Germany, 281, 282, And*.

**RIDDER, JOHN**, 27, M, Tailor, -, Germany, 433, 402, CHAS*. In HH of Herman Sturken, M, 38, born Germany.

**RIPMAN, MEENA**, 35, F, None listed, -, Germany, 847, 827, CHAS-. In HH of Sophia Selle 34, born Germany.

**RISLAND, C.**, 23, M, Boot maker, -, Germany, 128, 119, CHAS+. In HH of Martin Lanse, M, 34, born Germany.

**RISLAND, ELIZABETH**, 24, F, None listed, -, Germany, 128, 119, CHAS+. In HH of Martin Lanse, M, 34, born Germany.

**RISSLER, F.**, 30, M, Blacksmith, -, Germany, 163, 153, CHAS-.

ROADHOUSE, ELIZA, 18, F, None listed, -, Germany, 69, 61, CHAS+. In HH of William Hitchfield, M, 19, born Germany.

ROBERTS, FRANCES, 41, M, Master mariner, -, Germany, 28, 34, CHAS.

ROETTEN, F. ERKERIN, 50, M, Planter, -, Germany, 77, 77, BEAU+.

ROFF, HANS, 21, M, Clerk, -, Germany, 3, 3, CHAS-. In HH of John E. Lee, M, 29, born Germany.

ROLLETEN, JOHN, 31, M, Farmer, -, Germany, 77, 79, AND.

ROLLETEN, JOSEPH, 26, M, Farmer, -, Germany, 92, 94, AND.

ROLLOSIN, AUGUSTUS, 30, M, Tailor, -, Germany, 208, 189, CHAS*.

ROLLOSIN, HANNAH, 25, F, None listed, -, Germany, 208, 189, CHAS*. In HH of Augustus Rollosin, M, 30, born Germany.

ROLPHEN, H., 27, M, Shoemaker, -, Germany, 262, 245, CHAS+.

ROLPHIN, ANNA, 34, F, None listed, -, Germany, 980, 959, CHAS-. In HH of August Rolphin, M, 30, born Germany.

ROLPHIN, AUGUST, 30, M, Tailor, -, Germany, 980, 959, CHAS-.

ROSEBORO, PETER, 24, M, Shoemaker, -, Germany, 21, 17, CHAS+. In HH of Andrew Beauford, M, 36, born France.

ROSENBAUM, C., 75, M, None, -, Germany, 85, 95, CHAS. In HH of Harman Knee, M, 47, born Germany.

ROSENBAUM, GEORGE O., 37, M, Merchant, -, Germany, 36, 36, CHAS*.

ROSENBERG, GAZANA, 25, F, None listed, -, Germany, 285, 269, CHAS-. In HH of James Harrale, M, 30, born GA.

ROSENKRANTZ, CATHARIN, 25, F, None listed, -, Germany, 562, 554, CHAS%. In HH of Henry Bulwinkle, M, 45, born Germany.

ROSENTHAL, CAROLINE, 20, F, None listed, -, Germany, 509, 459, CHAS. In HH of William Young, M, 52, born Scotland.

ROSENTHAL, LEWIS, 30, M, Pedler, -, Germany, 509, 459, CHAS. In HH of William Young, M, 52, born Scotland.

ROTETTER, CAROLINE, 15, F, None listed, -, Germany, 1079, 1128, PICK. In HH of John Rottetter, M, 60, born Germany.

ROTETTER, JOHN, 60, M, Farmer, -, Germany, 1079, 1128, PICK.

ROTETTER, LUCY, 17, F, None listed, -, Germany, 1079, 1128, PICK. In HH of John Rottetter, M, 60, born Germany.

ROTETTER, MARIANNE, 55, F, None listed, -, Germany, 1079, 1128, PICK. In HH of John Rottetter, M, 60, born Germany.

ROTHMAN, JACOB, 29, M, Shoemaker, -, Germany, 25, 20, CHAS+. In HH of John Metzler, M, 34, born Germany.

ROWE, HENRY, 23, M, Locksmith, -, Germany, 86, 78, CHAS+. In Boarding House.

ROZELL, ESTHER, 11, F, None listed, -, Germany, 539, 548, RICH+. In HH of Mary Rozell, F, 43, born Germany.

ROZELL, JANE, 9, F, None listed, -, Germany, 539, 548, RICH+. In HH of Mary Rozell, F, 43, born Germany.

ROZELL, MARY, 43, F, None listed, -, Germany, 539, 548, RICH+.

ROZENBURG, RACHEL, 60, F, None listed, -, Germany, 350, 356, RICH. In HH of Selig J. Rozenburg, M, 39, born Germany.

ROZENBURG, SELIG J., 39, M, Merchant, -, Germany, 350, 356, RICH.

RUCKES, C., 24, M, Clerk, -, Germany, 172, 155, CHAS. In HH of Ann Marsh, F, 35, born SC.

RUDDEN, WILLIAM A., 25, M, Shoe/bootmaker, -, Germany, 1016, 1016, EDGE.

RUMPLE, ANNA, 28, F, None listed, -, Germany, 100, 92, CHAS+. In HH of G.H. Rumple, M, 43, born Germany.

RUMPLE, G.H., 43, M, Tavern Keeper, -, Germany, 100, 92, CHAS+.

RUNG, JOHN, 26, M, Shopkeeper, -, Germany, 596, 588, CHAS%. In HH of Henry Ehricks, M, 37, born Germany.

RUSH, MEETA, 22, F, None listed, -, Germany, 991, 970, CHAS-. In HH of Elizabeth Teape, F, 23, born England.

RUTHFORD, VALENTINE, 6, M, None listed, -, Germany, 261, 235, CHAS*. In HH of Mary McNeill, F, 47, born SC.

RUTZLER, ALICK, 4, M, None listed, -, Germany, 511, 469, CHAS+. In HH of John Rutzler, M, 45, born Germany.

RUTZLER, FRANK, 11, M, None listed, -, Germany, 511, 469, CHAS+. In HH of John Rutzler, M, 45, born Germany.

RUTZLER, JOHN, 45, M, Shoemaker, -, Germany, 511, 469, CHAS+.

RYAN, JOHN, 20, M, Laborer, -, Germany, 548, 540, CHAS%. In HH of Joana Mahony, F, 22, born Ireland.

S

SACHLEBIUN, AUGUSTUS, 27, M, Teacher, -, Germany, 896, 876, CHAS-.

SACHLEBIUN, LEONORA, 21, F, None listed, -, Germany, 896, 876, CHAS-. In HH of Augustus Sachlebiun, M, 27, born Germany.

SACHLEBIUN, LUDER, 25, M, Drayman, -, Germany, 896, 876, CHAS-. In HH of Augustus Sachlebiun, M, 27, born Germany.

SACKLMAN, F., 40, M, Teacher, -, Germany, 587, 545, CHAS+.

SAGER, JOHN, 20, M, Clerk, -, Germany, 254, 259, RICH. In HH of Harmon C. Frank, M, 28, born Germany.

SAHLMAN, H., 33, M, Grocer, -, Germany, 648, 607, CHAS+.

SAHLMAN, HENRY, 35, M, Shopkeeper, -, Germany, 40, 37, CHAS-. Listed as prisoner.

SAHLMAN, SOPHIA, 21, F, None listed, -, Germany, 648, 607, CHAS+. In

HH of H. Sahlman, M, 33, born Germany.
SAMSON, HENRY, 17, M, None listed, -, Germany, 452, 449, CHAS%. In HH of Herman Hasdale, M, 31, born Germany.
SANCFORD, NICHOLAS, JR., 29, M, Farmer, -, Germany, 112, 112, BEAU*.
SARBS, METTA, 20, F, None listed, -, Germany, 196, 180, CHAS*. In HH of Lewis Muller, M, 31, born Germany.
SASS, L.W., 54, M, Sexton German Lutheran Church, -, Germany, 100, 92, CHAS+. In HH of G.H. Rumple, M, 43, born Germany.
SATZEN, HENRY, 25, M, Clerk, -, Germany, 491, 446, CHAS. In HH of Henry Rancken, M, 26, born Germany.
SAVAGE, ANN, 39, F, None listed, B, Germany, 18, 16, CHAS-. In HH of Betsey Savage, F, 50 mulatto, born Germany {sic}. Birthplace listed as Germany, could be a transcription error in census.
SAVAGE, BETSEY, 50, F, None listed, M, Germany, 18, 16, CHAS-. Birthplace listed as Germany, could be a transcription error in census.
SAVAGE, FABRIEL, 42, M, Laborer, B, Germany, 18, 16, CHAS-. In HH of Betsey Savage, F, 50 mulatto, born Germany {sic}. Birthplace listed as Germany, could be a transcription error in census.
SAVAGE, MARGARET, 4, F, None listed, M, Germany, 18, 16, CHAS-. In HH of Betsey Savage, F, 50 mulatto, born Germany {sic}. Birthplace listed as Germany, could be a transcription error in census.
SCEPTS, CARL, 12, M, None listed, -, Germany, 58, 52, CHAS+. In HH of Fetz Hallenback, M, 28, born Germany.
SCHACKMAND, L., 45, M, Merchant, -, Germany, 720, 700, CHAS-.
SCHACTE, ELIZA, 30, F, None listed, -, Germany, 819, 802, CHAS%. In HH of John Schacte, M, 38, born Germany.
SCHACTE, JOHN, 38, M, Tavern Keeper, -, Germany, 819, 802, CHAS%.
SCHACTE, WILLIAM, 32, M, Tavern Keeper, -, Germany, 819, 802, CHAS%. In HH of John Schacte, M, 38, born Germany.
SCHAFFASEY, A., 54, M, Carpenter, -, Germany, 991, 970, CHAS-. In HH of Elizabeth Teape, F, 23, born England.
SCHAFFASEY, CHARLOTTE, 38, F, None listed, -, Germany, 991, 970, CHAS-. In HH of Elizabeth Teape, F, 23, born England.
SCHAFFASEY, ELIZA, 17, F, None listed, -, Germany, 991, 970, CHAS-. In HH of Elizabeth Teape, F, 23, born England.
SCHAFFASEY, LEWIS, 8, M, None listed, -, Germany, 991, 970, CHAS-. In HH of Elizabeth Teape, F, 23, born England.
SCHAFFASEY, WILLIAM, 19, M, Clerk, -, Germany, 991, 970, CHAS-. In HH of Elizabeth Teape, F, 23, born England.
SCHAFFER, HENRY, 16, M, Clerk, -, Germany, 815, 798, CHAS%. In HH of Frederick Henrickson, M, 40, born Germany.

SCHARMAN, TECKLAR, 18, F, None listed, -, Germany, 69, 61, CHAS+. In HH of William Hitchfield, M, 19, born Germany.

SCHARTWZ, ELIZABETH, 35, F, None listed, -, Germany, 503, 469, CHAS*. In HH of Jacob Schartwz, M, 41, born Germany.

SCHARTWZ, FREDRICK, 16, M, Clerk, -, Germany, 503, 469, CHAS*. In HH of Jacob Schartwz, M, 41, born Germany.

SCHARTWZ, JACOB, 41, M, Shopkeeper, -, Germany, 503, 469, CHAS*.

SCHARTWZ, JACOB, 15, M, None listed, -, Germany, 503, 469, CHAS*. In HH of Jacob Schartwz, M, 41, born Germany.

SCHARTWZ, WILHELM, 14, M, None listed, -, Germany, 503, 469, CHAS*. In HH of Jacob Schartwz, M, 41, born Germany.

SCHATTLES, NICHOLAS, 42, M, None listed, -, Germany, 237, 222, CHAS-. Poor House.

SCHAWB, HENRY, 55, M, Mail Carrier, -, Germany, 57, 57, CHAS~. Born : Bremen, Germany.

SCHECTER, F., 50, F, None listed, -, Germany, 165, 156, CHAS+.

SCHEIB, M., 24, M, Tailor, -, Germany, 16, 15, CHAS+.

SCHEREN, CATHARINE, 19, F, None listed, -, Germany, 71, 71, BEAU+. In HH of Jacob Scheren, M, 31, born Germany.

SCHEREN, JACOB, 31, M, Boot maker, -, Germany, 71, 71, BEAU+.

SCHERIFFA, LENA, 20, F, None listed, -, Germany, 433, 402, CHAS*. In HH of Herman Sturken, M, 38, born Germany.

SCHINEDER, N.R., 32, M, Tavern keeper, -, Germany, 379, 344, CHAS.

SCHINEDER, PALENA S., 29, , None listed, -, Germany, 379, 344, CHAS. In HH of N.R. Schineder, M, 32, born Germany.

SCHIPMAN, HAREM BESENT, 62, M, Planter, -, Germany, 37, 37, CHAS2.

SCHLESINGER, ANTHONY, 23, M, Clerk, -, Germany, 221, 226, RICH. Page out of order, follow HH 177/181. In HH of Elias Levy, M, 50, born Germany.

SCHLEYER, CLAUS, 37, M, Shopkeeper, -, Germany, 1050, 1028, CHAS%.

SCHLIMEYER, JOHN, 27, M, Clerk, -, Germany, 83, 83, BEAU. In HH of Henry Husman, M, 38, born Germany.

SCHLOUSUT?, JOSEPH, 30, M, Baker, -, Germany, 2031, 2034, EDGE. In HH of Antony Furgurson, M, 45, born NC.

SCHLYMEYER, HENRY, 50, M, Shopkeeper, -, Germany, 237, 237, BEAU.

SCHMIDT, C., 16, M, Clerk, -, Germany, 133, 133, CHAS%. In HH of George Barkman, M, 37, born Germany.

SCHNELL, H., 24, M, Upholsterer, -, Germany, 720, 700, CHAS-. In HH of L. Schackmand, M, 45, born Germany.

SCHNEPP, FREDERICK, 20, M, Clerk, -, Germany, 176, 159, CHAS. In HH of Peter Wineholtz, M, 24, born Germany.

SCHNEPP, HENRY, 28, M, Clerk, -, Germany, 176, 159, CHAS. In HH of

Peter Wineholtz, M, 24, born Germany.

SCHNIDER, ANNA C., 54, F, None listed, -, Germany, 641, 641, LEX. In HH of John Schnider 56, born Germany.

SCHNIDER, HENRY, 30, M, Farmer, -, Germany, 642, 642, LEX.

SCHNIDER, JOHN, 56, M, Blk. Smith, -, Germany, 641, 641, LEX.

SCHNIEDER, HENRY, 24, M, Shoemaker, -, Germany, 294, 271, CHAS+. In HH of W. Durnstucks, M, 28, born Germany.

SCHNIEDER, SUDER, 20, M, Clerk, -, Germany, 22, 22, CHAS%. In HH of J. Borchers, M, 37, born Germany.

SCHOL, DIEDERICK, 12, M, None listed, -, Germany, 117, 109, CHAS-. In HH of John Conrade, M, 40, born Germany.

SCHORB, J. R., 31, M, Teacher, -, Germany, 491, 491, FAIR.

SCHRICK, REBECCA, 40, F, None listed, -, Germany, 429, 388, CHAS+.

SCHRINER, CATHERINE, 52, F, None listed, -, Germany, 162, 153, CHAS+. In HH of John H. Schriner, M, 56, born Germany.

SCHRINER, JOHN H., 56, M, Merchant, -, Germany, 162, 153, CHAS+.

SCHRODER, BETA, 27, F, None listed, -, Germany, 219, 205, CHAS-. In HH of J.C. Mehrteus, M, 32, born Germany.

SCHRODER, C., 26, M, Upholsterer, -, Germany, 720, 700, CHAS-. In HH of L. Schackmand, M, 45, born Germany.

SCHRODER, HENRY, 22, M, Clerk, -, Germany, 219, 205, CHAS-. In HH of J.C. Mehrteus, M, 32, born Germany.

SCHRODER, JACOB, 45, M, Farmer, -, Germany, 1087, 1137, PICK.

SCHRODER, JOHN, 30, M, Grocer, -, Germany, 718, 709, CHAS%.

SCHRODER, MARGARET, 24, F, None listed, -, Germany, 1087, 1137, PICK. In HH of Jacob Schroder, M, 45, born Germany.

SCHRODER, MATILDA, 26, F, None listed, -, Germany, 718, 709, CHAS%. In HH of John Schroder, M, 30, born Germany.

SCHROEDER, C., 25, M, Shopkeeper, -, Germany, 336, 336, CHAS%. In HH of Diedrick Bullwinkle, M, 22, born Germany.

SCHROEDER, C., 24, M, Clerk, -, Germany, 133, 133, CHAS%. In HH of George Barkman, M, 37, born Germany.

SCHROEDER, F., 27, M, Shopkeeper, -, Germany, 85, 95, CHAS. In HH of Harman Knee, M, 47, born Germany.

SCHROEDER, J., 30, M, Shopkeeper, -, Germany, 355, 355, CHAS%.

SCHULK, MARTIN, 28, M, Baker, -, Germany, 285, 264, CHAS+. In HH of H. Wittschew, M, 23, born Germany.

SCHULTER, ANNE, 37, F, None listed, -, Germany, 852, 830, CHAS%. In HH of William Beckman, M, 38, born SC.

SCHULTER, ANNE, 13, F, None listed, -, Germany, 852, 830, CHAS%. In HH of William Beckman, M, 38, born SC.

SCHULTZ, HY., 24, M, Pedler, -, Germany, 323, 298, CHAS. In HH of F. Weanholz, M, 25, born Germany.

SCHULTZ, WILLIAM, 30, M, Grocer, -, Germany, 92, 92, CHAS%. In HH of Mary Pahler, F, 45, born SC.

SCHWAKER, AUGUST, 16, M, Clerk, -, Germany, 342, 316, CHAS. In HH of P. Mancko, M, 30, born Germany.

SCHWARTS, HARMAN, 21, M, Clerk, -, Germany, 66, 66, CHAS%. In HH of J.C. Welhert, M, 39, born Germany.

SCHWARTZ, ANDREAS, 34, M, Tailor, -, Germany, 303, 279, CHAS+.

SCHWARTZ, CATHERINE, 20, F, None listed, -, Germany, 527, 510, CHAS-. In HH of C.F. Kohncke, M, 45, born Germany.

SCHWARTZ, DEEDERICK, 22, M, Clerk, -, Germany, 99, 92, CHAS-. In HH of Luder Johnson, M, 35, born Germany.

SCHWARTZ, FREDK., 34, M, Clerk, -, Germany, 315, 299, CHAS-. In HH of Saml. A. Nelson, M, 31, born MA.

SCHWARTZ, HANS, 18, M, None listed, -, Germany, 303, 279, CHAS+. In HH of Andreas Schwartz, M, 34, born Germany.

SCHWARTZ, KATHERINE, 28, F, None listed, -, Germany, 303, 279, CHAS+. In HH of Andreas Schwartz, M, 34, born Germany.

SCHWARTZ, MARGARETTA, 22, F, None listed, -, Germany, 303, 279, CHAS+. In HH of Andreas Schwartz, M, 34, born Germany.

SCHWARTZ, FREDERICK, 43, M, None listed, -, Germany, 237, 222, CHAS-. Poor House.

SCHWARZ, PHILLIP, 51, M, Planter, -, Germany, 396, 403, PICK+.

SCHWERTZ, HARMAN, 21, M, Clerk, -, Germany, 52, 47, CHAS+. In HH of Theodore Cordes, M, 35, born Germany.

SCHWING, DIEDERICK, 12, M, None listed, -, Germany, 235, 220, CHAS-. In HH of Johan Schwing, M, 34, born Germany.

SCHWING, E., 43, M, Grocer, -, Germany, 171, 161, CHAS-.

SCHWING, ELIZA, 36, F, None listed, -, Germany, 235, 220, CHAS-. In HH of Johan Schwing, M, 34, born Germany.

SCHWING, JOHAN, 34, M, Shopkeeper, -, Germany, 235, 220, CHAS-.

SCHWING, META, 14, F, None listed, -, Germany, 235, 220, CHAS-. In HH of Johan Schwing, M, 34, born Germany.

SCHWING, SOPHIA, 40, F, None listed, -, Germany, 171, 161, CHAS-. In HH of E. Schwing, M, 43, born Germany.

SEAMAN, LEONARAD, 18, M, Gas fitter, -, Germany, 40, 37, CHAS-. Listed as prisoner, date 1850.

SEARLE, CHRISTIANA, 26, F, None listed, -, Germany, 886, 866, CHAS-. In HH of William Searle, M, 36, born England.

SEASTRUM, HENRY, 23, M, Baker, -, Germany, 211, 197, CHAS-. In HH of

Jacob Small, M, 30, born Germany.

SEBER, CLAUS, 12, M, None listed, -, Germany, 405, 403, CHAS%. In HH of C. Von Spechan, M, 28, born Germany.

SECKENDORFFE, GELLE, 22, F, None listed, -, Germany, 813, 793, CHAS-. In HH of Isaac Seckendorffe, M, 40, born Germany.

SECKENDORFFE, HANNAH, 45, F, None listed, -, Germany, 813, 793, CHAS-. In HH of Isaac Seckendorffe, M, 40, born Germany.

SECKENDORFFE, ISAAC, 40, M, Merchant, -, Germany, 813, 793, CHAS-.

SECKENDORFFE, ISAAC, 21, M, Shopkeeper, -, Germany, 813, 793, CHAS-. In HH of Isaac Seckendorffe, M, 40, born Germany.

SEDOFF, HENRY, 30, M, Shopkeeper, -, Germany, 336, 336, CHAS%. In HH of Diedrick Bullwinkle, M, 22, born Germany.

SEDOFF, JOHN, 15, M, None listed, -, Germany, 196, 179, CHAS. In HH of C. Ollen, M, 28, born Germany.

SEEVERS, HENRY, 35, M, Laborer, -, Germany, 677, 669, CHAS%.

SEEVERS, MARGARET, 33, F, None listed, -, Germany, 677, 669, CHAS%. In HH of Henry Seevers, M, 35, born Germany.

SEIGMONDS, H., 17, M, Clerk, -, Germany, 1133, 1112, CHAS%. In HH of H. Zehee, M, 48, born Germany.

SELTZER, CAROLINE, 32, F, None listed, -, Germany, 246, 221, CHAS*. In HH of Henry Seltzer, M, 30, born Germany.

SELTZER, HENRY, 30, M, Grocer, -, Germany, 246, 221, CHAS*.

SEMECKE, EDWARD, 35, M, Grocer, -, Germany, 11, 10, CHAS$.

SEMECKE, REBECCA, 30, F, None listed, -, Germany, 11, 10, CHAS$. In HH of Edward Semecke, M, 35, born Germany.

SENGNICK, A., 24, M, Clerk, -, Germany, 685, 665, CHAS-. In Victoria Hotel.

SERVERS, J.A.., 19, M, Clerk, -, Germany, 1360, 1360, BARN. In HH of J. Margenhoff, M, 26, born Germany.

SEVENER, EDWARD, 2, M, None listed, M, Germany, 530, 545, RICH. In HH of Mary Sevener, F, 80, born Germany.

SEVENER, ELIZABETH, 28, F, None listed, M, Germany, 530, 545, RICH. In HH of Mary Sevener, F, 80, born Germany.

SEVENER, JOSEPH, 26, M, Carpenter, M, Germany, 530, 545, RICH. In HH of Mary Sevener, F, 80, born Germany.

SEVENER, LUCY, 21, F, None listed, M, Germany, 530, 545, RICH. In HH of Mary Sevener, F, 80, born Germany.

SEVENER, MARIA, 5, F, None listed, M, Germany, 530, 545, RICH. In HH of Mary Sevener, F, 80, born Germany.

SEVENER, MARY, 80, F, None listed, M, Germany, 530, 545, RICH.

SEWES, AUGUSTUS N., 24, M, Painter, -, Germany, 86, 78, CHAS+. In Boarding House.

SHACKER, EDY, 22, M, Laborer, -, Germany, 548, 540, CHAS%. In HH of Joana Mahony, F, 22, born Ireland.

SHAFFER, MARTIN, 28, M, Merchant/clerk, -, Germany, 2021, 2027, EDGE. In HH of John Green, M, 40, born Germany.

SHANDRANE, ELIZABETH, 24, F, None listed, -, Germany, 130, 121, CHAS+. In HH of John Shandrane, M, 29, born Germany.

SHANDRANE, JOHN, 29, M, Boot maker, -, Germany, 130, 121, CHAS+.

SHANKS, M.A., 38, M, Farmer, -, Germany, 93, 93, EDGE.

SHARWICK, HENRY, 60, M, Customs Inspect, -, Germany, 376, 341, CHAS.

SHELLAR, CHARLES, 35, M, Cabinetmaker, -, Germany, 23, 19, CHAS+. In HH of James ONeal, M, 43, born Ireland.

SHERGER, JOHN H., 18, M, Clerk, -, Germany, 97, 89, CHAS+. In HH of A. Bischoff, M, 35, born Germany.

SHERRIDAN, JOHN, 26, M, Tailor, -, Germany, 58, 52, CHAS+. In HH of Fetz Hallenback, M, 28, born Germany.

SHERRISEN, JOHN, 62, M, Shopkeeper, -, Germany, 691, 683, CHAS%.

SHERRISEN, LOUISA, 58, F, None listed, -, Germany, 691, 683, CHAS%. In HH of John Sherrisen, M, 62, born Germany.

SHIBER, MADISON, 37, M, Confectioner, -, Germany, 537, 537, FAIR. In HH of J.U. Zucker, M, 48, born Switzerland.

SHIER, C.P., 40, M, Butcher, -, Germany, 1217, 1196, CHAS%.

SHIRA, LOUISA, 22, F, None listed, -, Germany, 1044, 1022, CHAS%. In HH of Peter Shira, M, 21, born Germany.

SHIRA, PETER, 21, M, Laborer, -, Germany, 1044, 1022, CHAS%.

SHIRER, JOHN, 28, M, Shoemaker, -, Germany, 565, 581, RICH.

SHIRER, MARY, 26, F, None listed, -, Germany, 565, 581, RICH. In HH of John Shirer, M, 28, born Germany.

SHOLKIE, GEORGE, 30, M, Tavern keeper, -, Germany, 747, 705, CHAS+.

SHULTZ, HENRY, 74, M, Founder/Hamburg, -, Germany, 2066, 2072, EDGE. Occupation: Founder of Hamburg. {Note: This section of Edgefield Co.,SC is the Town of Hamburg}

SHULZEEN, CATHERINE, 24, F, None listed, -, Germany, 153, 144, CHAS+. In HH of F. Shulzeen, M, 34, born Germany.

SHULZEEN, F., 34, M, Grocer, -, Germany, 153, 144, CHAS+.

SHULZEEN, HARMAN, 24, M, Clerk, -, Germany, 153, 144, CHAS+. In HH of F. Shulzeen, M, 34, born Germany.

SHUTLZE, CHARLES, 41, M, Shoemaker, -, Germany, 130, 130, BEAU.

SHUTLZE, MARGARET, 28, F, None listed, -, Germany, 130, 130, BEAU. In HH of Charles Shutlze, M, 41, born Germany.

SIEBER, CATHARINA, 12, F, None listed, -, Germany, 1091, 1069, CHAS%. In HH of Dedrick Sieber, M, 40, born Germany.

SIEBER, DEDRICK, 40, M, Carpenter, -, Germany, 1091, 1069, CHAS%.
SIEBER, MAPISA, 32, F, None listed, -, Germany, 1091, 1069, CHAS%. In
HH of Dedrick Sieber, M, 40, born Germany.
SIEBER, META, 9, F, None listed, -, Germany, 1091, 1069, CHAS%. In HH of
Dedrick Sieber, M, 40, born Germany.
SIEGLING, JOHN, 55, M, Music Store, -, Germany, 415, 398, CHAS-.
SIMMONS, CAROLINE, 28, F, None listed, -, Germany, 266, 271, RICH. In
HH of Lewis Simmons, M, 31, born England.
SIMPKIN, H., 18, M, Clerk, -, Germany, 660, 618, CHAS+. In HH of H. Lens,
M, 21, born Germany.
SINGLETARY, MARY A., 43, F, None listed, -, Germany, 94, 74, CHAS$. In
HH of D.M. Singletary, M, 43, born SC.
SINGLETREE, FREDERICK, 55, M, Shopkeeper, -, Germany, 502, 495,
CHAS%.
SINGON, GOLLIP, 34, M, Farmer, -, Germany, 1176, 1176, LEX.
SINGON, HANNAH, 31, F, None listed, -, Germany, 1176, 1176, LEX. In HH
of Gollip Singon, M, 34, born Germany
SLAHN, CHRISTOPHE, 31, M, Carpenter, -, Germany, 242, 220, CHAS. In
HH of Jacob Slahn, M, 56, born Germany.
SLAHN, CLAUDE, 58, F, None listed, -, Germany, 242, 220, CHAS. In HH of
Jacob Slahn, M, 56, born Germany.
SLAHN, JACOB, 56, M, Carpenter, -, Germany, 242, 220, CHAS.
SLAHN, JOHN JACOB, 24, M, Blacksmith, -, Germany, 242, 220, CHAS. In
HH of Jacob Slahn, M, 56, born Germany.
SLAHN, MARIA, 22, F, None listed, -, Germany, 242, 220, CHAS. In HH of
Jacob Slahn, M, 56, born Germany.
SLATER, TERESA, 16, F, None listed, -, Germany, 211, 197, CHAS-. In HH
of Jacob Small, M, 30, born Germany.
SLEMYER, C., 18, M, Clerk, -, Germany, 479, 437, CHAS. In HH of F.
Bullwinkle, M, 22, born Germany.
SLIMERMEYER, MARTHA, 23, F, None listed, -, Germany, 1148, 1127,
CHAS%. In HH of Carson Wortman, M, 30, born Germany.
SLINEKER, HENRY, 17, M, None listed, -, Germany, 336, 336, CHAS%. In
HH of Diedrick Bullwinkle, M, 22, born Germany.
SLIPPERGUSS, CATHERINE, 20, F, None listed, -, Germany, 468, 465,
CHAS%. In HH of Mary Ford, F, 60, born SC.
SMALL, JACOB, 30, M, Baker, -, Germany, 211, 197, CHAS-.
SMITH, CHRISTIAN, 56, M, Blacksmith, -, Germany, 501, 501, LEX.
SMITH, H., 32, M, Grocer, -, Germany, 425, 383, CHAS.
SMITH, H., 25, M, Shopkeeper, -, Germany, 670, 628, CHAS+.
SMITH, H.S., 26, F, None listed, -, Germany, 425, 383, CHAS. In HH of H.

Smith, M, 32, born Germany.

**SMITH, HELEN**, 20, F, None listed, -, Germany, 670, 628, CHAS+. In HH of H. Smith, M, 25, born Germany.

**SMITH, JAMES**, 20, M, Clerk, -, Germany, 165, 148, CHAS. In HH of J.C. Ottgen, M, 35, born Germany.

**SMITH, MARIA A.**, 7, F, None listed, -, Germany, 183, 166, CHAS. In HH of Sebastian H. Smith, M, 48, born Germany.

**SMITH, MARY**, 47, F, None listed, -, Germany, 589, 571, CHAS-. In HH of Hans Jager, M, 51, born Germany.

**SMITH, MARY H.**, 38, F, None listed, -, Germany, 183, 166, CHAS. In HH of Sebastian H. Smith, M, 48, born Germany.

**SMITH, MINALL**, 37, M, Planter, -, Germany, 1174, 1174, SUMT.

**SMITH, PETER**, 17, M, Laborer, -, Germany, 21, 21, CHAS^. In HH of Charles H. Wilson, M, 19, born SC.

**SMITH, SEBASTIAN**, 48, M, Cabinetmaker, -, Germany, 183, 166, CHAS.

**SMITZER, ANN**, 32, F, None listed, -, Germany, 1087, 1065, CHAS%. In HH of Charles Smitzer, M, 38, born Germany.

**SMITZER, CHARLES**, 38, M, Butcher, -, Germany, 1087, 1065, CHAS%.

**SMITZER, WILLIAM**, 14, F, None listed, -, Germany, 1087, 1065, CHAS%. In HH of Charles Smitzer, M, 38, born Germany.

**SNIPPE, A.**, 25, F, None listed, -, Germany, 754, 734, CHAS-. In HH of Bernard Volger, M, 30, born Germany.

**SNIPPE, ALLENE**, 16, F, None listed, -, Germany, 754, 734, CHAS-. In HH of Bernard Volger, M, 30, born Germany.

**SNOW, CHARLES**, 66, M, Farmer, -, Germany, 389, 389, LAU.

**SNOWERS, F.**, 22, M, Clerk, -, Germany, 502, 454, CHAS. In HH of H. Sturgis, M, 30, born Germany.

**SOLMAN, C.**, 37, M, Farmer, -, Germany, 973, 950, CHAS%.

**SOMMERS, ANDREW**, 54, M, Merchant, -, Germany, 1726, 1727, EDGE. In HH of Alexander Hunter, M, 46, Landlord, born VA.

**SOMMERS, ANN**, 39, F, None listed, -, Germany, 800, 780, CHAS-. In HH of E. Sommers, M, 49, born Germany.

**SOMMERS, E.**, 49, M, Merchant, -, Germany, 800, 780, CHAS-.

**SOMMERS, THOS.**, 18, M, Merchant, -, Germany, 1726, 1727, EDGE. In HH of Alexander Hunter, M, 46, Landlord, born VA. Thos. Sommers, born Hamburg, Germany.

**SONEWDRUCKER, EUSTICIA**, 64, F, None listed, -, Germany, 12, 12, RICH. In HH of Henry Sonewdrucker, M, 79, born Germany.

**SONEWDRUCKER, HENRY**, 79, M, None, -, Germany, 12, 12, RICH.

**SPALAIN, JACOB**, 35, M, Shoemaker, -, Germany, 1175, 1175, LEX.

**SPALAIN, RICKER**, 22, F, None listed, -, Germany, 1175, 1175, LEX. In HH of Jacob Spalain, M, 35, born Germany.

**SPEIGHT, CATHERINE**, 37, F, None listed, -, Germany, 892, 872, CHAS-. In HH of Frederick Speight, M, 40, born Germany.

**SPEIGHT, CATHERINE**, 11, F, None listed, -, Germany, 898, 878, CHAS-. In HH of Francis Speight, M, 47, born Germany.

**SPEIGHT, ELIZABETH**, 12, F, None listed, -, Germany, 892, 872, CHAS-. In HH of Frederick Speight, M, 40, born Germany.

**SPEIGHT, FRANCIS**, 47, M, Shoemaker, -, Germany, 898, 878, CHAS-.

**SPEIGHT, FREDERICK**, 40, M, Shoemaker, -, Germany, 892, 872, CHAS-.

**SPEIGHT, JULIET**, 14, F, None listed, -, Germany, 898, 878, CHAS-. In HH of Francis Speight, M, 47, born Germany.

**SPEIGHT, TERESA**, 40, F, None listed, -, Germany, 898, 878, CHAS-. In HH of Francis Speight, M, 47, born Germany.

**SPEIGHT, THOMAS**, 14, M, None listed, -, Germany, 892, 872, CHAS-. In HH of Frederick Speight, M, 40, born Germany.

**SPIEGAL, F.**, 12, M, Clerk, -, Germany, 1096, 1073, CHAS-. In HH of B.H. Fink, M, 26, born Germany.

**SPIETEL, F.**, 18, M, Watch maker, -, Germany, 746, 726, CHAS-.

**SPIKLE, CHRISTIANA**, 40, F, None listed, -, Germany, 1168, 1147, CHAS%. In HH of Edward Spikle, M, 34, born Germany.

**SPIKLE, EDWARD**, 34, M, Laborer, -, Germany, 1168, 1147, CHAS%.

**SPIKLE, FERDINAND**, 15, M, Clerk, -, Germany, 1168, 1147, CHAS%. In HH of Edward Spikle, M, 34, born Germany.

**SPIKLE, HENRY**, 8, M, Clerk, -, Germany, 1168, 1147, CHAS%. In HH of Edward Spikle, M, 34, born Germany.

**SPIKLE, MATILDA**, 19, F, None listed, -, Germany, 1168, 1147, CHAS%. In HH of Edward Spikle, M, 34, born Germany.

**SPIKLE, WILLIAM**, 17, M, None listed, -, Germany, 1168, 1147, CHAS%. In HH of Edward Spikle, M, 34, born Germany.

**SPINKIN, MARTIN**, 34, M, Store keeper, -, Germany, 453, 420, CHAS*.

**SPISKE, J.F.**, 25, M, Upholsterer, -, Germany, 720, 700, CHAS-. In HH of L. Schackmand, M, 45, born Germany.

**SPRASFOL, CATHERINE**, 10, F, None listed, -, Germany, 698, 690, CHAS%. In HH of Diedreck Sprasfol, M, 42, born Germany.

**SPRASFOL, DIEDRECK**, 42, M, Laborer, -, Germany, 698, 690, CHAS%.

**SPRASFOL, ELIZA**, 38, F, None listed, -, Germany, 698, 690, CHAS%. In HH of Diedreck Sprasfol, M, 42, born Germany.

**SPRASFOL, JOHN**, 16, M, None listed, -, Germany, 698, 690, CHAS%. In HH of Diedreck Sprasfol, M, 42, born Germany.

**SPRASFOL, MALINA**, 12, F, None listed, -, Germany, 698, 690, CHAS%. In HH of Diedreck Sprasfol, M, 42, born Germany.

SPRECKELS, BERTHOL, 20, M, Store keeper, -, Germany, 165, 165, CHAS%. In HH of John B. Otten, M, 29, born Germany.

SPRIGGS, CLAUS, 25, M, Grocer, -, Germany, 510, 468, CHAS+.

ST.RECORDS, GERD., 50, M, Grocer, -, Germany, 558, 524, CHAS*.

STAHLL, FRANCIS, 34, M, Clerk, -, Germany, 28, 26, CHAS-. In HH of Louis Mayer, M, 25, born Germany.

STAMS, HENRY, 20, M, Grocer, -, Germany, 160, 151, CHAS+.

STATE, FREDERICK, 58, M, Butcher, -, Germany, 772, 755, CHAS%.

STECKELEY, AMELIA, 37, F, None listed, -, Germany, 712, 704, CHAS%. In HH of John Steckeley, M, 40, born Germany.

STECKELEY, JACOB, 14, M, None listed, -, Germany, 712, 704, CHAS%. In HH of John Steckeley, M, 40, born Germany.

STECKELEY, JOHN, 40, M, Laborer, -, Germany, 712, 704, CHAS%.

STEELER, FRANCES, 31, M, Engineer, -, Germany, 379, 344, CHAS. In HH of N.R. Schineder, M, 32, born Germany.

STEELIES, B., 25, M, Grocer, -, Germany, 505, 498, CHAS%. In HH of H. Henken, M, 25, born Germany.

STEFFERS, W., 25, M, Grocer, -, Germany, 802, 785, CHAS%.

STEINMAN, F., 25, M, Grocer, -, Germany, 433, 392, CHAS+. In HH of H. Steinman, M, 28, born Germany.

STEINMAN, H., 28, M, Grocer, -, Germany, 433, 392, CHAS+.

STELLING, ELIZABETH A., 27, F, None listed, -, Germany, 458, 471, RICH. In HH of Jacob H. Stellling, M, 35, born Germany.

STELLING, IVER, 21, M, Shopkeeper, -, Germany, 82, 74, CHAS+. In HH of Joseph Pattena, M, 41, born Italy.

STELLING, JACOB H., 35, M, Miller, -, Germany, 458, 471, RICH.

STEMMERMANN, ALBERT, 23, M, Clerk, -, Germany, 610, 591, CHAS-. In HH of H. Stemmermann, M, 34, born Germany.

STEMMERMANN, H., 34, M, Grocer, -, Germany, 610, 591, CHAS-.

STEMMERMANN, THOMAS, 13, M, None listed, -, Germany, 610, 591, CHAS-. In HH of H. Stemmermann, M, 34, born Germany.

STENDER, AMELIA, 33, F, None listed, -, Germany, 817, 800, CHAS%. In HH of Henry Stender, M, 41, born Germany.

STENDER, C., 31, M, Grocer, -, Germany, 853, 831, CHAS%.

STENDER, ELIZABETH, 10, F, None listed, -, Germany, 853, 831, CHAS%. In HH of C. Stender, M, 31, born Germany.

STENDER, ELLEN, 26, F, None listed, -, Germany, 817, 800, CHAS%. In HH of Henry Stender, M, 41, born Germany.

STENDER, FREDERICK, 16, M, None listed, -, Germany, 817, 800, CHAS%. In HH of Henry Stender, M, 41, born Germany.

STENDER, GOTLIB, 5, M, None listed, -, Germany, 817, 800, CHAS%. In

127

HH of Henry Stender, M, 41, born Germany.

**STENDER, HARMAN**, 23, M, R.R. Conductor, -, Germany, 817, 800, CHAS%. In HH of Henry Stender, M, 41, born Germany.

**STENDER, HENRY**, 41, M, Clothing Store, -, Germany, 817, 800, CHAS%.

**STENDER, MARY**, 29, F, None listed, -, Germany, 853, 831, CHAS%. In HH of C. Stender, M, 31, born Germany.

**STEPFATER, ANDRE**, 36, M, Tailor, -, Germany, 257, 231, CHAS*. In HH of M.E. Joureaine, F, 48, born SC.

**STETTING, CATHERINE**, 24, F, None listed, -, Germany, 518, 468, CHAS. In HH of John Stetting, M, 38, born Germany.

**STETTING, E.H.**, 24, M, Grocer, -, Germany, 69, 67, CHAS*.

**STETTING, JOHN**, 38, M, Shopkeeper, -, Germany, 518, 468, CHAS.

**STIELGES, DIEDERICK**, 18, M, Clerk, -, Germany, 345, 328, CHAS-. In HH of Henry Biesarrer, M, 35, born Germany.

**STIEN, AMELIA**, 28, F, None listed, -, Germany, 386, 350, CHAS. In HH of Francis Stien, M, 45, born Germany.

**STIEN, FRANCES**, 18, M, None listed, -, Germany, 386, 350, CHAS. In HH of Francis Stien, M, 45, born Germany.

**STIEN, FRANCIS**, 45, M, Watch maker, -, Germany, 386, 350, CHAS.

**STIEN, ROSA**, 22, F, None listed, -, Germany, 136, 126, CHAS-.

**STIENKER, F.**, 28, M, Baker, -, Germany, 285, 264, CHAS+. In HH of H. Wittschew, M, 23, born Germany.

**STIENTO, F.**, 20, M, Clerk, -, Germany, 370, 343, CHAS*. In HH of John Herkamp, M, 38, born Germany.

**STORICH, ELIZABETH**, 37, F, None listed, -, Germany, 11, 11, CHAS+. In HH of Franz Baties, M, 38, born Germany.

**STORK, JOHN**, 35, M, Shoemaker, -, Germany, 322, 328, RICH.

**STRANS, GEORGE**, 50, M, Leather dealer, -, Germany, 800, 783, CHAS%.

**STRANS, MARGARET**, 32, F, Clerk, -, Germany, 147, 138, CHAS+.

**STRANS, MARIA**, 56, F, None listed, -, Germany, 800, 783, CHAS%. In HH of George Strans, M, 50, born Germany.

**STRATTON, GERTRUDE**, 36, F, None listed, -, Germany, 531, 497, CHAS*. In HH of Jacob Stratton, M, 42, born Germany.

**STRATTON, HANS JASEN**, 26, M, Clerk, -, Germany, 531, 497, CHAS*. In HH of Jacob Stratton, M, 42, born Germany.

**STRATTON, JACOB**, 42, M, Shopkeeper, -, Germany, 531, 497, CHAS*.

**STRATTON, THEADON**, 16, M, Clerk, -, Germany, 531, 497, CHAS*. In HH of Jacob Stratton, M, 42, born Germany.

**STRAUSS, ANTOINETTE**, 37, F, None listed, -, Germany, 842, 852, RICH+. In HH of George Strauss, M, 50, born Germany.

**STRAUSS, FANNY**, 29, F, None listed, -, Germany, 2115, 2115, ABB. In HH of Maurice Strauss, M, 33, born France.

STRAUSS, GEORGE, 50, M, Planter, -, Germany, 842, 852, RICH+.

STRICKFUSS, CHRISTIANA, 27, F, None listed, -, Germany, 429, 427, CHAS%. In HH of J.F. Strickfuss, M, 31, born Germany.

STRICKFUSS, J.F., 31, M, Grocer, -, Germany, 429, 427, CHAS%.

STRICKFUSS, JOHN T., 8, M, None listed, -, Germany, 429, 427, CHAS%. In HH of J.F. Strickfuss, M, 31, born Germany.

STROBB, JOHN, 24, M, Shoe/boot maker, -, Germany, 1726, 1729, EDGE.

STROHEKER, JOHN, 23, M, Clerk, -, Germany, 187, 191, RICH. In HH of Matthew Harding, M, 33, born Ireland.

STRONG, CHARLES, 38, M, Clerk, -, Germany, 50, 45, CHAS+. In HH of Frederick Allahaley, M, 27, born Germany.

STRONG, CHARLES, 24, M, Clerk, -, Germany, 162, 162, CHAS%. In HH of John Byer, M, 38, born Germany.

STRONG, GEORGE, 42, M, Laborer, -, Germany, 919, 896, CHAS%.

STRUCK, WILLIAM, 21, M, Shopkeeper, -, Germany, 173, 173, CHAS%. In HH of John H. Pringle, M, 32, born Germany.

STUFFELL, HENRY, 26, M, Machinist, -, Germany, 1059, 1036, CHAS-. In HH of Florance Hertwich, M, 26, born Germany.

STUFFELL, MARGARET, 24, F, None listed, -, Germany, 1059, 1036, CHAS-. In HH of Florance Hertwich, M, 26, born Germany.

STURGIS, H., 30, M, Grocer, -, Germany, 502, 454, CHAS.

STURKE, HARMAN, 34, M, Tailor, -, Germany, 800, 758, CHAS+.

STURKEN, DORAS, 28, F, None listed, -, Germany, 433, 402, CHAS*. In HH of Herman Sturken, M, 38, born Germany.

STURKEN, HERMAN, 38, M, Tailor, -, Germany, 433, 402, CHAS*.

STURKEN, L., 17, M, Clerk, -, Germany, 405, 403, CHAS%. In HH of C. Von Spechan, M, 28, born Germany.

SUANDALE, S., 40, M, Tailor, -, Germany, 2341, 2341, GREE. In HH of W.P.Turpun ? , M, 29, born SC.

SUARES, DIEDERICK, 24, M, Clerk, -, Germany, 89, 87, CHAS*. In HH of Lewis Miller, M, 27, born Germany.

SUBKIN, L., 24, M, Shopkeeper, -, Germany, 27, 32, CHAS.

SUSDORFF, GUSTAVIS, 30, M, Merchant, -, Germany, 836, 816, CHAS-. In Boarding House.

SWABB, HENRY, 45, M, Overseer, -, Germany, 1254, 1254, SUMT.

SWABB, HENRY, 42, M, Overseer, -, Germany, 1116, 1116, SUMT.

SWEETMAN, C., 22, M, Chymist, -, Germany, 523, 473, CHAS. In HH of John P. Neibuhr, M, 31, born Germany.

SWITZER, LENA, 20, F, None listed, -, Germany, 1014, 991, CHAS%. In HH of A.H. Hayden, M, 33, born CT.

**SWITZER, MARY**, 20, F, None listed, -, Germany, 1014, 991, CHAS%. In HH of A.H. Hayden, M, 33, born CT.

## T

**TAYLEE, CARLE**, 16, M, Clerk, -, Germany, 432, 415, CHAS-. In HH of Diederick Harvers, M, 30, born Germany.

**TAYLEE, JOANA**, 12, F, None listed, -, Germany, 432, 415, CHAS-. In HH of Diederick Harvers, M, 30, born Germany.

**TEACHEN, HENRY**, 24, M, Clerk, -, Germany, 92, 92, CHAS%. In HH of Mary Pahler, F, 45, born SC.

**TEASE, CARLOS**, 26, M, Baker, -, Germany, 285, 264, CHAS+. In HH of H. Wittschew, M, 23, born Germany.

**TEILEY, ANNA**, 21, F, None listed, -, Germany, 742, 722, CHAS-. In HH of F. Teiley, M, 27, born Germany.

**TEILEY, F.**, 27, M, Shoemaker, -, Germany, 742, 722, CHAS-.

**TENETT, JOHN F.**, 65, M, Fruiterer, -, Germany, 59, 53, CHAS+.

**TEPPY, ADOLPH**, 24, M, Clerk, -, Germany, 687, 679, CHAS%. In HH of William Teppy, M, 50, born Germany.

**TEPPY, ANGELINE**, 47, F, None listed, -, Germany, 687, 679, CHAS%. In HH of William Teppy, M, 50, born Germany.

**TEPPY, WILLIAM**, 50, M, Police officer, -, Germany, 687, 679, CHAS%.

**TERBET, F.H.**, 21, M, Shoemaker, -, Germany, 429, 388, CHAS+.

**THEU, F.W.**, 28, M, Gass fitter, -, Germany, 391, 355, CHAS.

**THEUS, HENRY**, 20, M, Clerk, -, Germany, 121, 112, CHAS+. In HH of J.B. Rankin, M, 29, born Germany.

**THOMAS, CHARLES**, 28, M, Ordinance man, -, Germany, 1005, 982, CHAS%. Under command of Major P. Hagnes, Comg. Off. U.S. Arnsel.

**THU, CATHARINE**, 30, F, None listed, -, Germany, 683, 675, CHAS%. In HH of John H. Thu, M, 35, born Germany.

**THU, JOHN H.**, 35, M, Shopkeeper, -, Germany, 683, 675, CHAS%.

**THUS, HENRY**, 25, M, Waiter, -, Germany, 326, 301, CHAS. On Steam Ship Southerner.

**TIDYMAN, G.S.**, 28, M, Shopkeeper, -, Germany, 196, 179, CHAS. In HH of C. Ollen, M, 28, born Germany.

**TIDYMAN, J.F.**, 30, M, Shopkeeper, -, Germany, 40, 37, CHAS-. Listed as prisioner, date 1850.

**TIEDMAN, CHARLES**, 17, M, Shopkeeper, -, Germany, 204, 204, CHAS%. In HH of Clause Meyer, M, 25, born Germany.

**TIEDMANN, ANN**, 35, F, None listed, -, Germany, 549, 541, CHAS%. In HH of O. Tiedmann, M, 40, born Germany.

TIEDMANN, CLAUS, 20, M, None listed, -, Germany, 549, 541, CHAS%. In HH of O. Tiedmann, M, 40, born Germany.

TIEDMANN, O., 40, M, Shopkeeper, -, Germany, 549, 541, CHAS%.

TIETYEW, DIEDERICK, 23, M, Shopkeeper, -, Germany, 171, 137, CHAS*.

TILMYER, H., 24, M, Clerk, -, Germany, 318, 293, CHAS. In HH of H. Bregnan, M, 24, born Germany.

TIMERMAN, HARMON, 38, M, Carpenter, -, Germany, 671, 663, CHAS%.

TIMERMAN, SOPHIA, 26, F, None listed, -, Germany, 671, 663, CHAS%. In HH of Harmon Timerman, M, 38, born Germany.

TINCKER, JOHN, 26, M, Shopkeeper, -, Germany, 609, 601, CHAS%.

TRAPMAN, LEWIS, 60, M, Merchant, -, Germany, 399, 372, CHAS*. In HH of Rev. J.S. Hanckel, M, 33, born SC.

TRIEST, FANNY, 12, F, None listed, -, Germany, 667, 647, CHAS-. In Boarding House.

TRIEST, JACOB, 7, M, None listed, -, Germany, 667, 647, CHAS-. In Boarding House.

TRIEST, JANET, 28, M, None listed, -, Germany, 667, 647, CHAS-. In Boarding House.

TRIEST, SAMUEL, 10, M, None listed, -, Germany, 667, 647, CHAS-. In Boarding House.

TRIEST, W., 32, M, Merchant, -, Germany, 667, 647, CHAS-. In Boarding House.

TRUCHAR, C., 25, M, Acct., -, Germany, 24, 24, KERS. In HH of Moses Drucker, M, 45, born Germany.

TRYIST, CAROLINE, 36, F, None listed, -, Germany, 259, 244, CHAS-. In HH of J. Tryist, M, 41, born Germany.

TRYIST, CHANCH, 34, F, None listed, -, Germany, 259, 244, CHAS-. In HH of J. Tryist, M, 41, born Germany.

TRYIST, FANNY, 12, F, None listed, -, Germany, 259, 244, CHAS-. In HH of J. Tryist, M, 41, born Germany.

TRYIST, J., 41, M, Clothing store, -, Germany, 259, 244, CHAS-.

TRYIST, JACOB, 8, M, None listed, -, Germany, 259, 244, CHAS-. In HH of J. Tryist, M, 41, born Germany.

TRYIST, MYER, 30, M, Clothing store, -, Germany, 259, 244, CHAS-. In HH of J. Tryist, M, 41, born Germany.

TRYIST, MYER, 19, M, Clerk, -, Germany, 259, 244, CHAS-. In HH of J. Tryist, M, 41, born Germany.

TRYIST, SAMUEL, 9, M, None listed, -, Germany, 259, 244, CHAS-. In HH of J. Tryist, M, 41, born Germany.

TUCKERMANN, WILLIAM, 21, M, Clerk, -, Germany, 770, 753, CHAS%. In HH of William Brigham, M, 38, born Germany.

**TUNNO, WILLIAM**, 70, M, Fisherman, B, Germany, 280, 254, CHAS*. In HH of E. Messner, M, 28, born Germany.

**TURNER, ALFRED**, 4, M, None listed, M, Germany, 20, 18, CHAS-. In HH of Ann Turner, F, 55 mulatto, born Germany {sic}. Birthplace: listed as Germany, could be a transcription error in census.

**TURNER, ANN**, 55, F, None listed, M, Germany, 20, 18, CHAS-. Birthplace listed as Germany, could be a transcription error in census.

**TURNER, ANNA**, 7, F, None listed, M, Germany, 20, 18, CHAS-. In HH of Ann Turner, F, 55 mulatto, born Germany {sic}. Birthplace listed as Germany, could be a transcription error in census.

**TURNER, BETSEY**, 44, F, None listed, M, Germany, 19, 17, CHAS-. In HH of Sarah Turner, F, 40 mulatto, born Germany {sic}. Birthplace listed as Germany, could be a transcription error in census.

**TURNER, ISABELL**, 10, F, None listed, M, Germany, 19, 17, CHAS-. In HH of Sarah Turner, F, 40 mulatto, born Germany {sic}. Birthplace listed as Germany, could be a transcription error in census.

**TURNER, JOHN**, 8, M, None listed, M, Germany, 20, 18, CHAS-. In HH of Ann Turner, F, 55 mulatto, born Germany {sic}. Birthplace listed as Germany, could be a transcription error in census.

**TURNER, JOHN**, 5, M, None listed, M, Germany, 19, 17, CHAS-. In HH of Sarah Turner, F, 40 mulatto, born Germany {sic}. Birthplace listed as Germany, could be a transcription error in census.

**TURNER, JULIA**, 12, F, None listed, M, Germany, 19, 17, CHAS-. In HH of Sarah Turner, F, 40 mulatto, born Germany {sic}. Birthplace listed as Germany, could be a transcription error in census.

**TURNER, JULIA**, 7, F, None listed, M, Germany, 19, 17, CHAS-. In HH of Sarah Turner, F, 40 mulatto, born Germany {sic}. Birthplace listed as Germany, could be a transcription error in census.

**TURNER, MARY**, 16, F, None listed, M, Germany, 19, 17, CHAS-. In HH of Sarah Turner, F, 40 mulatto, born Germany {sic}. Birthplace listed as Germany, could be a transcription error in census.

**TURNER, SARAH**, 40, F, None listed, M, Germany, 19, 17, CHAS-. Birthplace listed as Germany, could be a transcription error in census.

**TURNER, SUSAN**, 28, F, None listed, M, Germany, 20, 18, CHAS-. In HH of Ann Turner, F, 55 mulatto, born Germany {sic}. Birthplace listed as Germany, could be a transcription error in census.

**TURNER, THEODORE**, 3, M, None listed, M, Germany, 19, 17, CHAS-. In HH of Sarah Turner, F, 40 mulatto, born Germany {sic}. Birthplace listed as Germany, could be a transcription error in census.

# U

**URCHIN, ANNA**, 28, F, None listed, -, Germany, 48, 56, CHAS. In HH of John D Urchin, M, 29, born Germany.

**URCHIN, JOHN**, 22, M, Baker, -, Germany, 48, 56, CHAS. In HH of John D Urchin, M, 29, born Germany.

**URCHIN, JOHN D.**, 29, M, Baker, -, Germany, 48, 56, CHAS.

**URTMEYER, CONRAD**, 18, M, Clerk, -, Germany, 435, 394, CHAS+. In HH of Henry Olten, M, 26, born Germany.

**USTMAN, HENRY**, 28, M, Musician, -, Germany, 86, 78, CHAS+. In Boarding House.

# V

**VAN DELKIN, MARTHA**, 26, F, None listed, -, Germany, 720, 678, CHAS+.

**VAN HARDEN, JOHN**, 19, M, Shopkeeper, -, Germany, 601, 593, CHAS%.

**VAN HASSEL, C.**, 23, F, Milliner, -, Germany, 852, 832, CHAS-. In HH of A.G. Parker, F, 38, born Germany.

**VAN WELKIN, ANNA**, 24, F, None listed, -, Germany, 692, 684, CHAS%. In HH of John Van Welkin, M, 32, born Germany.

**VAN WELKIN, JOHN**, 32, M, Grocer, -, Germany, 692, 684, CHAS%.

**VAN ZOOSTEIN, FREDERICK**, 27, F, None listed, -, Germany, 448, 445, CHAS%. In HH of Martin Van Zoostein, M, 22, born Germany.

**VAN ZOOSTEIN, MARTIN**, 22, M, Baker, -, Germany, 448, 445, CHAS%.

**VANDELKIN, ANNA**, 24, F, None listed, -, Germany, 470, 467, CHAS%. In HH of C. Vandelkin, M, 24, born Germany.

**VANDELKIN, C.**, 24, M, Grocer, -, Germany, 470, 467, CHAS%.

**VANDELKIN, ELIZA**, 19, F, None listed, -, Germany, 470, 467, CHAS%. In HH of C. Vandelkin, M, 24, born Germany.

**VANDERLIPPE, FREDERICK**, 51, M, Farmer, -, Germany, 1122, 1100, CHAS%.

**VANDOHLEN, ALBERT**, 33, M, Merchant, -, Germany, 463, 421, CHAS+.

**VANGLAUGH, F.**, 35, M, Merchant, -, Germany, 2251, 2251, GREE. In HH of A.H. Rowand, M, 30, born NJ.

**VANGLAUGH, GERRITTA**, 28, F, None listed, -, Germany, 2251, 2251, GREE. In HH of A.H. Rowand, M, 30, born NJ.

**VARN, AARON**, 60, M, Farmer, -, Germany, 462, 462, COLL.

**VARNICKY, HENRY**, 28, M, Carpenter, -, Germany, 871, 848, CHAS%.

**VENER, DIEDERICK**, 12, M, None listed, -, Germany, 630, 611, CHAS-. In HH of John A. Kerp, M, 26, born Germany.

**VERDEMEYER, HENRY**, 21, M, Shoemaker, -, Germany, 742, 722, CHAS-. In HH of F. Teiley, M, 27, born Germany.

**VERPLANK, CLAUS**, 36, M, Clerk, -, Germany, 7, 7, CHAS%. In HH of Diederick Munch, M, 48, born Germany.

**VETTERHAU, LALACK**, 12, M, None listed, -, Germany, 81, 73, CHAS+. In HH of Marcus Vetterhau, M, 39, born Germany.

**VETTERHAU, MARCUS**, 39, M, Shopkeeper, -, Germany, 81, 73, CHAS+.

**VETTERHAU, PHILIP**, 16, M, None listed, -, Germany, 81, 73, CHAS+. In HH of Marcus Vetterhau, M, 39, born Germany.

**VETTERHAU, SOPHIA**, 39, F, None listed, -, Germany, 81, 73, CHAS+. In HH of Marcus Vetterhau, M, 39, born Germany.

**VICTCHIN, ANNA**, 20, F, None listed, -, Germany, 48, 58, CHAS.

**VICTUS, JOHN**, 18, M, Clerk, -, Germany, 69, 67, CHAS*. In HH of E.H. Stetting, M, 24, born Germany.

**VOGEL, LOUISA**, 37, F, None listed, -, Germany, 413, 424, RICH. In HH of Theodore Vogel, M, 30, born Germany.

**VOGEL, THEODORE**, 30, M, Shoemaker, -, Germany, 413, 424, RICH.

**VOGEL, WILLIAM**, 6, M, None listed, -, Germany, 413, 424, RICH. In HH of Theodore Vogel, M, 30, born Germany.

**VOGELSINGER, BECKER**, 24, M, Cabinetmaker, -, Germany, 706, 686, CHAS-. In HH of C. Vogelsinger, M, 42, born Germany.

**VOGELSINGER, C.**, 42, M, Clerk, -, Germany, 706, 686, CHAS-.

**VOGELSINGER, FREDERICK**, 17, M, Cabinetmaker, -, Germany, 706, 686, CHAS-. In HH of C. Vogelsinger, M, 42, born Germany.

**VOGELSINGER, MEENA**, 39, F, None listed, -, Germany, 706, 686, CHAS-. In HH of C. Vogelsinger, M, 42, born Germany.

**VOLGER, ANN**, 24, F, None listed, -, Germany, 754, 734, CHAS-. In HH of Bernard Volger, M, 30, born Germany.

**VOLGER, BERNARD**, 30, M, Tobacconist, -, Germany, 754, 734, CHAS-.

**VOLGER, CHRISTOPHER**, 35, M, Merchant, -, Germany, 190, 194, RICH.

**VOLLARS, JOHN H.**, 29, M, Clerk, -, Germany, 416, 388, CHAS*. In HH of John H. Renneker, M, 30, born Germany.

**VOLLERS, LEWIS**, 20, M, Upholsterer, -, Germany, 675, 655, CHAS-. In HH of T.H. LaRousselliere, M, 29, born SC..

**VOLMER, CHRISTOPHER**, 35, M, Tavern keeper, -, Germany, 968, 945, CHAS%.

**VON BEEN, JACOB**, 24, M, Grocer, -, Germany, 404, 368, CHAS.

**VON DOHLEN, A.**, 32, M, Grocer, -, Germany, 89, 81, CHAS+.

**VON DOHLEN, CLARA**, 26, M, Clerk, -, Germany, 89, 81, CHAS+. In HH of A. Von Dohlen, M, 32, born Germany.

**VON EBOMSON, DEDRICK**, 28, M, Farmer, -, Germany, 1077, 1126, PICK.

**VON GLAHN, B.**, 25, M, Merchant, -, Germany, 838, 818, CHAS-. In HH of T.M. Bristol, M, 30, born CT.

VON GLAHN, CARSON, 30, M, None listed, -, Germany, 898, 875, CHAS%. In HH of Dedrick Meinarders, M, 36, born Germany.

VON GLAHN, D., 26, F, None listed, -, Germany, 425, 383, CHAS. In HH of H. Smith, M, 32, born Germany.

VON GLAHN, H., 35, M, Shopkeeper, -, Germany, 512, 505, CHAS%. In HH of Edward Logan, M, 25, born SC.

VON GLAHN, MARTIN, 26, M, Grocer, -, Germany, 337, 320, CHAS-.

VON GLANN, AUGUST, 29, M, Merchant, -, Germany, 838, 818, CHAS-. In HH of T.M. Bristol, M, 30, born CT.

VON HADEHN, CHRISTOPHER, 24, M, None listed, -, Germany, 278, 278, CHAS%. In HH of Henry Mehrtens, M, 25, born Germany.

VON HOLLAND, H., 24, M, Clerk, -, Germany, 120, 120, CHAS%.

VON SANTEN, F., 20, M, Clerk, -, Germany, 847, 827, CHAS-. In HH of Sophia Selle 34, born Germany.

VON SPECHAN, C., 28, M, Shopkeeper, -, Germany, 405, 403, CHAS%.

VON SPRAGEN, ELEANOR, 28, F, None listed, -, Germany, 46, 41, CHAS+. In HH of Fred. Von Spragen, M, 33, born Germany.

VON SPRAGEN, FRED., 33, M, Tavern keeper, -, Germany, 46, 41, CHAS+.

VONDERLIETH, E., 33, M, Tailor, -, Germany, 108, 100, CHAS+.

VONDERLIETH, FLORINA C., 25, F, None listed, -, Germany, 108, 100, CHAS+. In HH of E. Vonderlieth, M, 33, born Germany.

VONDERLIETH, FLORINA W., 2, F, None listed, -, Germany, 108, 100, CHAS+. In HH of E. Vonderlieth, M, 33, born Germany.

VOSS, CARSTEIN, 44, M, Planter, -, Germany, 204, 204, CHAS3.

# W

WADELKIN, ANN, 22, F, None listed, -, Germany, 954, 931, CHAS%. In HH of Henry Wadelkin, M, 19, born Germany.

WADELKIN, HENRY, 19, M, Shopkeeper, -, Germany, 954, 931, CHAS%.

WAGENER, ELIZA, 28, F, None listed, -, Germany, 464, 447, CHAS-. In HH of John A. Wagener, M, 34, born Germany.

WAGENER, JOHN A., 34, M, Editor, -, Germany, 464, 447, CHAS-.

WAGENER, LISETTA, 9, F, None listed, -, Germany, 464, 447, CHAS-. In HH of John A. Wagener, M, 34, born Germany.

WAGENER, MARIA, 19, F, None listed, -, Germany, 464, 447, CHAS-. In HH of John A. Wagener, M, 34, born Germany.

WAGGONER, JOHN, 33, M, Lace Weaver, -, Germany, 546, 547, And*. In HH of Frederic Harbert, M, 39, born Germany.

WAGNER, FREDERICK, 18, M, Clerk, -, Germany, 51, 46, CHAS+. In HH of J.H. Wilkenning, M, 32, born Germany.

WAINEKIN, J., 32, M, Clerk, -, Germany, 179, 162, CHAS. In HH of Hans Jessen, M, 32, born Germany.

WALD, CATHERINE, 38, F, None listed, -, Germany, 21, 19, CHAS-. In HH of Frederick Wald, M, 50, born Germany.

WALD, FREDERICK, 50, M, Laborer, -, Germany, 21, 19, CHAS-.

WALD, WILLIAM, 16, M, Carpenter, -, Germany, 21, 19, CHAS-. In HH of Frederick Wald, M, 50, born Germany.

WALLACE, J.C., 23, M, Clerk, -, Germany, 493, 476, CHAS-. In HH of William Brunger, M, 30, born Germany.

WALSLEEN, THOS., 38, M, Clerk, -, Germany, 202, 190, CHAS+. In Boarding House.

WALTER, HENRY, 28, M, Musician, -, Germany, 202, 190, CHAS+. In Boarding House.

WARNICKER, WILLIAM, 30, M, Laborer, -, Germany, 1174, 1153, CHAS%.

WARNKER, HENRY E., 34, M, Shoemaker, -, Germany, 1159, 1138, CHAS%.

WARTMAN, T., 20, M, Clerk, -, Germany, 10, 10, CHAS. In HH of John Rankin, M, 22, born Germany.

WASSERMAN, WILLIAM, 27, M, Tailor, -, Germany, 465, 422, CHAS. In HH of Leslie O'Wen, M, 47, born Ireland.

WATERMAN, CHARLES, 30, M, Shopkeeper, -, Germany, 594, 586, CHAS%.

WATERMAN, JOHN, 25, M, None listed, -, Germany, 594, 586, CHAS%. In HH of Charles Waterman, M, 30, born Germany.

WEANHOLZ, F., 25, M, Pedler, -, Germany, 323, 298, CHAS.

WEBER, A. A., 52, M, Shoemaker, -, Germany, 236, 214, CHAS.

WEBER, ALPINE, 30, M, Shopkeeper, -, Germany, 750, 730, CHAS-.

WEBER, C. MULLER, 25, M, Shoemaker, -, Germany, 412, 385, CHAS*. In HH of John Weber, M, 38, born Germany.

WEBER, CAROLINE, 40, F, None listed, -, Germany, 364, 335, CHAS. In HH of Peter Weber, M, 50, born Germany.

WEBER, CHARLOTTE, 33, F, None listed, -, Germany, 916, 893, CHAS%. In HH of George Weber, M, 38, born Germany.

WEBER, EMILY, 6, F, None listed, -, Germany, 364, 335, CHAS. In HH of Peter Weber, M, 50, born Germany.

WEBER, FREDERICA, 26, F, None listed, -, Germany, 412, 385, CHAS*. In HH of John Weber, M, 38, born Germany.

WEBER, FREDERICK, 24, M, Boot maker, -, Germany, 143, 143, CHAS%. In HH of Jacob Hillan, M, 35, born Germany.

WEBER, GEORGE, 38, M, Laborer, -, Germany, 916, 893, CHAS%.

WEBER, GEORGE, 8, M, None listed, -, Germany, 916, 893, CHAS%. In HH of George Weber, M, 38, born Germany.

WEBER, JAMES, 1, M, None listed, -, Germany, 364, 335, CHAS. In HH of Peter Weber, M, 50, born Germany.

WEBER, JOHN, 38, M, Shoemaker, -, Germany, 412, 385, CHAS*.

WEBER, JOHN, 10, M, None listed, -, Germany, 364, 335, CHAS. In HH of Peter Weber, M, 50, born Germany.

WEBER, MADELINE, 35, F, None listed, -, Germany, 236, 214, CHAS. In HH of A.A. Weber, M, 52, born Germany.

WEBER, MARAGARET, 27, F, None listed, -, Germany, 750, 730, CHAS-. In HH of Alpine Weber, M, 30, born Germany.

WEBER, MARTIN, 8, M, None listed, -, Germany, 364, 335, CHAS. In HH of Peter Weber, M, 50, born Germany.

WEBER, PETER, 50, M, Shoemaker, -, Germany, 364, 335, CHAS.

WEBER, SAML., 24, M, Clerk, -, Germany, 101, 93, CHAS+. In Boarding House.

WEDMYER, FREDRICK, 27, M, Shopkeeper, -, Germany, 559, 551, CHAS%.

WEEDNA, WILHDMINE, 26, F, None listed, -, Germany, 2031, 2037, EDGE. In HH of Charles Weedna, M, 42, born Saxony. Wilhdmine, born Baden Germany

WEGAR, GERHARD, 42, M, Farmer, -, Germany, 532, 532, LEX.

WEHMAN, CATHERINE, 20, F, None listed, -, Germany, 648, 607, CHAS+. In HH of H. Sahlman, M, 33, born Germany.

WEHMAN, F., 24, M, Grocer, -, Germany, 384, 357, CHAS*.

WEIGIN, HENRY, 27, M, Mariner, -, Germany, 471, 468, CHAS%. In HH of Herman Meyer, M, 33, born Germany.

WEINBERG, FRANCIS, 42, F, None listed, -, Germany, 529, 544, RICH. In HH of Christian Kline, M, 38, born Germany.

WEINBERG, JACOB L., 26, M, Clerk, -, Germany, 253, 258, RICH. In HH of Charles J. Lindfors, M, 34, born Sweden.

WELBER, F., 25, M, Music Teacher, -, Germany, 23, 23, NEWB. In HH of J. Wilson 33, M, Hotel Keeper, born SC.

WELCHMAN, J., 20, M, Clerk, -, Germany, 793, 776, CHAS%. In HH of B. Burghman, M, 48, born Germany.

WELHERT, J.C., 39, M, Grocer, -, Germany, 66, 66, CHAS%.

WELLE, SOPHIA, 34, F, None listed, -, Germany, 847, 827, CHAS-.

WELLHAASEN, H.C., 27, M, Merchant, -, Germany, 81, 81, KERS.

WELSBAGER, CHARLES, 53, M, None, -, Germany, 372, 340, CHAS.

WELSBAGER, HENRIETTA, 54, F, None listed, -, Germany, 372, 340, CHAS. In HH of Charles Welsbager, M, 53, born Germany

WELTIES, D., 24, M, Clerk, -, Germany, 783, 766, CHAS%. In HH of Frederick Kracki, M, 41, born Germany.

WERKERMANN, H., 34, M, Merchant, -, Germany, 436, 395, CHAS+.

WERKERMANN, MARGARET, 24, F, None listed, -, Germany, 436, 395, CHAS+. In HH of H. Werkermann, M, 34, born Germany.
WERNER, DIEDERICK, 27, M, Clerk, -, Germany, 662, 642, CHAS-. In HH of Catherine Bochman, F, 25, born Germany.
WERNER, HARMAN, 30, M, Grocer, -, Germany, 112, 104, CHAS+.
WERTKIN, LEWIS, 33, M, Fruiterer, -, Germany, 55, 50, CHAS+.
WESTENDORFF, C.P.L., 60, M, Clerk, -, Germany, 365, 327, CHAS+.
WETZ, J., 35, M, Clerk, -, Germany, 721, 701, CHAS-. In HH of Edwin Bates, M, 23, born Canada.
WEYMAN, FREDERICK, 19, M, Cigar Manuf., -, Germany, 454, 451, CHAS%. In HH of W.H. Boring, M, 28, born VA.
WHEELER, JOHN, 49, M, Engineer, -, Germany, 666, 666, WILL. In HH of William Knox, M, 33, born SC.
WHITTER, HENRY, 21, M, Clerk, -, Germany, 775, 733, CHAS+. In Boarding House
WHITTING, HANNAH, 32, F, None listed, -, Germany, 307, 291, CHAS-.
WHITTING, JOANA, 14, F, None listed, -, Germany, 307, 291, CHAS-. In HH of Hannah Whitting, F, 32, born Germany.
WHITTING, WILLIAM, 16, M, Clerk, -, Germany, 307, 291, CHAS-. In HH of Hannah Whitting, F, 32, born Germany.
WHITTY, FREDK., 24, M, Clerk, -, Germany, 101, 93, CHAS+. In Boarding House.
WICKER, FREDRICK, 33, M, Drayman, -, Germany, 1028, 1006, CHAS%.
WICKER, LANA, 33, F, None listed, -, Germany, 1028, 1006, CHAS%. In HH of Fredrick Wicker, M, 33, born Germany.
WICKERS, CATHARINE R., 22, F, None listed, -, Germany, 57, 59, PICK. In HH of Frederick Wickers, M, 38, born Germany.
WICKERS, FREDERICK, 38, M, Farmer, -, Germany, 57, 59, PICK.
WICKIE, JOHN, 24, M, Shoemaker, -, Germany, 25, 20, CHAS+. In HH of John Metzler, M, 34, born Germany.
WICKIE, MARY, 22, F, None listed, -, Germany, 25, 20, CHAS+. In HH of John Metzler, M, 34, born Germany.
WIEBENS, HENRY, 61, M, Grocer, -, Germany, 489, 447, CHAS+.
WIECKERS, T., 25, M, Clerk, -, Germany, 11, 10, CHAS$. In HH of Edward Semecke, M, 35, born Germany.
WIEDERO, BUSH, 46, M, Tailor, -, Germany, 541, 507, CHAS*. In HH of John Ahrens, M, 35, born Germany.
WIERFELDER, S., 30, M, Shoemaker, -, Germany, 473, 439, CHAS*.
WILHURST, GODLIP, 40, M, Planter, -, Germany, 731, 740, RICH+.
WILKENNING, GALEINA, 30, F, None listed, -, Germany, 51, 46, CHAS+. In HH of J.H. Wilkenning, M, 32, born Germany.

**WILKENNING, J.H.**, 32, M, Grocer, -, Germany, 51, 46, CHAS+.

**WILKES, JOHN**, 40, M, Shoemaker, -, Germany, 236, 214, CHAS. In HH of A.A. Weber, M, 52, born Germany.

**WILKIN, CATHERINE**, 30, F, None listed, -, Germany, 176, 159, CHAS. In HH of Peter Wineholtz, M, 24, born Germany.

**WILLIAME, H.**, 40, M, Priv. U.S.A., -, Germany, 47, 43, CHAS$. In HH of John Ewing, M, 50, born MA.

**WILLIAMS, JOHN**, 69, M, Shoemaker, -, Germany, 2081, 2081, ABB.

**WILLIAMS, JOHN**, 35, M, Mariner, -, Germany, 1, 1, CHAS+. In HH of John P. Blum, M, 28, born Germany.

**WILLIAMS, MATILDA**, 30, F, None listed, -, Germany, 1, 1, CHAS+. In HH of John P. Blum, M, 28, born Germany.

**WILLIAMS, OLLVIA**, 19, F, None listed, -, Germany, 148, 139, CHAS+. In HH of Joseph Williams, M, 32, born Italy.

**WILLING, LAWRENCE**, 50, M, Farmer, -, Germany, 2123, 2127, EDGE.

**WILTN, HENRY CHRISTOPHER**, 30, M, RR Conductor, -, Germany, 1190, 1169, CHAS%.

**WINEBERG, JOHN**, 38, M, Shopkeeper, -, Germany, 825, 805, CHAS-.

**WINEBERG, JULIA**, 28, F, None listed, -, Germany, 825, 805, CHAS-. In HH of John Wineberg, M, 38, born Germany.

**WINEHOLTZ, AUGUSTA**, 23, F, None listed, -, Germany, 176, 159, CHAS. In HH of Peter Wineholtz, M, 24, born Germany.

**WINEHOLTZ, PETER**, 24, M, Shopkeeper, -, Germany, 176, 159, CHAS.

**WINGES, DIEDERICK**, 34, M, Laborer, -, Germany, 772, 755, CHAS%. In HH of Frederick State, M, 58, born Germany.

**WINKERMAN, A.**, 28, M, None listed, -, Germany, 470, 467, CHAS%. In HH of C. Vandelkin, M, 24, born Germany.

**WINTERS, CHRISTINE**, 9, F, None listed, -, Germany, 866, 843, CHAS%. In HH of John Winters, M, 38, born Germany.

**WINTERS, DIEDERICK**, 12, M, None listed, -, Germany, 866, 843, CHAS%. In HH of John Winters, M, 38, born Germany.

**WINTERS, JOHN**, 38, M, Carpenter, -, Germany, 866, 843, CHAS%.

**WINTERS, MARGARET**, 34, F, None listed, -, Germany, 866, 843, CHAS%. In HH of John Winters, M, 38, born Germany.

**WINTHRON, DEDRICK**, 11, M, None listed, -, Germany, 632, 641, RICH+. In HH of John Winthron, M, 48, born Germany.

**WINTHRON, JOHN**, 48, M, Planter, -, Germany, 632, 641, RICH+.

**WINTHRON, MARGARET**, 41, F, None listed, -, Germany, 632, 641, RICH+. In HH of John Winthron, M, 48, born Germany.

**WINTHRON, MARGARET**, 17, F, None listed, -, Germany, 632, 641, RICH+. In HH of John Winthron, M, 48, born Germany.

**WINTHRON, SOPHIA**, 14, F, None listed, -, Germany, 632, 641, RICH+. In HH of John Winthron, M, 48, born Germany.

**WITCHELL, FREDERICK**, 20, M, Clerk, -, Germany, 72, 64, CHAS+. In HH of John Barre, M, 56, born France.

**WITHE, AUGUSTE**, 4, M, None listed, -, Germany, 198, 180, CHAS. In HH of P.F. Wethe, M, 40, born Germany.

**WITHE, GELDON**, 32, F, None listed, -, Germany, 198, 180, CHAS. In HH of P.F. Wethe, M, 40, born Germany.

**WITHE, LUCY**, 8, F, None listed, -, Germany, 198, 180, CHAS. In HH of P.F. Wethe, M, 40, born Germany.

**WITHE, P.F.**, 40, M, Shoemaker, -, Germany, 198, 180, CHAS.

**WITTPEN, FREDERICA**, 14, F, None listed, -, Germany, 745, 725, CHAS-. In HH of Frederick Wittpen, M, 43, born Germany.

**WITTPEN, FREDERICK**, 43, M, Seedsman, -, Germany, 745, 725, CHAS-.

**WITTPEN, JOANA**, 43, F, None listed, -, Germany, 745, 725, CHAS-. In HH of Frederick Wittpen, M, 43, born Germany.

**WITTSCHEN, NEIL**, 20, M, Shopkeeper, -, Germany, 609, 601, CHAS%. In HH of John Tincker, M, 26, born Germany.

**WITTSCHEW, H.**, 23, M, Baker, -, Germany, 285, 264, CHAS+.

**WITTSCHEW, LIPEY**, 19, F, None listed, -, Germany, 285, 264, CHAS+. In HH of H. Wittschew, M, 23, born Germany.

**WOLFE, JACOB**, 24, M, Merchant, -, Germany, 539, 539, FAIR. In HH of Saling Wolfe, M, 32, born Prussia.

**WOLFF, SIMON**, 42, M, Merchant, -, Germany, 160, 160, CHAS3.

**WOOLFALL, HERMAN**, 28, M, Upholsterer, -, Germany, 444, 441, CHAS%. In HH of William Blesman, M, 30, born Germany.

**WOOLFE, SERENA**, 22, F, None listed, -, Germany, 414, 373, CHAS+. In HH of W. Woolfe, M, 23, born Germany.

**WOOLFE, W.**, 23, M, Shoemaker, -, Germany, 414, 373, CHAS+.

**WOOLFFE, J.M.**, 28, M, Shopkeeper, -, Germany, 801, 781, CHAS-.

**WOORSEN, JOSEPHINE**, 12, F, None listed, -, Germany, 473, 470, CHAS%. In HH of Lambert Woorsen, M, 35, born Ireland.

**WOORSEN, LAMBERT**, 35, M, Plasterer, -, Germany, 473, 470, CHAS%.

**WORTMAN, CARSON**, 30, M, Mariner, -, Germany, 1148, 1127, CHAS%.

**WORTMAN, CATHARINE**, 30, F, None listed, -, Germany, 1180, 1159, CHAS%. In HH of Henry Wortman, M, 42, born Germany.

**WORTMAN, GAZENU**, 23, F, None listed, -, Germany, 1148, 1127, CHAS%. In HH of Carson Wortman, M, 30, born Germany.

**WORTMAN, HENRY**, 42, M, Shopkeeper, -, Germany, 1180, 1159, CHAS%.

**WREDEN, BENJAMIN**, 38, M, Grocer, -, Germany, 385, 383, CHAS%.

**WREDEN, SUSAN**, 32, F, None listed, -, Germany, 385, 383, CHAS%. In HH

of Benjamin Wreden, M, 38, born Germany.
WULBURN, HENRY, 21, M, Grocer, -, Germany, 199, 187, CHAS+.

## Z

ZANDERS, CHRISTINA, 40, F, None listed, -, Germany, 1133, 1112, CHAS%. In HH of H. Zehee, M, 48, born Germany.
ZAUGBAUM, FRED., 26, M, Prof of Music, -, Germany, 877, 856, CHAS-. In HH of Rufus Fairchild, M, 40, born PA.
ZEHEE, ANNA, 15, F, None listed, -, Germany, 1133, 1112, CHAS%. In HH of H. Zehee, M, 48, born Germany.
ZEHEE, H., 48, M, Grocer, -, Germany, 1133, 1112, CHAS%.
ZEHEE, JOHN, 19, M, Clerk, -, Germany, 1133, 1112, CHAS%. In HH of H. Zehee, M, 48, born Germany.
ZEHEE, WILLIAM, 22, M, Boiler maker, -, Germany, 1133, 1112, CHAS%. In HH of H. Zehee, M, 48, born Germany.
ZELEO, WILLIAM, 38, M, Shopkeeper, -, Germany, 795, 778, CHAS%.
ZERBET, DIEDERICK, 17, M, Clerk, -, Germany, 35, 35, CHAS%. In HH of Henry Zerbet, M, 31, born Germany.
ZERBET, HENRY, 31, M, Shopkeeper, -, Germany, 35, 35, CHAS%.
ZERWATAKEE, FREDERICA, 35, F, None listed, -, Germany, 695, 687, CHAS%. In HH of John Zerwatakee, M, 37, born Germany.
ZERWATAKEE, JOHN, 37, M, Grocer, -, Germany, 695, 687, CHAS%.
ZIMMERMAN, A., 23, M, Priv. U.S.A., -, Germany, 47, 43, CHAS$. In HH of John Ewing, M, 50, born MA.
ZIMMERMAN, CHARLES C.A., 50, M, Teacher, -, Germany, 657, 668, RICH.
ZIMMERMAN, HERMAN, 38, M, Carpenter, -, Germany, 413, 385, CHAS*.
ZIMMERMAN, SOPHIA, 26, F, None listed, -, Germany, 413, 385, CHAS*. In HH of Herman Zimmerman, M, 38, born SC.
ZUMKELLER, ANDREW, 32, M, Shopkeeper, -, Germany, 512, 505, CHAS%. In HH of Edward Logan, M, 25, born SC.

❖

# BORN IN ITALY (52)

## A

ANGELO, JAMES, 35, M, Fruiterer, -, Italy, 358, 320, CHAS+.
ANNLINO, LEONARDO, 28, M, Seaman, -, Italy, 326, 301, CHAS . On Steam Ship Southerner.

**ANTONY, WILLIAM**, 37, M, Mariner,-, Italy, 334, 308, CHAS . In HH of William Bennett, M, 40, born NY.

**AUGUSTINE, NICHOLAS**, 27, M, Statuary Moulde,  -, Italy, 330, 297, CHAS+ . Occupation: Statuary Moulder.

## B

**BARRANEL, ANTONIO**, 23, M, Mariner,-, Italy, 330, 297, CHAS+. In HH of Nicholas Augustine, M, 27, born Italy.

**BONNEFACE, LEWIS**, 32, M, Rigger, -, Italy, 76,  68, CHAS+. In HH of D.L. McCarthy, M, 30, born Ireland.

**BOSSON, FRANCIS**, 44, M, Fruiterer,-, Italy, 210,  190, CHAS*.

**BROUDINE, AUGUSTINE**, 16, M, Fruiterer, -, Italy, 42,  37, CHAS+. In HH of Anthony Drago, M, 26, born Gibraltar.

**BURROW, EML.**, 28, M, Fruiterer, -, Italy, 262,  247, CHAS-.

## C

**CAMEALE, ANGELO**, 34, M, Fruiterer, -, Italy, 84,  76, CHAS+.

**COSTELLEN, JOSEPH**, 35, M, Fisherman, -, Italy, 384,  384, Will . In HH of William Johnson, M, 63, born SC.

**CURRIER, C.**, 38, M, Fruiterer, -, Italy, 54,  49, CHAS+.

## D

**DECOSTA, J.F.**, 48, M, Musician,-, Italy, 221,  199, CHAS . In HH of Alexr. Gordon, M, 50, born Scotland.

**DRAGO, ANDREW**, 26, M, Merchant, -, Italy, 666, 646, CHAS-. In HH of Blanco Drago, F, 50, born Italy.

**DRAGO, ANTONIO**, 25, M, Merchant,-, Italy, 666, 646, CHAS-. In HH of Blanco Drago, F, 50, born Italy.

**DRAGO, BLANCO**, 58, F, None listed,-, Italy, 666, 646, CHAS-.

**DRAGO, CAROLINE**, 16, F, None listed,-, Italy, 666, 646, CHAS-. In HH of Blanco Drago, F, 50, born Italy.

**DRAGO, OLIVIA**, 18, F, None listed,-, Italy, 666, 646, CHAS-. In HH of Blanco Drago, F, 50, born Italy.

## F

**FORRE, A. DELLA**, 70, M, Saw Mill,-, Italy, 351, 351, CHAS%.

**FRANCES, JOHN**, 44, M, Fisherman, -, Italy, 76,  68, CHAS+. In HH of D.L. McCarthy, M, 30, born Ireland.

**G**

GAMBALE, A., 39, M, Merchant,-, Italy, 225, 201, CHAS*.

GASTEY, ARNISE, 38, M, Laborer,-, Italy, 237, 222, CHAS- . In Poor House.

**J**

JACOB, MATHEW, 55, M, Shopkeeper,-, Italy, 83, 75, CHAS+. In HH of Nicholas Tallerand, M, 53, born Italy.

JACOB, PETER, 19, M, Clerk, -, Italy, 83, 75, CHAS+. In HH of Nicholas Tallerand, M, 53, born Italy.

JOSEPHS, S.J., 22, M, Mariner,-, Italy, 90, 102, CHAS .

JUDAS, CHARLES, 40, M, Cutter, -, Italy, 40, 37, CHAS- . Listed as prisoner.

JUDGEE, CHARLES, 39, M, Cutler, -, Italy, 318, 292, CHAS+.

**L**

LENAR, JOSEPH, 32, M, Clerk, -, Italy, 400, 360, CHAS+.

LEWIS, P., 23, M, Shopkeeper,-, Italy, 263, 246, CHAS+.

**M**

MAY, MARY, 34, F, None listed,-, Italy, 142, 133, CHAS+. In HH of John May, M, 60, born RI.

MCHUGH, PETRONELLA, 25, F, None listed,-, Italy, 392, 375, CHAS-. In HH of Mary McHugh, F, 46, born Ireland.

MONTEVEDA, GEAVANA, 20, M, Seaman, -, Italy, 326, 301, CHAS . On Steam Ship Southerner.

MOROSO, ANTHONY, 30, M, Fruit merchant, -, Italy, 319, 293, CHAS*

MORRELLO, JANE, 45, F, None listed,-, Italy, 659, 639, CHAS-. In HH of N. Morrello, M, 50, born Gibralter

MUSSO, A., 30, M, Fruiterer, -, Italy, 62, 56, CHAS+.

**N**

NATALE, P., 40, M, Tavern keeper, -, Italy, 64, 57, CHAS+.

**P**

PADRON, FERDENAND, 42, M, Rigger, -, Italy, 783, 741, CHAS+.

PALMEDA, CHARLES, 30, M, Physician, -, Italy, 801, 759, CHAS+. In HH of A.D. Waters, M, 36, born Canada

PATTENA, JOSEPH, 41, M, Fruiterer, -, Italy, 82, 74, CHAS+.

PERGEN, L., 25, M, Shopkeeper,-, Italy, 95, 95, CHAS%.

**PETAH, JOSEPH**, 31, M, Shopkeeper,-, Italy, 1130, 1109, CHAS%.
**PETAH, MARIA**, 25, F, None listed,-, Italy, 1130, 1109, CHAS%. In HH of
Joseph Petah, M, 31, born Italy.
**PETERS, CAROLINE**, 32, F, None listed,-, Italy, 362, 333, CHAS . In HH of
George Peters, M, 42, born Antwerp.

**R**
**RASNEL, ANTONIO**, 33, M, Labour, -, Italy, 132, 132, GEOR .
**RASNEL, JOANA**, 19, F, None listed,-, Italy, 132, 132, GEOR . In HH of
Antonio Rasnel, M, 33, born Italy.

**S**
**SALVO, CORADO**, 63, M, Clerk, -, Italy, 225, 201, CHAS*. In HH of A.
Gambale, M, 49, born Italy.
**SALVO, J.**, 48, M, Painter,-, Italy, 991, 970, CHAS- . In HH of Elizabeth
Teape, F, 23, born England.
**SLAVICK, J.L.**, 27, M, Rigger, -, Italy, 212, 190, CHAS*.

**T**
**TALLERAND, NICHOLAS**, 53, M, Clerk, -, Italy, 83, 75, CHAS+.

**V**
**VADET, JOSEPH**, 25, M, Mariner,-, Italy, 330, 297, CHAS+. In HH of
Nicholas Augustine, M, 27, born Italy.

**W**
**WHYTE, JOSEPH**, 70, M, Confectioner, -, Italy, 786, 766, CHAS-.
**WILLIAMS, JOSEPH**, 32, M, Mariner,-, Italy, 148, 139, CHAS+.

❖

# BORN IN FRANCE - 244

**A**
**ALLISON, MARY**, 70, F, None listed, -, France, 473, 431, CHAS. In HH of
George Allison, M, 32, born PA.
**ALMER, HENRY**, 32, M, Artist, -, France, 355, 317, CHAS+.
**ALMER, LEWIS**, 13, M, None listed, -, France, 355, 317, CHAS+. In HH of
Henry Almer, M, 32, born France.

144

ALMER, MARIA, 10, F, None listed, -, France, 355, 317, CHAS+. In HH of Henry Almer, M, 32, born France.

ALMER, SOPHIA, 30, F, None listed, -, France, 355, 317, CHAS+. In HH of Henry Almer, M, 32, born France.

ANDRE, JOSEPH, 25, M, Gardener, -, France, 1325, 1325, BARN.

# B

BAEER, CHARLES, 57, M, Harness maker, -, France, 113, 126, CHAS.

BAEER, ELIZA, 12, F, None listed, -, France, 113, 126, CHAS. In HH of Charles Baeer, M, 57, born France.

BAILEY, FRANCES, 25, M, Cook, -, France, 952, 929, CHAS%.

BAILEY, GUMFREY, 50, F, None listed, -, France, 952, 929, CHAS%. In HH of Frances Bailey, M, 25, born France.

BARBOT, A., 65, M, Merchant, -, France, 40, 48, CHAS.

BARRE, JOHN, 59, M, Wine merchant, -, France, 934, 914, CHAS-.

BARRE, JOHN, 56, M, Wine merchant, -, France, 72, 64, CHAS+.

BEAUFORD, ANDREW, 36, M, Shoemaker, -, France, 21, 17, CHAS+.

BEDAUGH, A., 57, M, Merchant, -, France, 306, 306, CHAS3.

BERGER, A., 40, M, Dancing Master, -, France, 139, 130, CHAS+. In HH of Joseph Fry, M, 40, born Germany.

BERGER, OCTAVIA, 14, F, None listed, -, France, 139, 130, CHAS+. In HH of Joseph Fry, M, 40, born Germany.

BERNARD, ALFRED, 16, M, Clerk, -, France, 992, 971, CHAS-. In HH of S.B. Bernard, M, 38, born France.

BERNARD, CLEMENTINE H., 36, F, None listed, -, France, 992, 971, CHAS-. In HH of S.B. Bernard, M, 38, born France.

BERNARD, ESTHER, 14, F, None listed, -, France, 992, 971, CHAS-. In HH of S.B. Bernard, M, 38, born France.

BERNARD, S.B., 38, M, Merchant, -, France, 992, 971, CHAS-.

BLANCHAN, CECELIA, 41, F, None listed, -, France, 854, 832, CHAS%. In HH of Edward Blanchan, M, 40, born France.

BLANCHAN, EDWARD, 40, M, Carpenter, -, France, 854, 832, CHAS%.

BLANCHAN, ELIZABETH, 38, F, None listed, -, France, 854, 832, CHAS%. In HH of Edward Blanchan, M, 40, born France.

BLANCHAN, JULIANA, 28, F, None listed, -, France, 854, 832, CHAS%. In HH of Edward Blanchan, M, 40, born France.

BLANCHAN, MARY ANN, 60, F, None listed, -, France, 854, 832, CHAS%. In HH of Edward Blanchan, M, 40, born France.

BLANCHAN, STAMSLAUS, 37, M, Carpenter, -, France, 854, 832, CHAS%. In HH of Edward Blanchan, M, 40, born France.

**BLAYDEN, O.**, 27, M, Clerk, -, France, 843, 823, CHAS-. In HH of O. Lhomdieu, M, 31, born NJ.

**BLONDEAU, E.**, 70, M, None, -, France, 447, 406, CHAS+.

**BLONDEAU, MARY C.**, 55, F, None listed, -, France, 447, 406, CHAS+. In HH of E. Blondeau, M, 70, born France.

**BOLLIN, CHARLES J.**, 28, M, RR agent, -, France, 635, 653, RICH.

**BONNEAU, TEARA**, 70, F, None listed, -, France, 467, 424, CHAS. In HH of Mary Chapeaux, F, 45, born SC.

**BONNOUE, J.**, 45, M, Dancing master, -, France, 373, 335, CHAS+.

**BOUDET, PAULINE**, 20, F, None listed, -, France, 1, 1, CHAS%. In HH of William Aiken, M, 44, born SC.

**BOULAIN, MARIA**, 81, F, None listed, -, France, 417, 389, CHAS*. In HH of Peter B. Lalane, M, 32, born NY.

**BOULAIN, PETER B.**, 81, M, None listed, -, France, 417, 389, CHAS*. In HH of Peter B. Lalane, M, 32, born NY.

**BOURDENAND, JOHN**, 40, M, Tobacconist, -, France, 733, 691, CHAS+.

**BOUTON, ANGELINA**, 23, F, None listed, -, France, 211, 198, CHAS+. In HH of Antoine Bouton, F, 25, born France.

**BOUTON, ANTOINE**, 25, F, None listed, -, France, 211, 198, CHAS+.

**BRANDT, H.F.**, 40, M, Confectioner, -, France, 761, 741, CHAS-.

**BURTIE, FRANCIS**, 35, M, Shoemaker, -, France, 347, 353, RICH. In HH of Jane E. Reeder, F, 37, born MA.

## C

**CALLEN, STEPHEN**, 24, M, Clerk, -, France, 379, 344, CHAS. In HH of N.R. Schineder, M, 32, born Germany.

**CAMMAN, JOHN**, 41, M, Farmer, -, France, 1011, 1012, AND*.

**CARRIBO, HENRY**, 75, M, None, -, France, 603, 606, MAR.

**CHALON, F.**, 70, M, Farmer, -, France, 992, 969, CHAS%.

**CHANDLER, R.W.**, 31, M, Watch maker, -, France, 379, 344, CHAS. In HH of N.R. Schineder, M, 32, born Germany.

**CLASTRIERE, STEPHEN**, 55, M, Carpenter, -, France, 630, 648, RICH. In HH of John N. Scofield, M, 35, born NY.

**CLINCH, ANDREW**, 75, M, Farmer, -, France, 1315, 1315, NEWB.

**COLRUSTZ, SYLVIA**, 28, F, None listed, -, France, 493, 447, CHAS. In HH of Peter Leure, M, 53, born France.

**CONSAR, ANN**, 25, F, None listed, -, France, 256, 241, CHAS-. In HH of Nathl. M. Gailbraith, M, 35, born SC.

**CONSAR, LEWIS**, 28, M, Musician, -, France, 256, 241, CHAS-. In HH of Nathl. M. Gailbraith, M, 35, born SC.

CORDES, ELIZA C., 30, F, None listed, -, France, 52, 47, CHAS+. In HH of Theodore Cordes, M, 35, born Germany.

CORNIA, FRANCIS, 90, M, None, -, France, 789, 747, CHAS+.

CORNIA, MARY, 78, F, None listed, -, France, 789, 747, CHAS+. In HH of Francis Cornia, M, 90, born France.

COSTAMAGNA, MARY, 60, F, None listed, -, France, 860, 818, CHAS+. In HH of Gustavis Follen, M, 33, born SC.

## D

DADEN, L.H., 35, M, Jeweller, -, France, 671, 651, CHAS-.

DALES, FRANCES, 56, F, None listed, -, France, 645, 604, CHAS+.

DALORY, ANTHONY, 45, M, Cabinetmaker, -, France, 132, 135, RICH.

DECHAMP, GEORGE, 23, M, Tailor, -, France, 414, 425, Rich. In HH of James H. Wells, M, 56, born GA.

DELAMOTE, R., 50, M, French Council, -, France, 293, 270, CHAS.

DELANNAY, JULES, 36, M, Professor of Languages, -, France, 468, 451, CHAS-.

DELAY, JANE, 83, F, None listed, -, France, 667, 647, CHAS-. In Boarding House.

DELPORTE, ADELLE, 29, F, None listed, -, France, 639, 598, CHAS+. In HH of Simon Delporte, M, 34, born France.

DELPORTE, SIMON, 34, M, Merchant, -, France, 639, 598, CHAS+.

DEMONTELLE, H., 40, M, Teacher, -, France, 680, 638, CHAS+. In HH of Elizabeth Cantwell, F, 40, born SC.

DENAN, ADELAIDE, 46, F, None listed, -, France, 817, 797, CHAS-. In HH of Thomas E. Denan, M, 45, born France.

DENAN, THOMAS E., 45, M, Clerk, -, France, 817, 797, CHAS-.

DENNIS, JOHN A., 33, M, Confectioner, -, France, 492, 486, CHAS%.

DENNIS, LEWIS, 58, M, Carpenter, -, France, 237, 222, CHAS-. Poor House.

DEVINEAU, ANN M., 30, F, None listed, -, France, 820, 800, CHAS-. In HH of E. Devineau, M, 40, born SC.

DIVENEAU, JOSEPH, 63, M, Dealer, -, France, 35, 30, CHAS+.

DOLOZ, ADELAIDE, 50, F, None listed, -, France, 728, 737, RICH+.

DOLOZ, ADELAIDE, 17, F, None listed, -, France, 728, 737, RICH+. In HH of Adelaide Doloz, F, 50, born France.

DOLOZ, EUGENIA, 24, F, None listed, -, France, 728, 737, RICH+. In HH of Adelaide Doloz, F, 50, born France.

DOLOZ, FRANCIS, 22, M, Carriage maker, -, France, 728, 737, RICH+. In HH of Adelaide Doloz, F, 50, born France.

DOLOZ, JOSEPHINE, 20, F, None listed, -, France, 728, 737, RICH+. In HH

of Adelaide Doloz, F, 50, born France.
**DOVILLIERS, EUGENE**, 30, M, Artist, -, France, 738, 747, RICH+. In HH of Michel Dovilliers, M, 70, born France.
**DOVILLIERS, MICHEL**, 70, M, Planter, -, France, 738, 747, RICH+.
**DOVILLIERS, ZOE**, 46, F, None listed, -, France, 738, 747, RICH+. In HH of Michel Dovilliers, M, 70, born France.
**DUSBAN, A., MRS.**, 58, F, None listed, -, France, 114, 114, BEAU.

# F

**FAUKENBERG, C.**, 25, M, French Council, -, France, 293, 270, CHAS. In HH of R. DeLamote, M, 50, born France.
**FEBRE, LAURA**, 78, F, None listed, -, France, 1085, 1063, CHAS%. In HH of John Michel, M, 59, born St. Domingo.
**FENGAS, H.P.**, 42, M, Professor, -, France, 203, 186, CHAS*. Occupation: Professor of languages.
**FISCHER, CATHERINE**, 36, F, None listed, -, France, 189, 172, CHAS. In HH of F. Fischer, M, 32, born France.
**FISCHER, F.**, 32, M, Shoemaker, -, France, 189, 172, CHAS.
**FLORIN, CHARLES**, 40, M, Clerk, -, France, 325, 299, CHAS*.
**FLORIN, WILHELLMINA**, 36, F, None listed, -, France, 325, 299, CHAS*. In HH of Charles Florin, M, 40, born France.
**FOLLEN, JOSEPH**, 78, M, None listed, -, France, 860, 818, CHAS+. In HH of Gustavis Follen, M, 33, born SC.
**FOUCANNIO, FRANCES**, 30, M, Merchant, -, France, 497, 451, CHAS. In Boarding House.
**FRANCOIS, SAMUEL**, 37, M, Clerk, -, France, 72, 64, CHAS+. In HH of John Barre, M, 56, born France.
**FREIDEL, CHARLES**, 44, M, Daguerreotype artist, -, France, 5, 5, AND. In HH of William Hubbard, M, 51, Innkeeper, born SC.
**FREVET, LEWIS H.**, 33, M, Painter, -, France, 853, 863, RICH+.
**FULLON, P.N., REV.**, 33, M, Clergyman, -, France, 480, 446, CHAS*. In HH of Rt. Revd. Jgn. A. Reynolds, M, 51, born KY.
**FURLONG, JOHN**, 73, M, None, -, France, 364, 347, CHAS-. In HH of Eustine Vente, M, 35, born France.

# G

**GAINBOW, CATHERINE**, 30, F, None listed, -, France, 862, 820, CHAS+. In HH of W.H. Gainbow, M, 35, born France.
**GAINBOW, W.H.**, 35, M, Professor of languages, -, France, 862, 820, CHAS+.

GALLIOT, ALEXIS, 65, M, Tobacconist, -, France, 99, 91, CHAS+.
GANTHIER, F., 50, M, Music professor, -, France, 1081, 1059, CHAS%.
GANTHIER, LOUISA, 48, F, None listed, -, France, 1081, 1059, CHAS%. In
HH of F. Ganthier, M, 50, born France.
GODFREY, A., 37, M, Tailor, -, France, 196, 184, CHAS+.
GOVENEUR, PETER, 44, M, Cutter, -, France, 383, 347, CHAS.
GREZET, FRANCIS, 53, M, Carpenter, -, France, 5, 5, COLL.
GUTHIER, EMILY, 50, F, None listed, -, France, 451, 434, CHAS-. In HH of
F. Guthier, M, 59, born France.
GUTHIER, F., 59, M, Professor of music, -, France, 451, 434, CHAS-.

H
HARRIS, HENRY, 30, M, Teacher, -, France, 504, 504, Fair. In HH of J.F.
Gamble, M, 42, Hotel keeper, born NC. Henry Harris, born Paris. At the
Winnsboro Hotel.
HARTZOG, JOHN F., 40, M, Wheelwright, -, France, 305, 305, ORNG*.
HAYNSWORTH, MARY H., 60, F, None listed, -, France, 1852, 1852, SUMT.
In HH of Henry Haynsworth, M, 38, born SC.
HERBERT, MICHAEL, 39, M, Custom ho{house} boat, -, France, 185, 174,
CHAS+. Occupation: Custom House Boatman.
HIEMAN, ABRAM, 38, M, Farmer, -, France, 785, 786, ORNG+. In HH of
James Staily, M, 31, born SC.
HOPKINSON, EMMA, 5, F, None listed, -, France, 97, 97, CHAS^. In HH
of James Hopkinson, M, 36, born NJ.
HORAS, FRANCIS, 8, M, None listed, -, France, 465, 462, CHAS%. In HH
of John Horas, M, 59, born France.
HORAS, FRITZ, 5, M, None listed, -, France, 465, 462, CHAS%. In HH of
John Horas, M, 59, born France.
HORAS, HENRY, 11, M, None listed, -, France, 465, 462, CHAS%. In HH of
John Horas, M, 59, born France.
HORAS, JOHN, 59, M, Shopkeeper, -, France, 465, 462, CHAS%.
HORAS, JOHN, 13, M, None listed, -, France, 465, 462, CHAS%. In HH of
John Horas, M, 59, born France.
HUARD, C.P., 55, F, None listed, -, France, 291, 268, CHAS.
HUCHES, JOHN, 14, M, None listed, -, France, 406, 366, CHAS+. In HH of
Theodore Huches, M, 37, born SC.
HUCHET, ZOE, 50, F, None listed, -, France, 249, 234, CHAS-. In HH of
Eugene Huchet, M, 34, born SC.
HUGHES, MARY, 40, F, None listed, -, France, 399, 359, CHAS+. In HH of
Elias Hughes, M, 34, born VA.

**HUOT, LOUIS**, 23, M, Med. Student, -, France, 597, 614, RICH. In HH of Samuel Fair, M, 46, born SC.

**I**

**INGNOT, CHARLES**, 50, M, Ferry keeper, -, France, 66, 57, CHAS$.

**J**

**JOHN, CAROLINE**, 30, F, None listed, -, France, 237, 215, CHAS. In HH of Edward John, M, 35, born France.

**JOHN, EDWARD**, 35, M, Shoemaker, -, France, 237, 215, CHAS.

**JOHN, MARIA LOUISA**, 70, F, None listed, -, France, 549, 515, CHAS*. In HH of Saml. H. Patterson, M, 46, born SC.

**L**

**LABUTAT, ISIDORE**, 69, M, Musician, -, France, 1035, 1012, CHAS-.

**LACAPAGNE, EDWARD**, 42, M, Merchant, -, France, 985, 964, CHAS-.

**LACHARTRE, JAMES**, 40, M, Merchant, -, France, 357, 329, CHAS. In HH of E. Groves, F, 50, runs boarding house, born SC.

**LADAVIZE, R.**, 55, M, Shopkeeper, -, France, 182, 166, CHAS*.

**LAFAYETTE, EDWARD**, 35, M, Merchant, -, France, 562, 521, CHAS+.

**LAFONCARDE, ANTIONETTE**, 13, F, None listed, -, France, 969, 949, CHAS-. In HH of Zoe Grant, F, 40, born St. Domingo.

**LALUE, F.**, 38, M, Clerk, -, France, 357, 329, CHAS. In HH of E. Groves, F, 50, runs boarding house, born SC.

**LAMBLE, JAMES**, 31, M, Engineer, -, France, 27, 27, GEOR.

**LANCHICOAT, HENRY**, 32, M, Pilot, -, France, 128, 128, GEOR.

**LAPRINCE, JOHN**, 45, M, Rigger, -, France, 276, 256, CHAS+. In HH of A. Gilbert, M, 40, born MA.

**LAUREY, H.**, 28, M, Clerk, -, France, 827, 807, CHAS-.

**LEBUFF, FRANCIS**, 39, M, Painter, -, France, 413, 373, CHAS.

**LECLARE, ADOLPHUS**, 44, M, Merchant, -, France, 127, 118, CHAS+. In Boarding House.

**LEURE, PETER**, 53, M, Clerk, -, France, 493, 447, CHAS.

**LINGS, B.D.**, 38, M, None listed, -, France, 123, 123, BEAU. In HH of Daniel Mun, M, 26, born Germany.

**LOCASTE, JNO.**, 44, M, Planter, -, France, 1551, 1551, BARN.

**LOPON, NICHOLAS**, 30, M, Stage Driver, -, France, 1511, 1511, BARN.

**LOUIS, D.**, 31, M, Merchant, -, France, 69, 70, ORNG+.

**LOYAL, LEWIS C.**, 28, M, Carpenter, -, France, 668, 660, CHAS%.

**LUBY, PETER**, 24, M, None listed, -, France, 653, 645, CHAS%. In HH of

Edward Welling, M, 35, born SC.

LUBY, ROSELLE, 40, F, None listed, -, France, 653, 645, CHAS%. In HH of Edward Welling, M, 35, born SC.

LUMENA, JANE, 60, F, None listed, -, France, 820, 800, CHAS-. In HH of E. Devineau, M, 40, born SC.

# M

MALLET, FREDERICK, 36, M, Laborer, -, France, 109, 101, CHAS+.

MALLET, MARY, 30, F, None listed, -, France, 109, 101, CHAS+. In HH of Frederick Mallet, M, 36, born France.

MANGET, FELICIA, 36, F, None listed, -, France, 741, 750, RICH+. In HH of Victor Manget, M, 37, born France.

MANGET, JOHN A., 11, M, None listed, -, France, 741, 750, RICH+. In HH of Victor Manget, M, 37, born France.

MANGET, SAMUEL, 9, M, None listed, -, France, 741, 750, RICH+. In HH of Victor Manget, M, 37, born France.

MANGET, VICTOR, 37, M, Professor of Languages - Female Institute, -, France, 741, 750, RICH+.

MANGET, VICTOR E., 13, M, None listed, -, France, 741, 750, RICH+. In HH of Victor Manget, M, 37, born France.

MAPILLON, FELICE, 59, M, Shopkeeper, -, France, 469, 466, CHAS%.

MARION, ANN, 45, F, None listed, -, France, 701, 681, CHAS-. In HH of John O. Dener, M, 40, born SC.

MARION, JOSEPHINE, 44, F, None listed, -, France, 701, 681, CHAS-. In HH of John O. Dener, M, 40, born SC.

MASSELEAU, A., 39, M, Baker, -, France, 54, 54, KERS.

MATHUSSEN, FRANCES J., 60, F, None listed, -, France, 421, 379, CHAS. In HH of C.F. Mathussen, M, 72, born Germany.

MATIERE, LOUISA, 50, F, None listed, -, France, 360, 331, CHAS.

MATTEES, JOSEPH, 40, M, Boot maker, -, France, 339, 313, CHAS. In HH of Thomas Sarrar, M, 35, born France.

MCMANES, MARGARET, 22, F, None listed, -, France, 325, 300, CHAS. In HH of Nathaniel McManes, M, 29, born MD.

MEALER, MARY, 21, F, None listed, -, France, 984, 963, CHAS-. In HH of Charles McElleron, M, 30, born Ireland.

METAVA, FRANCIS, 73, M, None listed, -, France, 611, 604, CHAS%.

MICHEL, LA AMBLE, 50, M, None, -, France, 113, 113, CHAS%. In HH of T.D. Mitchell, M, 27, born SC.

MOISES, P., 66, M, Overseer, -, France, 115, 115, NEWB.

MORA, ADEL, 14, F, None listed, -, France, 452, 409, CHAS. In HH of Lewis

Mora, M, 40, born France.

**MORA, FRANCENA**, 36, F, None listed, -, France, 452, 409, CHAS. In HH of Lewis Mora, M, 40, born France.

**MORA, LEWIS**, 40, M, Shoemaker, -, France, 452, 409, CHAS.

**MORAN, EDWARD**, 48, M, None, -, France, 1129, 1108, CHAS%.

**MORAN, MARY**, 42, F, None listed, -, France, 1129, 1108, CHAS%. In HH of Edward Moran, M, 48, born France.

**MORSEMAN, CELENIS**, 60, F, None listed, -, France, 417, 376, CHAS+. In HH of William Maiseman {sic}, M, 34, born Ireland.

**MOTTAT, EDWARD**, 37, M, Merchant, -, France, 241, 226, CHAS-.

**MULLER, ANTHONY**, 29, M, Clerk, -, France, 174, 178, RICH.

**MULLER, MARY L.**, 18, F, None listed, -, France, 174, 178, RICH. In HH of Anthony Muller, M, 29, born France.

**MURAT, JOSEPH**, 40, M, Painter, -, France, 542, 557, RICH. Date 1849 by name. In Lunatic Asylum.

**N**

**NAYEL, VINCENT**, 52, M, Baker, -, France, 402, 375, CHAS*.

**NESPINESS, FELICITY**, 89, F, None listed, -, France, 383, 345, CHAS+. In HH of Wm. R. Green, M, 32, born CT.

**NUEFFER, M.**, 31, M, Music Professor, -, France, 127, 118, CHAS+. In Boarding House.

**P**

**PANSIN, CHRISTOPHER**, 45, M, Shopkeeper, -, France, 670, 650, CHAS-.

**PATAT, AMELIA**, 24, F, None listed, -, France, 1156, 1135, CHAS%. In HH of Anna Patat, F, 58, born France.

**PATAT, ANNA**, 58, F, None listed, -, France, 1156, 1135, CHAS%.

**PATAT, FRANCES**, 30, F, None listed, -, France, 1156, 1135, CHAS%. In HH of Anna Patat, F, 58, born France.

**PATAT, JOSEPH**, 33, M, Confectioner, -, France, 1156, 1135, CHAS%. In HH of Anna Patat, F, 58, born France.

**PATAT, JOSEPHINE**, 18, F, None listed, -, France, 1156, 1135, CHAS%. In HH of Anna Patat, F, 58, born France.

**PECAULT, JANE**, 16, F, None listed, -, France, 741, 721, CHAS-. In HH of Catherine Drose, F, 45, born SC.

**PELERUN, AUGUST**, 31, M, Merchant, -, France, 821, 801, CHAS-.

**PELERUN, SOPHIA**, 33, F, None listed, -, France, 821, 801, CHAS-. In HH of August Pelerun, M, 31, born France.

**PEROUNET, LUCIEN**, 35, M, Grocer, -, France, 29, 25, CHAS$.

PEROUNET, M., 30, F, None listed, -, France, 29, 25, CHAS$. In HH of Lucien Perounet, M, 35, born France.

PETERS, HARRIOT, 30, F, None listed, -, France, 38, 46, CHAS. In Boarding House.

PETERSON, JANE, 30, F, None listed, -, France, 480, 476, CHAS%. In HH of Catherine Sherry, F, 30, born Ireland.

PETIT, F., 55, M, Confectioner, -, France, 1002, 980, CHAS-.

PHILSBURY, ANTIONETTE, 40, F, None listed, -, France, 363, 372, Rich. In HH of Samuel Pilsbury, M, 47, born SC.

PINCHA, ARMET, 70, F, None listed, -, France, 291, 268, CHAS. In HH of C.P. Huard, F, 55, born France.

POINTE, ADEL, 47, F, None listed, -, France, 633, 614, CHAS-. In HH of Emele Pointe, M, 60, born France.

POINTE, EMELE, 60, M, None, -, France, 633, 614, CHAS-.

POINTE, ISIDORE, 19, M, Fruit Merchant, -, France, 633, 614, CHAS-. In HH of Emele Pointe, M, 60, born France.

POINTELL, J., 40, M, Saddler, -, France, 465, 422, CHAS. In HH of Leslie O'Wen, M, 47, born Ireland.

POLICE, E., 35, F, None listed, -, France, 457, 414, CHAS. In HH of H. Police, M, 50, born France.

POLICE, H., 50, M, Merchant, -, France, 457, 414, CHAS.

POLICI, EMILY, 28, F, None listed, -, France, 1093, 1071, CHAS%. In HH of Ivan Polici, M, 30, born France.

POLICI, IVAN, 30, M, Tinner, -, France, 1093, 1071, CHAS%.

PRINCE, A.L., 65, M, Book Keeper, -, France, 89, 81, CHAS+. In HH of A. Von Dohlen, M, 32, born Germany.

R

RAINE, CLAUDE, 55, M, None listed, -, France, 159, 142, CHAS. In HH of V. Datrieuse, F, 50, born St. Domingo.

RANDIN, F., 22, M, Seaman, -, France, 326, 301, CHAS. On Steam Ship Southerner.

RANDIN, F.N., 45, M, Seaman, -, France, 326, 301, CHAS. On Steam Ship Southerner.

RENIEE, C., 55, F, None listed, -, France, 360, 331, CHAS. In HH of Louisa Matiere, F, 50, born France.

REQUISE, JOSEPH, 26, M, Painter, -, France, 391, 355, CHAS. In HH of F.W. Theus, M, 28, born Germany.

REYMOND, M., 28, F, None listed, -, France, 1146, 1125, CHAS%. In HH of Harris Simons, M, 43, born Ireland. Marie Ramsay Simons age8/12 yr.

**ROGER, THOMAS J.**, 51, M, Merchant, -, France, 34, 31, CHAS-.

**RUFFER, HENRY**, 50, M, Laborer, -, France, 472, 469, CHAS%.

**RUFFER, MADELINE**, 46, F, None listed, -, France, 472, 469, CHAS%. In HH of Henry Ruffer, M, 50, born France.

**RUPELE, ANGELINE**, 50, F, None listed, -, France, 542, 557, RICH. Date 1850 by name. In Lunatic Asylum.

**S**

**SALVO, FRANCES**, 58, F, None listed, -, France, 225, 201, CHAS*. In HH of A. Gambale, M, 49, born Italy.

**SALVO, LOUISA**, 19, F, None listed, -, France, 481, 477, CHAS%. In HH of P.S. Salvo, M, 25, born SC.

**SARRAR, THOMAS**, 35, M, Boot maker, -, France, 339, 313, CHAS.

**SASSARD, J.**, 54, M, Master mariner, -, France, 593, 551, CHAS+.

**SCHIRER, MARY**, 50, F, None listed, -, France, 134, 125, CHAS+. In HH of J.B. Nixon, M, 31, born NY.

**SEBARA, HONORA**, 20, M, Confectioner, -, France, 761, 741, CHAS-. In HH of H.F. Brandt, M, 40, born France.

**SEYBT, AMY**, 76, F, None listed, -, France, 212, 217, RICH.

**SEYBT, GEORGE**, 37, M, Tailor, -, France, 33, 33, NEWB.

**SHATENGER, W.**, 30, M, Gilder, -, France, 317, 291, CHAS+. In HH of Tim Kennedy, M, 71, born Ireland.

**SINCLAIR, THERESA**, 25, F, None listed, -, France, 22, 20, CHAS$. In HH of Danl. Sinclair, M, 26, born NY.

**SLIPPERGREL, CHRISTIAN**, 30, M, Druggist, -, France, 466, 463, CHAS%.

**SOLOMONS, RACHEL**, 51, F, None listed, -, France, 1849, 1849, SUMT.

**SONBEDA, PETER**, 44, M, Mariner, -, France, 193, 177, CHAS*.

**STAIMER, A.**, 28, F, None listed, -, France, 164, 164, SUMT. In HH of V. Staimer, M, 45, born France.

**STAIMER, V.**, 45, M, Shoemaker, -, France, 164, 164, SUMT.

**STELLER, PETER**, 38, M, Mariner, -, France, 598, 556, CHAS+. In HH of Peter Mazyck, M, 38, born SC.

**STRAUSS, MAURICE**, 33, M, Merchant, -, France, 2115, 2115, ABB.

**SUMMERVILLE, ELIZA**, 22, F, None listed, -, France, 270, 251, CHAS+. In HH of Richard M. Collins, M, 40, born Ireland.

**T**

**TOWELL, JAMES**, 50, M, Well digger, -, France, 1061, 1061, BARN.

**TURET, F.**, 78, M, None, -, France, 761, 741, CHAS-. In HH of H.F. Brandt, M, 40, born France.

**V**

VENOT, J.T., 29, M, Tailor, -, France, 300, 274, CHAS*. In HH of E.W. Edgerton, M, 45, born CT.
VENTE, EUSTINE, 35, M, M.D., -, France, 364, 347, CHAS-.
VERDIER, SIMON, 70, M, Planter, -, France, 739, 739, COLL.
VIDAL, JOHN, 58, M, Merchant, -, France, 650, 609, CHAS+.
VIDAL, LEWIS, 40, M, Farmer, -, France, 320, 320, COLL*.
VIDAL, MARY, 46, F, None listed, -, France, 650, 609, CHAS+. In HH of John Vidal, M, 58, born France.
VOLLARD, E., 25, F, None listed, -, France, 301, 278, CHAS. In HH of Carl Epping, M, 28, born Germany.

**W**

WELKER, VALENTINE, 26, M, Overseer/factor, -, France, 130, 130, LEX.
WINEAU, E., 60, F, None listed, -, France, 820, 800, CHAS-. In HH of E. Devineau, M, 40, born SC.
WOODLY, ANNE, 45, F, None listed, -, France, 573, 565, CHAS%. In HH of James Woodly, M, 41, born NY.

**Y**

YON, MARY A., 68, F, None listed, -, France, 31, 28, CHAS-.

❖

# BORN IN SPAIN (22)

**A**

ANTONIO, F., 42, M, Mariner,-, Spain, 868, 848, CHAS-.

**C**

CAARAU, JACINTA, 13, M, None listed,-, Spain, 687, 645, CHAS+. In HH of P.A. Avelhie, M, 47, born SC..
CASTELLA, JOSE, 32, M, Cigar maker,-, Spain, 295, 272, CHAS+.
CORDERO, JOHN, 28, M, Police Officer,-, Spain, 119, 121, RICH.
CRICKEY, LEWIS, 26, N, Laborer,-, Spain, 94, 106, CHAS. In HH of Michael Bolger, M, 29, born Ireland.

## F

**FREGOZA, CORENO**, 30, F, None listed,-, Spain, 868, 848, CHAS- . In HH of F. Anonio, M, 42, born Spain.

**FREGOZA, SENO**, 39, M, None listed,-, Spain, 868, 848, CHAS- . In HH of F. Anonio, M, 42, born Spain.

**FREIDEL, ANGELICA**, 38, F, None listed,-, Spain, 5, 5, AND . In HH of William Hubbard, M, 51, Innkeeper, born SC.

## G

**GONRALVO, ANTONIO**, 38, M, Fisherman, -, Spain, 76, 68, CHAS+ . In HH of D.L. McCarthy, M, 30, born Ireland.

**GONZALUS, B.**, 55, M, Merchant,-, Spain, 835, 793, CHAS+ .

## L

**LORENZO, ANTONIO**, 40, M, Spanish Consol,-, Spain, 126, 117, CHAS+ . In HH of Louisa Hernander, F, 21, born Cuba.

## M

**MADENA, ORSA**, 60, M, Shoemaker,-, Spain, 449, 449, GREE.

## P

**PALMER, JOZE**, 26, M, Mariner,-, Spain, 139, 123, CHAS. In HH of Barthohs Costwick, M, 50, born Austria.

**PERRARA, EMANEUL**, 25, M, Mariner,-, Spain, 139, 123, CHAS. In HH of Barthohs Costwick, M, 50, born Austria.

**PERRERA, IVAN**, 29, M, Waiter, -, Spain, 326, 301, CHAS. On Steam Ship Southerner.

**POLLENA, JOSE**, 30, M, Rigger, -, Spain, 204, 192, CHAS+ . In HH of Mary M. Maher, F, 52, born Ireland.

## R

**RAVINA, J.D.**, 58, M, Professor,-, Spain, 393, 376, CHAS- . Occupation: Professor of Languages.

## S

**SCHRESTON, PETER**, 27, M, Speculator,-, Spain, 270, 270, CHAS3.

## T

**THOMAS, JAMES**, 50, M, None listed,-, Spain, 437, 389, CHAS.

**TREISER, CONARD**, 36, M, Carpenter, -, Spain, 94, 95, ORNG+ .

## W

WATKINS, GAUDALOUP, 50, M, Laborer,-, Spain, 991, 992, AND*. In HH
of Alfred Fortune, M, 47, born NC.
WILLIAMS, CHARLES, 13, M, None listed,-, Spain, 148, 139, CHAS+ . In
HH of Joseph Williams, M, 32, born Italy.

❖

## BORN IN RUSSIA (10)

## A

ALBUM, CHARLES, 30, M, Oysterman , -, Russia , 135, 115, CHAS$.

## B

BURNETT, MATILDA, 25, F, None listed, -, Rushia (sic), 1043, 1043, SUMT.
In HH of R.J. Burnett, 27, merchant, born in Rushia (sic).
BURNETT, R.J., 27, M, Merchant, -, Rushia (sic), 1043, 1043, SUMT.

## L

LIVINGSTON, HANNAH, 50, F, None listed, -, Russia , 71, 63, CHAS+. In
HH of Lewis S. Livingston, M, 52, born Russia.
LIVINGSTON, LEWIS S., 52, M, Shopkeeper, -, Russia , 71, 63, CHAS+.
LORYEA, AARON, 29, M, Tailor, -, Russia , 263, 248, CHAS-.

## S

SCHUR, BARNET, 22, M, Clerk, -, Russia, 362, 335, CHAS*. In HH of David
Schur, M, 50, born Russia.
SCHUR, BELLA, 44, F, None listed, -, Russia, 362, 335, CHAS*. In HH of
David Schur, M, 50, born Russia.
SCHUR, DAVID, 50, M, Clerk Heb.{Hebrew} Ruwwig Congregation, 362,
335, CHAS*.
SCHUR, HENRIETTA, 24, F, None listed, -, Russia, 362, 335, CHAS*. In HH
of David Schur, M, 50, born Russia.

❖

# BORN IN DENMARK - (25)

**B**

**BENSEMAN, F.W.**, 50, M, Mariner, -, Denmark, 43, 40, CHAS- .

**C**

**CHRISTIANSEN, JASPER**, 46, M, Grocer, -, Denmark, 997, 976, CHAS- .
**CLAUSON, THOS. C.**, 45, M, Pedlar, -, Denmark, 31, 31, NEWB . In HH of
James Flick 37, M, Painter, born Ireland.
**CRADDOCK, P.O.**, 28, M, Teacher, -, Denmark, 323, 323, BEAU* . In HH of
James W. Riley, M, 31, born SC.

**D**

**DERICKSON, HENRY**, 38, M, Carpenter, -, Denmark, 265, 265, CHAS% .

**E**

**EHRICKSON, CHARLES**, 33, M, Carpenter, -, Denmark, 263, 263, CHAS%.
**EPPRISAN, NELS**, 34, M, Carpenter, -, Denmark, 1679, 1679, EDGE . {Note:
follows fam No. 1625- out of order}

**F**

**FISCHER, GEORGE**, 32, M, Mariner, -, Denmark, 362, 333, CHAS. In
Boarding House.

**G**

**GIFFER, HANS**, 44, M, Tailor, -, Denmark, 471, 437, CHAS*.

**H**

**HORST, C.F.**., 37, M, Mechanic, -, Denmark, 564, 564, CHES .
**HORST, J.E.**, 33, F, None listed, -, Denmark, 564, 564, CHES . In HH of C.F.
Horst, M, 37, born Denmark.

**J**

**JACOBI, M.**, 18, M, None listed, -, Denmark, 694, 674, CHAS-. In HH of W.J.
Jacobi, M, 53, born Prussia.
**JACOBS, JACOB SIMON**, 56, M, Shopkeeper, -, Denmark, 41, 36, CHAS+.
**JACOBS, PHILIP S.**, 38, M, Jewish Minister, -, Denmark, 223, 228, RICH .
{Page out of order, follow HH 177/181.}

JACOBSON, DAVID, 18, M, Overseer, -, Denmark, 218, 218, BEAU+.

**K**
KEMPEL, ELIZABETH, 21, F, None listed, -, Denmark, 985, 964, CHAS-. In HH of Edward Lacapagne, M, 42, born France.

**L**
LINDEN, JOHN, 35, M, Mariner, -, Denmark, 362, 333, CHAS . In Boarding House.
LUNGBALLE, D.M., 52, M, Shopkeeper, -, Denmark, 102, 102, BEAU .

**M**
MESDORFF, JACOB, 50, M, Mariner, -, Denmark, 449, 416, CHAS*.
MOREFELD, M.A., 65, F, None listed, -, Denmark, 52, 52, COLL . In HH of Mrs. Mary Gilling 40, teacher, born SC.

**N**
NELSON, CHRIS., 60, M, Tavern keeper, -, Denmark, 218, 196, CHAS .

**R**
RICHTER, THEODORE, 15, M, Mariner, -, Denmark, 218, 196, CHAS . In HH of Chris. Nelson, M, 60, born Denmark.

**S**
SCHONEBOE, FREDERICK, 39, M, Police Officer, -, Denmark, 482, 466, CHAS-.

**T**
TOPPE, CHARLES R., 39, M, Clerk, -, Denmark, 997, 976, CHAS-. In HH of Jasper Christiansen, M, 46, born Denmark.

**W**
WILLIAMS, HENRY, 50, M, Engineer, -, Denmark, 498, 491, CHAS%.

❖

# BORN IN SWEDEN ( 29)

## A

**AGRIEL, CHARLES**, 37, M, Grocer, -, Sweden, 762, 742, CHAS-.
**ANDERSON, CHARLES**, 22, M, Mariner, -, Sweden, 426, 384, CHAS. In HH of Justice Palmer, M, 50, born VA.

## B

**BAHR, NICHOLAS**, 40, M, None listed, -, Sweden, 513, 506, CHAS%.
**BECKMAN, GEORGE**, 45, M, Mariner, -, Sweden, 654, 613, CHAS+.
**BENKERT, W.M.**, 32, M, Druggist, -, Sweden, 730, 710, CHAS-. In HH of J.P.M. Epping, M, 33, born Germany.
**BROWN, ROGER**, 27, M, Clerk, -, Sweden, 395, 377, CHAS-. In Boarding House.

## C

**CANE, ALFRED**, 29, M, Sugar maker, -, Sweden, 299, 276, CHAS.

## D

**DUNFORD, JACOB**, 45, M, Fisherman, -, Sweden, 112, 104, CHAS+. In HH of Harman Werner, M, 30, born Germany.

## F

**FLODORER, JOHN**, 58, M, Shopkeeper, -, Sweden, 529, 495, CHAS*.
**FLODORER, MARY ANN**, 54, F, None listed, -, Sweden, 529, 495, CHAS*. In HH of John Flordorer, M, 58, born Sweden.

## H

**HAMMERSCOLD, GEORGE**, 43, M, Clerk, -, Sweden, 651, 651, UNION. In HH of John Mintz, M, 45, born NC.
**HOGAN, MICHAEL**, 30, M, Boarding house, -, Sweden, 300, 277, CHAS.
**HORNHOLM, E.**, 29, M, Tailor, -, Sweden, 747, 727, CHAS-.

## J

**JOHNSTON, CHARLES**, 39, M, Mariner, -, Sweden, 132, 122, CHAS*.

## L

**LINDFORS, CHARLES J.**, 34, M, Merchant, -, Sweden, 253, 258, RICH.

160

**LOVEGREEN, H.S.**, 52, M, None listed, -, Sweden, 965, 945, CHAS-.

**M**

**MOLINE, DANIEL**, 46, M, Coach Painter, -, Sweden, 772, 730, CHAS+.

**N**

**NELSON, ALEXR.**, 24, M, Mariner, -, Sweden, 362, 333, CHAS. In Boarding House.
**NELSON, HENRY**, 33, M, Mariner, -, Sweden, 362, 333, CHAS. In Boarding House.
**NELSON, MAGNES**, 20, M, Mariner, -, Sweden, 362, 333, CHAS. In Boarding House.

**P**

**PETERSON, CHRISTIAN**, 39, M, Laborer, -, Sweden, 28, 35, CHAS.

**R**

**READ, WILLIAM**, 29, M, Rigger, -, Sweden, 520, 486, CHAS*. In HH of John H. Burke, M, 43, born SC.
**ROSE, FREDERICK**, 44, M, Mariner, -, Sweden, 449, 406, CHAS.

**T**

**TALLISON, AARON**, 27, M, Upholsterer, -, Sweden, 988, 967, CHAS-. In HH of Eliza Dallwig, F, 23, born MD.
**THOMPSON, JOHN T.**, 56, M, Farmer, -, Sweden, 183, 183, LEX.
**THOMPSON, WILLIAM**, 45, M, Mechanic, -, Sweden, 352, 352, BEAU-.

**W**

**WESTMAN, J.**, 28, M, Clerk, -, Sweden, 762, 742, CHAS-. In HH of Charles Agriel, M, 37, born Sweden.
**WICKENBERG, A.**, 22, F, None listed, -, Sweden, 289, 266, CHAS. In HH of F.D. Wickenberg, M, 32, born Sweden.
**WICKENBERG, F.D.**, 32, M, Merchant, -, Sweden, 289, 266, CHAS.

❖

161

# BORN IN SWITZERLAND (18)

**A**

**AVERIC, GUSTAVUS**, 50, M, Grocer, -, Switzerland, 20, 19, CHAS$

**B**

**BERT, JULIA AN**, 52, F, None listed, -, Switzerland, 502, 460, CHAS+. In HH of Jane Chisolm, F, 38, born SC
**BIANCIA, ACHILLE**, 33, M, Shoemaker, -, Switzerland, 32, 27, CHAS+
**BOESCH, J.U.**, 30, M, Brass Founder, -, Switzerland, 335, 301, CHAS+.
**BOESCH, NICHOLAS**, 28, M, Dyer, -, Switzerland, 220, 197, CHAS*.

**F**

**FENRICH, HENRICH**, 26, M, Founder, -, Switzerland, 999, 978, CHAS-. In HH of Otto Switzer, M, 38, born Switzerland.
**FRY, JACOB**, 31, M, Farmer, -, Switzerland, 118, 118, SPART..
**FRY, JAMES**, 62, M, Farmer, -, Switzerland, 3027, 3027, SPART

**H**

**HOHL, JNO. J.**, 43, M, Baker, -, Switzerland, 77, 77, LEX.

**L**

**LINGG, ALOIS**, 40, M, Baker, -, Switzerland, 75, 75, BEAU+.

**M**

**MARGRAF, BERTHA**, 30, F, None listed, -, Switzerland, 231, 236, RICH. In HH of Henry Margraf, M, 32, born Germany.
**MARTEY, ABRAHAM**, 43, M, Merchant, -, Switzerland, 186, 175, CHAS+. In HH of Elizabeth Martey, F, 38, born Switzerland.
**MARTEY, ELIZABETH**, 38, F, None listed, -, Switzerland, 186, 175, CHAS+
**MEYER, HENRY**, 57, M, Merchant, -, Switzerland, 144, 128, CHAS.

**S**

**SLAETT, HENRY**, 45, M, Laborer, -, Switzerland, 471, 468, CHAS%. In HH of Herman Meyer, M, 33, born Germany.
**SWITZER, OTTO**, 38, M, Watchmaker, -, Switzerland, 999, 978, CHAS-.

**W**

**WALKER, EMANUEL**, 42, M, Blacksmith, -, Switzerland, 471, 468, CHAS%.
In HH of Herman Meyer, M, 33, born Germany.

**Z**

**ZUCKER, J. U.**, 48, M, Confectioner, -, Switzerland, 537, 537, FAIR .

❖

❖❖❖

## Name Index:

### A



### B

**D**

William M., 10
Douglas
  Joseph, 46
Doyle
  James, 75
Drago
  Anthony, 142
Drose
  Catherine, 152
Drucker
  Moses, 29
Dubois
  Eleanor, 20
  Jesse, 39
Dunbar
  Paul, 25, 52, 55
Durnstucks
  W., 120

**E**

Eason
  James M., 104
Easton
  Geo. L., 10
Edgerton
  E.W., 155
Ehricks
  Henry, 69, 117
Eilhardt
  Gottlieb, 70, 76
Elias
  David, 10
Ellerhorst
  H.D., 71
Enston
  Wm., 10
Epler
  D., 110
Epping
  Carl, 155
  J.P.M., 112, 160

Ewing
  John, 7, 8, 38,
    45, 65, 68,
    75, 139, 141
  Major P., 58
  Mary, 43

**F**

Fair
  Samuel, 150
Fairchild
  Rufus, 141
Fell
  Elizabeth, 67
Ficken
  J.F., 74
Figeroux
  B., 80
Fink
  A., 4, 11, 22, 23,
    59
Finken
  Albert, 61
Flick
  James, 158
Folk
  John D., 109
  John W., 24
Follen
  Gustavis, 147,
    148
Ford
  Mary, 124
Fortune
  Alfred, 156
Fowler
  Joseph, 13
  William H., 3, 7,
    34, 102
Frank
  B.H., 126

Harmon C., 79,
  117
  John, 79
Frazer
  Charles P., 96
Fresonthick
  George, 32, 33
Fry
  Joseph, 145
Furgurson
  Antony, 119

**G**

Gabriel
  Joseph, 106
Gailbraith
  Nathl. M., 146
Gambale
  A., 154
Gamble
  J.F., 63, 149
Garber
  John, 99
Garden
  Benjn., 75, 108
Garrett
  George, 5
Garrison
  Henry, 12
Gerdts
  H., 99
Gessel
  H., 111, 114
Gibson
  Alexander, 44
  W.B., 34
Gilbert
  A., 150
Gilling, Mrs.
  Mary, 159
Givenrath

**H**

**J**



**K**

**N**

Neales
Jesse S., 56
Neibuhr
John P., 88
Nelles
P.D., 54
Nelson
Chris, 159
J., 32
Saml. A., 121
Newman
Nicholas, 97
Nichols
James, 3
Niebuhr
John P., 129
Nienmeths
J.H., 80
Niliams
F., 90
Nixon
J.B., 154
Norman
Charles, 110
Norris
William, 33

**O**

O'Conner
D.O., 43
Oetjen
H., 71, 105
Ogeman
John, 93
Ohen
Dedrick, 83
Oldenberg
Henry, 111
Oldenbuttle
G., 104
H., 63

Ollen
C., 92, 130
Olten
Henry, 133
ONeal
James, 123
Ostendosff
John H., 35, 69
Otten
John B., 127
Ottgen
J.C., 125
O'Wen
Leslie, 153
Lewlie, 136

**P**

Pahler
Mary, 121, 130
Palmer
Justice, 160
William S., 21
Pancknin
C.H., 79
Parker
A.G., 63, 82, 133
Wm., 3
Parks
Richard, 100
Patey
James, 25, 26
Pattena
Joseph, 56, 127
Patterson
Saml. H., 150
Pelerun
August, 5
Pelska
Eleanor, 82
Pepples
Wyley, 35

Perounet
Lucien, 153
Perouonet
Lucien, 12
Petch
Julius D., 25
Peters
Antwerp, 144
Petigrw
James L., 10
Philips
Stephen, 98
Piedemann
Henry, 91
Piexolla
Grace, 41
Pike
Daniel, 26
Pilsbury
Samuel, 153
Pluger
Henry, 78
Police
H., 153
Porcher
Peter, 52
Powell
Henry, 112
Thomas, 55
Prince
George, 101
Jacob, 113
Sarah, 27

**Q**

Quackenbush
T.L., 34

**R**

Rancken
Henry, 106

## S

T



V

175

Jonathan, 37
Zehee
  H., 122
Zeleo
  William, 98
Zerbet
  Henry, 96
Zucker
  J.U., 123

## Occupation Index:

### A

Accountant, 28, 50,
  53, 56, 131
Apothecary, 79
Apprentice, 3
Apt. Burser, 98
Architect, 85
Army, 7, 8
Artist, 35, 144, 148
Auctioneer, 20

### B

Baker, 8, 15, 16, 29,
  38, 40, 48,
  51, 53, 60,
  63, 64, 69,
  70, 73, 74,
  75, 79, 81,
  93, 94, 96,
  97, 98, 112,
  114, 115,
  119, 122,
  124, 128,
  130, 133,
  140, 151,
  152, 162

Bank clerk, 54
Bank officer, 56
Bar keeper, 102
Barber, 27
Bell hanger, 25
Blacksmith, 1, 3, 13,
  14, 32, 36,
  39, 40, 41,
  42, 45-47,
  51, 57, 59,
  61, 62, 68,
  75, 79, 83,
  92, 109, 113,
  116, 120,
  124, 163
Block maker, 38
Boarding house, 3,
  7, 160
Boarding house
  keeper, 27,
  32, 34
Boiler maker, 36,
  47, 74, 141
Book keeper, 153
Book seller, 24, 93
Bootmaker, 1, 12,
  36, 48, 51,
  55, 77, 84,
  86, 89, 90,
  105, 112,
  113, 115,
  117, 119,
  123, 129,
  136, 151,
  154
Brass founder, 162
Brick mason, 45
Bricklayer, 6, 9, 20,
  21, 36, 69,
  83
Brick maker, 21

Bridge contractor,
  54
Broker, 2
Builder, 82
Butcher, 12, 72, 85,
  123, 125,
  127

### C

Cabinetmaker,
  10, 11, 14, 16,
  23, 24, 29, 31,
  32, 39, 43, 50,
  52, 57, 62, 71,
  97, 99, 104, 115,
  123, 125, 134,
  147
Carpenter, 3, 5, 6, 8,
  9, 11, 15, 16,
  19, 20-22,
  26, 32, 34,
  37, 38, 41,
  42-46, 49,
  51, 54-56,
  67, 74, 81,
  82, 95, 97,
  101, 109,
  118, 124,
  131, 133,
  139, 145-
  147, 150,
  156, 158
Carriage maker, 19,
  26, 56, 147
Carriage trimmer,
  67
Carter, 86
Carver, 25
Chemist, 75, 79, 95,
  129

**D**



**E**



**F**

179

**Place Index:**

## T



## V



## W

www.ingramcontent.com/pod-product-compliance
Lightning Source LLC
Chambersburg PA
CBHW070427270326
41926CB00014B/2976